THE MOVING MARKET

CONTINUITY AND CHANGE IN THE BOOK TRADE

Liber Eccles YN *Cathed: Dunelm*

Vible Caſherick;

GOAILL STIAGH YN

CHENN CHONAANT,

AS YN

CONAANT NOA:

VEIH

Ny CHIED GHLARAGHYN,

Dy kiaralagh chyndait ayns GAILCK;

Ta ſhen dy ghra,

CHENGEY ny MAYREY ELLAN. VANNIN.

Pointit dy ve lhaibht ayns KIALTEENYN.

So they read in the BOOK, in the Law of GOD diſtinctly, and gave the Senſe, and cauſed them to underſtand the Reading. *Nehem.* viii 8.

John  *Ware*

17 97. *the Donor*

WHITEHAVEN:

PRENTIT LIORISH JUAN WARE AS E VAC.

M,DCC,LXXV.

Title-page of New Testament of Manx Bible (Whitehaven: John Ware, 1775) reduced to 65% (see p xiii, n 6)

The Moving Market

Continuity and Change in the Book Trade

Edited by
Peter Isaac and Barry McKay

OAK KNOLL PRESS
DELAWARE

PRINT NETWORKS

This series, edited by Peter Isaac and Barry McKay, publishes papers given at the annual Seminars on the British Book Trade

1. *Images & Texts*
2. *The Reach of Print*
3. *The Human Face of the Book Trade*
4. *The Mighty Engine*
5. *The Moving Market*

Library of Congress Cataloging-in-Publication Data
The moving market: continuity and change in the book trade /
Edited by Peter Isaac and Barry McKay.
p.cm. -- (Print networks; 5)
Papers presented at the Eighteenth Seminar on the British Book Trade
Newcastle upon Tyne, 2000.
Includes bibliographical references and index.
ISBN 1-58456-052-5

1. Book industries and trade -- Great Britain -- History --Congresses.
I. Isaac, Peter C.G. II. McKay, Barry. III Seminar on the British Book Trade
(18th: 2000: Newcastle upon Tyne, England) IV. Series.
Z325.M8 2001
381'.45002'0941 -- dc21

2001021025

Composed in MONOTYPE *Bulmer* by Peter Isaac & Barry McKay
Printed in England by St Edmundsbury Press, Bury St Edmunds

Contents

Contributors

Hugh Amory is the author of numerous publications on the bibliography of Henry Fielding and the history of the book in eighteenth-century England and America.

Iain Beavan, Senior Curator (Projects) in Historic Collections, University of Aberdeen, has written widely on the Scottish book trade, and in particular on the nineteenth-century period. His most recent research has centred on the Edinburgh publishing and bookselling firm of Oliver & Boyd.

Maureen Bell, Senior Lecturer in the English Department of the University of Birmingham, teaches Renaissance literature, early women's writing and the history of the book. Her research interests include women in the early-modern book trade and the provincial trade in the seventeenth century. She is currently working on Vol 4 of the *Cambridge History of the Book in Britain* and on 'A Chronology and Calendar of Documents related to the London Book Trade 1641–1700'.

Diana Dixon lectured at the College of Librarianship Wales and Loughborough University before taking early retirement in 1997. Currently she is researching the bibliographic control of English provincial newspapers at University College, London. She contributes the 'Annual Review of Work in Newspaper History' to *Media History*.

John Hinks was a librarian for thirty years before researching the history of the book trades in Leicester for a PhD at Loughborough University. He has recently edited *Aspects of Leicester* (Barnsley: Wharncliffe Books, 2000) to which he contributed a chapter 'Thomas Cooper and Leicester's Chartist press'.

David Hounslow is a former children's bookseller.

Peter Isaac, Emeritus Professor of Civil & Public Health of the University of Newcastle upon Tyne, set up the research group on the History of the Book Trade in the North in 1965, and, in 1985, began the compilation of the British Book Trade Index. He was President of the Bibliographical Society 1994–1996.

Philip Henry Jones, a lecturer in the Department of Information & Library Studies of the University of Wales Aberystwyth, has made a special study of the nineteenth-century Welsh-language book trade. He edited, with Eiluned Rees, *A Nation and its Books* (1998).

Wallace Kirsop is Honorary Professorial Fellow in French Studies at Monash University and General Editor of *A History of the Book in Australia* (to appear in three volumes from 2001 to 2003).

Barry McKay, an antiquarian bookseller who specializes in bibliography and the art and history of the book, has been engaged in research on the book trade in Cumbria and into chapbooks. He is joint editor of the *Print Network* series.

Lisa Peters was the British Book Trade Seminar Fellow for 2000, and is a Research Student in the Department of Information & Library Studies at the University of Wales Aberystwyth, studying Wrexham newspapers from 1848 to 1914. She has degrees from the Universities of Surrey and Wales, and previously worked in the National Library of Wales, Aberystwyth.

Janet Phipps began work at the Times Bookshop in 1952, before moving to the Trade Counter of a lawbook supplier. She has been an editorial assistant on several technical journals, and has worked for foreign and oriental printers. She became a school librarian, and gained a degree. Since retirement one of her voluntary jobs is to sort and price books for the Samaritans' secondhand bookshop.

Michael Powell is Librarian of Chetham's Library, Manchester. He has published on the local history and bibliography of Manchester and its region, and is surrently carrying out research on collectors and owners of books in the Northwest.

Sydney J Shep is Research Fellow and Printer at Wai-te-ata Press, Victoria University of Wellington. Dr Shep recently received a three-year Marsden grant from the Royal Society of New Zealand to investigate the history of colonial paper and papermaking in New Zealand, and continues to research topics in the history of the book and visual culture.

Richard B Sher, Distinguished Professor of History at New Jersey Institute of Technology in Newark, New Jersey, USA, is completing a study of the role of the book trade in the Scottish Enlightenment.

Jeffrey Smith, a graduate of the Universities of Newcastle upon Tyne and Northumbria at Newcastle, was awarded his PhD for his research 'James Losh: his ideas in relation to his circle and his time'. His biography *James Losh: Man of Ideas* is in press with Northern Universities Press. He is currently working on 'The River People', a biography of Geordies over 2000 years, and 'The Eye of the North: Cultural life in Georgian Newcastle'.

Terry Wyke, Senior Lecturer in Economic History at Manchester Metropolitan University, has published widely on the history of Manchester, including recent papers on venereal disease in eighteenth-century Manchester, and on Mrs Gaskell's *Mary Barton*. He is at present working on an account of sculpture in Greater Manchester for the Public Monuments and Sculpture Association Recording Project.

Editorial

Ave atque vale or 'meat and potatoes'

IN HIS EARLY STUDY of the English provincial book trade John Feather sums up his view of the situation in these words: 'The provincial printers... were left with little more than the scraps from the London table',[1] which many of us working in the field accepted without question. In consequence I and most of my fellow hewers of wood and drawers of water presented the results of our work apologetically and with blushes; we were helots working in the wilderness – or so we thought.

However, in April 1980 at the invitation of John Horden, at that time Director of the University of Leeds Institute of Bibliography and Textual Criticism, a Seminar on provincial printing (at that time perhaps the central interest of provincial book-trade studies) was held in Leeds. This half-day function was attended by some thirty workers in the field, and by bringing them together was catalytic in stimulating and encouraging more 'organized' provincial studies, which had been going on sporadically for a century or more. After a hiccupy start this Seminar is now an annual three-day affair attracting participants from overseas as well as from all parts of the UK. The value of our efforts was recognized when Robert Cross, of St Paul's Bibliographies, himself a distinguished bibliographer, started to publish the Seminar proceedings in the annual volumes of the *Print Networks* series.[2]

In 1965 a few librarians, bibliographers, both professional and amateur, and booksellers in the Northeast of England formed a research group *The History of the Book Trade in the North.*[3] Our original aim was to compile an authoritative bibliography of the region's publications, but we soon saw that this was both too narrow and years out of date. We extended our horizons, giving a very catholic definition to 'book trade'. In the last thirty-five years we have put out more than a hundred Working and Miscellaneous Papers, including several substantial books.[4]

The 'pantechnicon' title for our studies, 'book trade', has had the unfortunate consequence that the production and distribution of *books* has been overemphasized, with the result that, in the published literature, the metropolis overshadows the richness of the provincial trade. In a later article John Feather wrote[5] 'The first and central point is a very simple one: the country trade was distributive rather than productive, despite the fact that some books were indeed produced' (I had to resist the impulse to italicize this last putting-down phrase!).[6] The London publisher could not have flourished without the distribution network provided by the provincial book trade, but only the largest country bookseller could have survived on the sale of books alone. Jobbing printing, newspaper printing, publishing and distribution – the local newspaper-distribution networks were of great importance to the London trade – the production and sale of sermons and chapbooks, the sale of nostrums, and the production of 'some books... indeed' were essential to his existence. An extra-metropolitan view suggests that the provincial trade was more important to London publishers than the latter were to the provinces; and some illuminating, but perhaps too cursory, analyses based on the *English Short-Title Catalogue* confirm this.[7]

Many early provincial studies, arising from the author's pride in his region, resulted in the compilation of bibliographies listing publications *about* the region rather than of work published *in* that region. Somewhat later research to redress the balance has led to the criticism of provincial book-trade studies as being too concerned with enumeration.[8] Whatever the truth of this criticism the 'enumerators' have provided the straw for the bricks for such massive constructions as *The History of the Book in Britain* (duly capitalized). And many of us will recall reading polysyllabic theoretical historical analyses, which appeared like a pyramid balanced on its point, which was the tiny amount of solid information from which the generalizations had been drawn.

Until fairly recently many, perhaps most, book-trade studies, provincial and metropolitan, were, in a sense, extensions of analytical bibliography, dealing with the book as a physical object. But books are more than objects; they are written by people, produced by people, distributed by people, bought by people, and possibly read by people. Book historians now more generally accept the underlying tenor of Richard Sher's contribution to our Sixteenth Seminar:[9]

> I want to focus here on the importance of going beyond the bibliographical record whenever the sources permit. As much as bibliography, in the broadest sense of that term, can tell us about the making, selling, and collecting of books, and as vital as it is for that reason, it is constrained by its inability, except in rare instances, to humanize the study of book history. By this I mean showing how stories about books are also stories about authors, readers, and members of the book trade, seen as flesh-and-blood individuals with their own interests, aspirations, motives, strengths, and weaknesses.

This theme – the human face of the book trade – is taken up by several of the contributors to this volume. First and foremost Richard Sher's splendidly cast account of Andrew Millar shows how family background and beliefs led almost ineluctably to his becoming a bookseller, and a very successful one at that. Maureen Bell, likewise, shines a spotlight on a Derbyshire yeoman and his book-buying peregrinations; here is a recognizable person with his particular interests. Sydney Shep paints a fascinating picture of a devoted missionary printer, translated to the Antipodes, compelled to improvise for lack of materials that a metropolitan printer would have regarded as essential. In my paper I describe the relationships among artists, engravers, publishers, printers and commentators in the production of a single work, *The Landscape Illustrations of the Bible* – relationships too often causing the kind of friction that we can all recognize in our own lives. Although Iain Beavan is giving an account of Scottish booksellers' societies, he never loses sight of John Joseph Griffin, a bonny fighter against coercion. Michael Powell and Terry Wyke, who have previously held up to our gaze the penurious secondhand bookseller of Manchester, James Weatherley,[10] now analyse his account book of the 1830s and show how financially fragile his business was, not helped by his drinking. This, the authors' third paper at these Seminars, continues to give readers a picture of the 'underbelly' of the Manchester book trade. These papers all depend on the use of archives, surely quite essential if we are to have a chance to glimpse the 'human face'. Wallace Kirsop describes the successful career of the Dubliner Samuel Mullen and how he built a great business for the book-hungry people of metropolitan Melbourne; for lack of archival material Dr Kirsop has imaginatively used newspaper advertisements and catalogues. These papers came over to those of us who were able to be at the Eighteenth Seminar with a sense of immediacy, which is retained in these published accounts.

Jeffrey Smith introduced the Seminar, meeting as it was in Newcastle upon Tyne, to four notables from the late eighteenth and early nineteenth century, to give colour to that town's cultural context; each, in his own way, was a contributor to or beneficiary of the book trade. In Janet Phipps's lively paper the 'human face' was that of the author herself; having begun work at the Times Bookshop in 1952 Janet Phipps had a firsthand association with books and readers which she brought to bear on an exploration of book availability in Ipswich, her present home town.

John Hinks, historian of the book trade in Leicester, took us back to the trade's earliest years in that town before the development of printing. Philip Henry Jones continued his study of Welsh-language publishing, demonstrating from the records how difficult it was to carry on such work in the First World War, with its shortages of material and, perhaps even more important, of skilled labour. It would be of interest to know how other small publishers fared in the war, but the demand for waste paper too often caused the destruction of the very records we need for such study.

Even today with other sources of news,- radio, television and internet -, newspapers still have a vital role to play. Diana Dixon describes how newspapers came to the new town of Middlesbrough in the nineteenth century. As today's politicians know well, the opinions formed by newspapers are important to them, but, as Lisa Peters, the Seminar Fellow for 2000, shows in her article on the *Wrexham Guardian*, politics alone, even supported by political subvention, is not enough to keep a paper going.

Children (and semi-literate adults) were served by simple guides to reading and spelling,[11] catechisms, chapbooks and similar slight works. Although some metropolitan publishers, eg the Newberys, put out such material in very large numbers, their low cost often called for their production closer to their market, and many provincial printer/publishers produced great quantities. Much use in careless hands has resulted in their present great rarity, so that it is not easy to study them as they deserve – another 'blank' for the provincial book trade. David Hounslow, in his paper which gave us the title for this volume, examines in detail the transmission and transmogrification of the images in children's books on London street cries. Barry McKay describes a lottery book which he bought a few years ago, and goes on to discuss the use of playthings as tools for learning, a concept clearly in the mind of provincial publishers of battledores and simple spelling books.

There is still a very great deal to do to get a full picture of the provincial book trade. One of our main sources is the local Directory and similar material, but this will list only the master. In turn this produces two kinds of blank: it omits journeymen and apprentices, and, more importantly, it almost always fails to show the vital role played by women. The position of married women as *feme covert* meant that they had a legal status indistinguishable from that of their husband. But often, probably usually, the wife played an essential part in her husband's business. This is exemplified by a Newcastle mother and daughter: Anne Fisher (Mrs Thomas Slack) and her daughter, Sarah Hodgson. Anne Fisher not only wrote important teaching books, she also ran Thomas's printing/publishing business while he was away, and produced her own annual *Ladies' Memorandum Book*. Sarah Hodgson was perhaps even more important; Bewick described her husband Solomon as dissipated, and Sarah was the backbone of the business, developing it successfully after his early death.[12] Some fifteen years ago I started to compile the *British Book Trade Index* to collect in a computer database simple biographical information about all members of the book trade; it is to be hoped that this can be made widely available and so help to throw light on these lacunae.[13]

It comes over clearly from these Seminars that students of the book trade, originally a small band of amateurs but now more numerous and certainly more 'professional', get much pleasure (is it too trivial to call it 'fun'?) from their studies, and have, as I indicated earlier, made major contributions to larger work. In particular, historians of the provincial trade are slowly demonstrating the untruth of the unspoken belief that everything memorable in the book trade happens in the 'golden triangle' of London, Oxford and Cambridge. But our sources are commonly less accessible and we depend for success on luck, serendipity and, especially, good friends. There is a freemasonry among book historians outside the metropolis. This was well put by Trevor Howard-Hill in his percipient 1993 lecture 'After the war, with its social leveling, it became possible for people to come out of the provincial closet… and to admit [he should, perhaps, have said 'claim'] that many people of worth had come from outside the established centers of influence'.[14] Already, indeed, we have shown that John Feather's 'scraps from the London table' are indeed 'meat and potatoes'[15] – a substantial meal.

This is the fifth volume in the *Print Networks* series (sixth including the precursor *Six Centuries of the Book Trade in Britain* of 1990) of which I have been the first-named editor and compositor, and, being ten years over the biblical span, it seems timely to hand over the editorial blue pencil to my very good friend and generous supporter, Barry McKay. I have greatly enjoyed my five-year stint, and thank both my fellow-editor and all the friendly authors, who have contributed so much to *Print Networks*. I look forward to being able to make some small input to future volumes.

Wylam

Peter Isaac
January 2001

NOTES

1. John Feather, *The Provincial Book Trade in Eighteenth-Century England* (Cambridge: Cambridge University Press, 1985), 120.

2. The proceedings of the Eighth Seminar, held in Durham in July 1990, had earlier been published by St Paul's Bibliographies, Winchester, in 1990, edited by Peter Isaac, under the title *Six Centuries of the Provincial Book Trade in Britain.*

3. J C Day & W M Watson, 'History of the Book Trade in the North: the first twenty-five years', Isaac, *Six Centuries*, 187–97.

4. I briefly discuss this work in 'The English provincial book trade: a Northern mosaic', *Papers of the Bibliographical Society of America* (in press).

5. John Feather, 'The country book trade', in [ed] Robin Myers & Michael Harris, *Spreading the Word: The Distribution Networks of Print 1550–1850* (Winchester: St Paul's Bibliographies, 1990), 165–83 (165).

6. Without leaving the North several notable works immediately come to mind: the many editions of Anne Fisher's *A New Grammar* and *The Pleasing Instructor*, printed and published by her husband, the Newcastle printer Thomas Slack, from 1750 onwards; the first complete Bible in Manx printed and published by John Ware in Whitehaven in 1775; the first book to be printed in Arabic outside London and the university towns of Oxford and Cambridge, the Revd Edward Moises, *The Persian Interpreter*, printed and published by Solomon Hodgson in Newcastle in 1792; and Thomas Bewick's *A General History of Quadrupeds* (1st edn, 1790) and *A History of British Birds* (1st edn, 1804/5).

7. Such analyses are not assisted by the regrettable *ESTC* rule which limits the number of names shown in imprints.

8. See, for example, F W Ratcliffe, 'The contribution of book-trade studies to scholarship', Isaac, *Six Centuries*, 1–11.

9. Richard B Sher, 'William Buchan's *Domestic Medicine*: laying book history open', in [ed] Peter Isaac & Barry McKay, *The Human Face of the Book Trade: Print Culture and its Creators* (Winchester: St Paul's Bibliographies; New Castle, DE: Oak Knoll Press, 1999), 45–64 (46).

10. Michael Powell & Terry Wyke, 'Penny capitalism in the Manchester book trade: the case of James Weatherley', in [ed] Peter Isaac & Barry McKay, *The Reach of Print: Making, Selling and Using Books* (Winchester: St Paul's Bibliographies; New Castle, DE: Oak Knoll Press. 1998), 135–56.

11. For example, William Markham's *An Introduction to Spelling and Reading English*, first published in 1728, and still being put out in the provinces a century later.

12. For a fuller account of this redoubtable pair see Isaac 'English provincial book trade'.

13. For a description see Peter Isaac, 'The British Book Trade Index', *The Local Historian*, 24.2 (May 1994), 102–11.

14. T H Howard-Hill, *Getting a Grip on the Book in Britain* (Center for the History of the Book, Pennsylvania State University, 1993).

15. I am grateful to Warren McDougall for this colourful phrase.

Books and Culture in Late Eighteenth- and Early Nineteenth-Century Newcastle

JEFFREY SMITH

NEWCASTLE UPON TYNE, where this Seminar is being held, has long been an important publishing and cultural centre. This paper is intended to put this in context through an account of four notables of the period, who were involved in the cultural life of the city. They are a composer and writer, Charles Avison; a writer, publisher and political activist, the Revd James Murray; an artist, engraver and publisher, Thomas Bewick; and a book collector, diarist, and literary critic, James Losh. I could have added more, or made a different selection; the city had a rich crop of cultural personalities at that time.

In my chosen period, Newcastle was bustling. It was home to a range of Dissenters – Presbyterians of various sorts, Baptists, Methodists, and Quakers – who provided most of the energetic businessmen, doctors, lawyers, and industrialists who led the community. They built schools, hospitals, banks, and turned the river on both sides into a hive of industry. One of their creations was the Newcastle Literary and Philosophical Society, which, following the example of Manchester, became an influential centre for the discussion of literature, science and industry. George Stephenson demonstrated his miner's lamp there, and Lord Armstrong, the gunmaker, was an influential and generous member.

Once the legal restraints on printing were relaxed, this small town of some 26 000 people found a profitable home for over sixty printers, publishers, and booksellers – almost a hotbed, you might say, of intellectual activity.

It was far enough from London to dance to its own tune, but not so far as to ignore what was fashionable in the metropolis. By 1780 it had four newspapers – *Newcastle Chronicle, Newcastle Journal, Newcastle Weekly Chronicle* and *Newcastle Courant* – and from time to time it also produced magazines like the *Newcastle Magazine*, which were avidly read. The London papers came by stagecoach. James Losh (whom we shall meet later) noted in his diary when they were delayed because of bad weather[1] – not one of our better attributes!

Among the printers, publishers and booksellers you will recognise the names of Robert Akenhead, Joseph Barber, Ralph Beilby, William Charnley and John Bell among the most prominent. Most of them combined the printing business with other occupations. For example John Bell was a land-surveyor, Ralph Beilby a glass painter, and Joseph Barber ran a popular lending library, as well as being a druggist, and optical-instrument maker. Their premises were often meeting places and centres of cultural conversation. Their contribution to the cultural life of the town was considerable.

CHARLES AVISON

This brings us to the first of the men of the period, through whose eyes we will experience life in Newcastle, and who exemplify cultural life in this northern town – Charles Avison. He was a composer, organist and writer on music. Born in Newcastle in 1709, he chose to spend his life there, and died in 1770. He was active in the town as an organist, teacher of music, concert promoter and composer. He is mentioned in Robert Browning's *Parleyings,*[2] and Dr Charles Burney 'owned' that Avison was the first and almost the only writer to connect aesthetic ideas with music.[3] *An Essay on Musical Expression* was first published in 1752.[4] It was sufficiently popular to prompt a second 'enlarged' edition in the following year. It was advertised in the *Newcastle Journal* together with a concert of music.[5] The idea of offering books or music at concerts is obviously not just a modern 'pop'-music merchandising ploy! Oddly enough, considering the number of printers locally, this 'enlarged' edition was printed in London.

Avison's compositional output was small, but widely played during his lifetime. His ensemble pieces needed a group of a dozen or fifteen performers and were best played in a large room rather than a hall. They were on a much smaller scale than many of the pieces commonly performed by other composers of the time. St Nicholas's Church – now a cathedral – was considered to be one of the most spacious parish churches in the country, and Avison's appointment there made him the leading musician in the district.[6]

This appointment would no doubt improve his income from teaching music, as this advertisement in the *Newcastle Courant* suggests[7]

> Mr Avison begs to acquaint his friends that Mondays and Fridays are set apart for his teaching in Newcastle... he proposes to attend young ladies on the harpsichord between the hours of nine and one in the forenoon: and from two to six in the evening he will teach the violin and German flute: and where all his scholars may be assured of

> every assistance in his power to serve them. The terms are half-a-guinea per month (or eight lessons) and one guinea Entrance.

Avison also took apprentices; an advertisement in the same paper warned anyone 'be it at anyone's peril to receive or entertain him', after the said George Williams absconded.[8] The road to being an organist might not have been a happy one.

JAMES MURRAY

The next 'bookman' of our selection, is a man of a very different stamp. The Revd James Murray was a Scottish Congregationalist minister of a very independent and politically radical cast of mind, who achieved a popularity in Newcastle with its inhabitants that says much in a time when Scotsmen were not the flavour of the month. He came to Newcastle in 1760, only fifteen years after the '45 rebellion, and at the invitation of a group of Presbyterian Dissenters.

Educated at Edinburgh University, Murray had been appreciated by the congregation of a church in Alnwick for his pronounced anti-presbytery views, so much so that when his unsympathetic senior minister cast him out, he found a ready home south. He was soon to become the local leader of men of anti-establishment views, and to become the mentor of Thomas Spence, whose agrarian ideas were to impress Marx.

Professor Ashraf in her book on Spence describes Murray:[9]

> His success was spectacular. Sermons and weekday lectures announced in a newspaper drew packed audiences. High Bridge [his church] achieved a reputation for advanced opinion.

Murray was the author of many works, seeking to increase his £50 ministerial fee by this means, and by teaching. Most of his titles reflects his desire to spread his dissenting views; titles such as *The Freeman's Magazine, Protestant Package, Questions to the Philosophical Society, Sermons to Asses, A Grave answer to Mr. Wesley's Calm Address to our American Colonies* and *An Impartial History of the War in America.*[10] The major political crisis that stirred the mid- to late-eighteenth century was reflected in the Northeast, and in it Murray found ample scope for his intellectual and radical talents.

People who knew him, including Thomas Bewick, described Murray as 'playful' or 'facetious' in company, but in deadly earnest in defence of principle. The two moods mixed in his sermons – clowning, even reference to ladies' legs at one minute, and grim admonition on the next. The Bible story in his hands was history not mystery, and mostly about sinful people. Murray made them living types, added entertaining detail, justified ridicule and laughter in service of truth. Simple language and matter-of-factness corresponded to his crusade against hypocritical piety and 'enthusiasm'.

Murray's portrait shows a long, bony, serious face with a large nose. His voice was said to be harsh, his gestures wild and clumsy, and whilst he sermonised he continually took snuff which fell in showers on his gown and audience. Sneezing was followed by laughter, for it is not to be supposed that suppressed sniggers would have been the right response. Welford, who lived nearer his time, described him as

> a man of middle size and well-proportioned, his air firm and erect, and his expression commanding. He possessed solidity of judgement, depth of thinking, and brilliancy of wit. His satire was not like the keen, polished, and poisoned shafts of Junius, shot secretly in the dark – no! his dart was naked and barbed. He was a dauntless champion of liberty, and fearlessly set at defiance the frowns of power.[11]

Murray was involved in the Town-Moor affair – another eighteenth-century Newcastle fracas. Thomas Spence said that it had been a lesson which he never forgot.[12] Conflict between the Mayor and Aldermen (the Common Council) and the body of middling and lesser freemen and artisans went back to Tudor times. The Mayor had long ceased to be elected and 'nowhere had the oligarchical government by a select body been more completely established than at Newcastle'.[13] Embezzlement long continued to be an open scandal, often at the expense of charitable foundations. In 1771, 89 acres of the Town Moor were illegally advertised and eventually let for cultivation on easy terms with additional privileges of tenancy. The legal action that Murray instigated caused the Common Council a humiliating climb-down.

The dust was hardly settled when Murray again had Newcastle society reading his every word – the General Election of 1774. Junius's invective was tame compared with Murray's merciless exposure of the public and private records of the members for Newcastle in his two publications *The Contest,* which he wrote himself, and *The Freeman's Magazine,* which he edited. Awakening political consciousness was reflected in the rise of patriotic clubs. Murray, a non-voter of course, had already been involved in the warnings to the public published in London newspapers repudiating the actions of the members for Newcastle on the issues of arbitrary power. The wording of the Pledge presented by the burgesses to the Parliamentary candidates has always been attributed to him.[14]

The Burgesses' programme as put forward in their Instructions, Petition and election pledges, begins with the right to mandate MPs and the absolute right of constituents to recall them 'if they do not behave as they ought'.[15] The immediate aim was to replace 'men of such dubious characters' as the present representatives. The elected members must be forced to obtain the repeal of 'laws contrary to liberty'. The pledge was for the support of shorter Parliaments and a 'more equitable representation of the people', and in the first place the immediate enfranchisement of 'the whole body of Newcastle freeholders'. It reflected the growth of a new middle class owning property in the town.

The spirit of the petition may be guessed from the shock to Sir Walter Blackett, frequently Lord Mayor and resident MP. His biographer connects the incident with the marked decline in his popularity and calls it a particularly painful exhibition of 'ingratitude' among recent humiliations which preyed on his mind and hastened his end.[16] The sharpest criticism came from Murray who exposed his whole political record – his support for unpopular measures in the House, election rigging, monopolizing the representation of the town, misuse of public funds, and finally his true character displayed in scheming to rob the freemen of their last rights, down to the grass for the widow's cow.

In our last look at Murray it is illuminating to consider his three-volume history *An Impartial History of the Present War in America,* originally in parts by subscription and printed locally.[17] Whilst quick to acknowledge his subjection to his sovereign, he is not uncritical of the King's part in the disastrous breach with the colonists, though some of this he attributes to 'secret influence', by implication Lord Bute, his unpopular Scottish adviser. His sympathy was wholly with the Americans, a position that was largely opposite to national feeling that the Americans were not sovereign and should be taxed by the British Parliament.

Stern and dreaded as Murray was when defending civil or religious liberty, he was of a most cheerful disposition, kindly and charitable – as these two anecdotes of the time show:[18]

> As he was coming from Alnwick to Newcastle on a rainy day, he overtook a poor man who had no coat. Happening to have two on at the time, Mr. Murray took one off and put it on the poor man's back, with the observation that 'it was a pity he should have two coats on and the man none, indeed it was not fair'.
>
> A Scotch drover came into his chapel rather late one Sunday, and leaning on the edge of the pew, stood contented and listening to the sermon. Mr. Murray caused a pew to be opened to him, exclaiming at the same time 'if that man had had a powdered head and a fine coat on his back, you would have thrown open twenty pews to receive him'.

I'm still puzzled why Murray was wearing two coats!

THOMAS BEWICK

Thomas Bewick needs no introduction – I merely claim him as our own. As singular in his own way as Murray and Avison, Bewick straddles the eighteenth and nineteenth centuries, and his stride is a big one.

An uncompromisingly local man, he was born in August 1753 to a farmer at Cherryburn, near Eltringham, who also leased the Mickley-Bank colliery. Newcastle was where Bewick was to go to learn and practise the arts and crafts that were to make him famous.

He began early to demonstrate his artistic talents, drawing on the edges of his slate, and decorating the gravestones of the church and the walls of the houses of his neighbours. His grandmother left him twenty pounds for an apprenticeship and in 1757 he was bound to Ralph Beilby of the famous Beilby family of glass-painters. Bewick records that 'I liked my master, I liked the business'.[19] He was glad he did not have to leave the countryside and the beauties he loved.

In 1768, Dr Charles Hutton, the mathematician, employed Ralph Beibly to execute the diagrams for the first edition of his work on mensuration. Hutton procured the boxwood from London, with the tools for cutting the diagrams, and instructed Beilby and Bewick how to cut and square the blocks, and to cut and engrave lines upon them. 'Thus then', observes Hutton, 'I was the instructor of the very ingenious Mr. Bewick in this branch of engraving, which he has carried to such a high state of perfection'.[20] On the completion of this job, young Bewick addressed himself with uncommon ardour and perseverence to the task of obtaining a complete insight into and mastery of the art of wood-engraving.

The first book with pictorial woodcuts by Berwick entitled *The Youth's Instructor and Entertaining Story-Teller* was published by Thomas Saint in 1774. Many of the cuts in this work are beautiful, and testify to the advance the young artist had already made in his profession. 'The first of October 1774 arrived at last, and, for the first time in my life', he commented,'I felt myself at liberty'.[21] His servitude was ended and he became his own master. In 1775 a cut of the *Huntsman and Old Hound* was considered so meritorious that Beilby submitted it to the Society for the Promotion of the Fine Arts. Bewick was offered the choice between a gold medal or seven guineas; he chose the latter and gave them to his mother.

In 1776 he set off for London, and during the nine months he spent there he was plentifully employed, but he found the habits of the metropolis too much for his simple tastes, and he missed his beloved countryside. He said he would rather 'enlist for a soldier or go herd sheep at five shillings per week as long as he lived, than be tied to live in it'.[22] Bewick returned home and entered into partnership with Beilby, and his brother John Bewick was taken on as an apprentice.

By 1784 Bewick had improved his drawing and acquired a greater freedom in the use of his tools. A volume of *Select Fables* produced by Saint's Press can be fairly compared with the best of the cuts in his last work *Fables of Aesop.*[23] On Tuesday 15 November 1785 Bewick began to engrave the first wood blocks for his *History of Quadrupeds* with the figure of a dromedary. He began to embody his famous vignettes at the foot of some of the pages. Their bitter and often humorous social commentary are one of the marks of his work. On page 403 of the *Quadrupeds* (eg 5th edn, 1807) is the drawing of an unfortunate man who had been incarcerated in the prison of the Old Castle for thirty years for debt. In his *Memoir* Bewick recounts the origin of this volume:[24]

> Having from the time that I was a schoolboy been displeased with the figures in children's books... and having very often turned the matter over in my mind of making improvements... I at last came to a determination of making the attempt.
> On this occasion, being little acquainted with the nature of such undertakings, we consulted Mr. Solomon Hodgson, bookseller and editor of the *Newcastle Chronicle*... he warmly encouraged us to proceed... I began the business of cutting the blocks with the figure of a dromedary... my father died the same day. While I was busied in drawing and cutting the figures of animals, and also in designing and engraving the vignettes, Mr Beilby, being of a bookish or reading turn, proposed, in his evenings at home, to write or compile the descriptions... The greater part of the woodcuts were drawn and engraved at night, after the day's work of the shop was over.

The book was advertised on a handbill, with specimens of the illustrations.

In 1789 Bewick was commissioned by Marmaduke Tunstall Esq. of Wycliffe-on-the-Tees to engrave a drawing of the Chillingham Wild Bull. Bewick always considered it his masterpiece. Impressions of the Bull on parchment are a rarity. By this time Bewick was a master at engraving on wood.

From a letter of 8 August 1791 from Thomas Bewick to his wife[25] we learn that a *History of Birds* to correspond with the *Quadrupeds* was at that early period well known in London.

The dissolution of his partnership with Beilby was, as might be expected considering Bewick's prominence, a subject of discussion in the family immediately after the publication of that work. Bewick was involved in a fine edition of the poems of Goldsmith and Parnell, published by William Bulmer in London in 1795. The selection of the illustrations consisted of *The Traveller, The Deserted Village* and *The Hermit*. The excellence of the typography, printing and paper was only exceeded by the extraordinary beauty and novelty of the illustrations.[26] In it are combined the talents of the two brothers, together with the talents of Robert Johnson and his cousin John.[27] In 1797, the first volume of Bewick's great work the *History of British Birds* became an immediate popular success, and today is still regarded as a masterpiece.

JAMES LOSH

And so to the last of our quartet, James Losh. Born in 1763 to a Cumberland landed family, a Cambridge graduate, he became a barrister, Recorder of Newcastle, but more importantly from this point of view he was a compulsive diarist, a great reader of classical and modern literature and a book collector. After his death in 1833, the following notice appeared in the *Newcastle Chronicle*, Saturday 15 March 1834:

> On the third of March, 1834, and the following four days an event occurred in Newcastle upon Tyne the like of which it had never seen before, and was never likely to see again. The sale in Small's salerooms of a private library of books of the late Mr. James Losh of The Grove, Jesmond. The sale was spread over five days. Even a cursory glance at the items in the printed catalogue is sufficient to indicate that this was no ordinary bibliophile's collection: the variety and range of subjects are unusual.

The sale and the catalogue were the responsibility of Emerson Charnley, bookseller.

Losh came to Newcastle in 1799, where his brothers William and George were already in business. William at that time owned the Walker Ironsworks which was to employ George Stephenson of railway fame as foreman. His name appeared on railway patents alongside his more famous employee. Losh came with his wife to set up as a barrister, having been employed on the Northern Circuit briefly in 1784. He was a close friend of the Lakeland poets William Wordsworth, Samuel Taylor Coleridge and Robert Southey. When he came north from the Bristol area he had spent several years in their company, at their most creative time. In early 1798 Wordworth, his sister and Coleridge were about to embark on their well-documented trip to Germany. They were anxious to have Losh accompany them:[28]

> 11 March 1798
>
> Coleridge is now writing at the same table. I need not say how ardently he joins me in this wish, and how deeply interested he is in everything relating you. We have a delightful scheme in agitation, which is rendered still more delightful by a probability which cannot exclude from my mind that you may be induced to join in the party – I am dear Losh you affectionate friend. W. Wordsworth.

Losh was not able to join the expedition, but this friendship was to last for the rest of his life.

His religious commitment did not prevent him from joining his contemporaries in the many social occasions that made up the life of the middle and professional class of his time. Early in his new life he writes:

> 3 August 1801
>
> Ball in the evening. The room full of genteel-looking well-dressed people. Some but not many handsome women. I had a pleasant evening...

Losh very quickly became a member of the Newcastle Literary and Philosophical Society, and then for thirty years its vice-chairman, often chairing its meetings and using his developing gifts as an arbitrator to preserve its frequently-challenged smooth running. At the time when he was struggling to set up a law practice he yet found time to pursue charitable ventures:

> 21 December 1800
>
> Charity school.
>
> 25 June 1801
>
> At infirmary. I spoke several times on things proposed at the meeting. Meeting at the Soup kitchen.

Losh thought the law savage in its treatment of debtors and bankrupts. He was both compassionate in his frequent dealings with them, and fearful of a similar fate himself. As his family increased – he had eight surviving children – it was a constant struggle to maintain a genteel standard of life. Yet – and another credit to his integrity – he never used his access to the high and the mighty for his own benefit. His relationship with people like Earl Grey, Henry Brougham in politics, and a similar selection of eminent men in law, was close and his reputation high.

As the leader of the regional Whigs, Losh was heavily involved in local and national politics, and frequently acted as a conduit of local opinion to people like Grey when the latter was Prime Minister. His advice was sought and he gave it freely, well aware that as a Unitarian he could not seek political appointment until the repeal of the Test and Corporation Acts. As an active member of the Unitarian community he aided his minister the Revd William Turner in many excellent schemes for the education of the young. In 1810, he took a leading part in the establishment of the Jubilee Schools, and other infant schools.

18 December 1809

I attended a meeting today for the purpose of establishing schools in the Lancaster or Bell's plan. A committee was appointed with the powers to build and regulate the schools for one year after its completion... Schools of this description I consider of the first importance to the morals and happiness of the poor, and I trust no circumstances will prevent me from forwarding most zealously their establishment and support.

Losh's days were not all law practice and good works, however. His diaries are witness to the number of dinners, balls, theatre visits, excursions, and private dinner parties he went to. Typical are the following:

24 June 1802

Play at night; *Jane Shore.* This is a poor play, but Mrs Siddons played the part of Shore admirably. Young Siddons was not good as Hastings. In my opinion he will never make a fine actor.

19 July 1821

Coronation fete. Dinner with 150 at Mansion House. A splendid entertainment. Turkey, venison, old hock, champagne. Two oxen roasted whole, three parts ale, and one part port wine. The beef was spoiled in the roasting, and almost wholly spoiled by the clumsy manner in which it was distributed. The 'mob' did not do any serious mischief, but the great majority were obviously malcontents. They either laughed at the whole business or felt indignant at the idle expense that was incurred by the Corporation, without contributing to their amusement or comfort.

After the battle of Trafalgar and the death of Nelson, a ball and supper were held in Newcastle to honour the naval victories and the newly created Lord Collingwood, who was born in Newcastle, and whose family lived in Morpeth.

We close our consideration of the culture of Newcastle, having looked at Avison the composer and musician, Murray the writer and political activist, Bewick the artist and engraver, and Losh the social leader and diarist with an entry that sums up the independent provincial attitude to the visit of a national figure to a northern town proud of itself and its radical politics:

28 September 1827

This day was mainly spent in observing (and in some degree participating in) the means adopted for receiving the Duke of Wellington with due honours. The *Great Captain* is a most consumate general, I think no person can reasonably doubt that, and that he has a powerful claim upon the gratitude of the nations seems equally clear. But when we consider it is now 13 years since his last great victory was obtained and that he has the character of being a cold and profligate man, that he has no splendid talents as a statesman or an orator, and that he has attached himself to what is justly called a narrow-minded and illiberal party in this country, we shall not wonder that he was received by the people of Newcastle (to say the least of it) without anything like enthusiasm.

CONCLUSION

My paper ends with a question: what was it about Newcastle that held these 'bookmen' in thrall? Avison resisted the London that would bring J C Bach and Mozart to it; Bewick worked successfully in London for a short time and returned home for the rest of his life; Murray, came down from Edinburgh and did not follow his pupil Thomas Spence to the capital; and Losh, who knew the elite of London's intellectual society, was always glad to come home; and included among them the author of this paper who has lived here nearly seventy years. One answer, at least, is that Newcastle was far enough from London to be an important cultural and publishing centre, proud of its achievements and independence.

NOTES

The rather crude sketches are reproduced (somewhat reduced in size) from Richard Welford, *Men of Mark 'Twixt Tyne and Tweed*, 3 vols (Newcastle: Walter Scott, 1895): Avison 1, 156; Bewick 1, 265; Losh 3, 84; & Murray 3, 214.

1. Diaries of James Losh (Carlisle Public Library).
2. P M Horsley, 'Charles Avison: the man and his milieu', *Music and Letters* (Jan 1974), 6.
3. Charles Burney, *A General History of Music* (London, 1789), 7; and Horsley, 'Avison', 22.
4. Ruth Sansbury, *Charles Avison: an Essay in Musical Expression* (unpublished MA thesis, University of Northumbria at Newcastle, 1995), 1.
5. *Newcastle Journal*, 11 August 1752.
6. Arthur Milner, 'Charles Avison', *Musical Times*, 95 (1954), 28.
7. *Newcastle Courant*, 16 April 1734.
8. *Newcastle Courant*, 17 February 1738.
9. P M Ashraf, *The Life and Times of Thomas Spence* (Newcastle, 1983), 17–19.
10. James Murray, *The Freeman's Magazine* (Newcastle, 1774); *Protestant Package* (Newcastle, 1778); *Questions to the Philosophical Society* (Newcastle, 1775); *Sermons to Asses* (London, 1771); *A Grave Answer to Mr. Wesley's Calm Address to our American Colonies* (Newcastle, 1777); *An Impartial History of the Present War in America*, 2 vol (Newcastle, 1778/1781).
11. Richard Welford, *Men of Mark 'Twixt Tyne and Tweed* (Newcastle, 1895), 3, 217.
12. Thomas Spence, *The Restorer of Society to its Natural State* (London, 1807), 27.
13. T F Gibson, *The Borough History of Newcastle upon Tyne* (Newcastle, 1875), 41, 43–4.
14. Ashraf, *Spence*, 38.
15. Ashraf, *Spence*, 38.
16. Ashraf, *Spence*, 37.

17. See note 10.
18. Welford, *Men of Mark*, 3, 215.
19. Thomas Bewick, *A Memoir of Thomas Bewick Written by Himself*, [ed] Iain Bain (Oxford, 1975), 36.
20. Robert Robinson, *Thomas Bewick: his Life and Times* (Newcastle, 1887), 28.
21. Robinson, *Bewick*, 45.
22. Robinson, *Bewick*, 51.
23. See Robinson, *Bewick*, 39.
24. Bewick, *Memoir*, 105–7.
25. Robinson, *Bewick*, 93.
26. Robinson, *Bewick*, 95. [Bewick's genius has never been more satisfactorily demonstrated than by Bulmer's typographical skill in this publication – *Ed.*]
27. William Andrew Chatto & John Jackson, *A Treatise on Wood Engraving* (London: Chatto & Windus, new edn, 1861), 513–4.
28. Mary Moorman, *William Wordsworth: a Biography – the Early Years 1770–1803* (Oxford, 1957), 207; see also note 1.

The First World War and Welsh-language Publishing

PHILIP HENRY JONES

FOLLOWING A PERIOD of considerable prosperity during the third quarter of the nineteenth century, Welsh-language publishing was in decline well before the outbreak of the First World War. This was partly the result of a combination of demographic and educational changes which eroded the potential readership for Welsh-language material; the 1921 census was the first to show a fall (of some 50 000) in the number of Welsh speakers. The decline was also hastened by new currents of thought, notably the spread of socialist ideas, usually through the medium of English, which were generally inimical to the largely chapel-based Welsh literary culture. There were also growing tensions within the field of Welsh literature as a younger generation of university-educated authors and scholars poured scorn upon the linguistic, literary, and critical standards of the nineteenth century. In 1922, for example, G J Williams dismissed most Welsh religious books as '*pamphlets*' and '*ephemeral works*' rather than true literature. '*Most of the books*', he maintained, '*published fifty years ago, expositions, religious biographies, essays, and sermons are rotting in cupboards, wholly forgotten*'.[1] Precisely those works that had brought a degree of prosperity to Welsh-language publishing during its golden age were now condemned out of hand.

The Welsh-language book trade was poorly placed to face a major challenge, most printer-publishers being small-scale local concerns. Of the two major publishers Gee & Son of Denbigh had lost impetus after the premature death of Howel Gee in 1903. In 1914, following a decade of indecisive family management, it was taken over by Welsh Weekly Newspapers, a company dominated by Seymour and Gomer Berry and Viscountess Rhondda. Gee thus became essentially a newspaper publishing concern. It received so little attention from its new owners throughout the war years that D S Davies, Thomas Gee's son-in-law who managed affairs in Denbigh, could write bitterly in 1918 'I am glad to hear that Mr Berry has at last taken an interest in the Baner. He has been so busy making money that he has not given a thought to this Journal however his support comes too late'.[2]

The other major firm, Hughes & Son of Wrexham, had adapted to the changing environment more successfully by exploiting the growing market for Welsh schoolbooks and consolidating its position as the leading publisher of Welsh music. It also profited from the growing popularity of drama in Wales by publishing Welsh plays and charging licence fees for their performance. Even so, Hughes found that the demand for Welsh books was decreasing well before 1914. Its response was to concentrate on reprinting proved successes and to reduce the number of new Welsh titles it published – a sure recipe for decline in the longer term.

The new problems arising during the war and in the immediate post-war years thus exacerbated long-standing difficulties. The precise nature of these problems is best documented in the archives of Hughes a'i Fab of Wrexham, which can be supplemented by material relating to the Gee-published newspaper, *Baner ac Amserau Cymru*.

Once the immediate financial panic caused by the outbreak of war had died down, there was a general expectation that the war would be a short one – the belief that 'it would be all over by Christmas'. Although it had become clear by the end of 1914 that Britain would be involved in a lengthy conflict, there was still a general belief that 'business as usual' was possible.[3] Even so, newspapers soon began to experience a decrease in advertising. The journalist Picton Davies, employed in 1914 by the Caernarfon weekly *Yr Herald Cymraeg*, recalled that '*The first blow was a shocking decrease in the advertisements of London commercial concerns, one of our main sources of finance*'.[4] Welsh publishing firms were also quick to reduce their press advertising; as early as January 1915 Hughes apologised to the Aberdare weekly *Y Darian* for not placing advertisements in it for some time and added ominously that it could not do so 'at present time owing to the war'.[5]

By the end of 1914 over a million men had joined the armed forces, and pre-war unemployment had been replaced by a shortage of labour. During 1915 and 1916, as the war made increasing demands upon a wide range of raw materials, and as manufacturers and importers began to engage in pre-emptive price increases (or in straightforward profiteering), a period of creeping inflation set in. The book trade soon began to experience unwelcome price rises. As early as August 1915 Hughes complained that Ballantyne had markedly increased its prices: before the war, Ballantyne had charged the firm £2.10*s*.0*d* for printing 500 copies of the song 'Gwlad yr Eisteddfodau' (*Land of Eisteddfods*) but was now asking £3.6*s*.0*d*.[6]

Despite a sharp increase in the cost of living, full employment and considerable overtime working limited wage demands during the early years of the war.[7] Shortly after the war, the trend of wages in printing was outlined by A L Bowley using figures based on the minimum time-rates paid to male compositors on jobbing or weekly news.[8] Before the introduction of a national scale in 1919, weekly wage rates varied considerably from 39/- in London to 25/- in Folkestone, the rate being normally related to the size of the town. Although Bowley quoted figures for a few places in Wales such as Cardiff and Swansea, these related to men employed on English-language newspapers. Precisely how much compositors in Welsh-language offices earned remains unclear. Partly because of the limited degree of unionisation (apart from at Wrexham and Caernarfon), Welsh rates were low: at the beginning of the twentieth century printers in some towns in North Wales were earning as little as 22/- to 24/- per week.[9] The following table, based on Bowley's figures for Lincoln, may be taken to represent typical small-town rates.[10] Weekly wages rose slowly to the end of 1916, but then increased rapidly so that by October 1918 they stood at over twice the 1914 figure.

Date	Wage
1914 July	30/-
1915 Nov	32/-
1916 Dec	35/-
1917 June	38/-
1917 Oct	42/-
1918 April	47/-
1918 June	51/-
1918 Oct	61/-

As well as having to pay their own workers more, firms such as Hughes which contracted work out to other concerns found that these passed on their increased costs. In June 1917, Hughes complained that 'Setting O[ld] N[otation] costs half as much again as it did'.[11] As well as increasing their prices, firms resorted to more insidious methods of offsetting increased costs. Thus after increasing their charges in October 1915, trade binders introduced charges for warehousing publishers' stocks of unbound sheets from May 1916 onwards.[12] From July 1917 onwards printers similarly charged for the storage of unbound sheets and the rental of standing type.[13] Hughes reacted to these adverse developments by terminating in the course of 1916 a relationship with Ballantyne which had begun in 1868.

The rush to volunteer and the apparently insatiable demand for labour for the munitions industry meant that Hughes was experiencing a serious shortage of hands even before the introduction of conscription for men aged between eighteen and forty-five in May 1916. In February 1916 the firm complained 'We are considerably handicapped – like most other firms – these days [by] scarcity of labour & difficulty in getting material from manufacturers'.[14] The problem was exacerbated by the attitude of the Typographical Association which was strongly opposed to 'dilution'. Although it grudgingly relaxed some rules 'as war emergency' in July 1916, it ensured that any extra work went to its members and was adamant in its refusal to accept female or unskilled labour.[15] Its refusal to allow employers to replace apprentices joining the forces further aggravated the labour shortage.[16]

Since printing was deemed to be a non-essential trade, it suffered from periodic combings-out of its workforce; thus in January 1917 all fit men up to the age of fifty-six were to be called up. By then, the number of men employed in printing had declined by almost 50%, leading to an acute labour shortage, particularly of key employees such as machine-minders and keyboard-operators.[17] Thus Hughes lost its stereotyper to the army in April 1917.[18] In July 1917 it gloomily reported 'We are in the same position as last year "too much work for the number of men now employed & others likely to go" ',[19] and by September things had worsened: 'We may say that owing to our staff having been reduced – we have only one man in our Binding Dept., not even a boy to help him – we have fallen badly in arrears with our own stock & are quite out of a good number of books'.[20] Setting music was also greatly delayed: 'Unfortunately we cannot bind ourselves to deliver at a given date as we have practically only two men on the music. One of these is called away more than half his time & should Government work come in they can demand preference'.[21] A final frantic comb-out of labour following the German offensive of March 1918 further reduced staff numbers so that in July 1918 the firm had to tell an enquirer that it could not 'undertake to do any Old Notation'.[22] Since the binding department was also facing further staffing reductions, Hughes had to inform the organizer of the National Eisteddfod Gymanfa Ganu (*Singing Festival*) that the firm needed to have the exact wording of lettering for a complimentary copy of the festival programme by return of post, 'our Finisher (who does the lettering) having had his papers to join up today'.[23]

The shortage of labour also severely delayed the completion of work contracted out to other firms. In April 1918 Hughes complained that 'we find it almost impossible to get any work through the hands of our engravers, we sent them some MSS months ago, & they cannot even now give us any promise as to when they will be able to turn them out. It takes several months for us to get <u>reprints</u> from them, this is due to their staffs being greatly reduced through the calls of the army'.[24]

The enormous scale of casualties in the First World War has tended to obscure the fact that killing the enemy was a grossly inefficient process which created a very heavy demand for metals also required by the printing industry. As a result of the demand for lead for shrapnel, a conference was called in December 1917 to secure the release of superfluous type metal and stereo plates.[25] By the end of 1916 the use of copper otherwise than for munitions was prohibited and process-engravers had to surrender old blocks and electros to secure new supplies.[26] A lively market in copper scrap developed and Hughes found it had to fend off enthusiastic enquirers, one being told in March 1917:

> Replying to yours re copper scrap – we have little if any scrap – the blocks held by us are used time after time for successive editions of books – some are ordered for customers & are passed on to them after completing the job for which they were ordered.

We may have a few perhaps that have been used in magazines from time to time & which might be used as scrap.[27]

Regulations were progressively tightened and in September 1918 Hughes stated that 'In compliance with the request of the Ministry of Munitions we a short time ago had to scrap a large number of our Plates & Blocks'.[28]

Binding materials were also in short supply and became increasingly expensive. In April 1916 Hughes informed a customer that the firm was no longer able to letter the side of books since 'Gold and other Materials have gone up so much'.[29] By July 1917 it had become so difficult to secure binding cloth that Hughes claimed 'It is impossible now to get sufficient cloth of one colour to bind all the 2000 copies'.[30] The greatest problem, however, was the supply of strawboard. By April 1917 it was scarcely to be had and its price had risen from £4.10*s*.0*d* to £35 per ton. In November the Calvinistic Methodist Bookroom was told 'As was pointed out to you by Mr Hughes when we were binding last lot of *Perorydd* Solfa, boards have advanced ten times the previous cost and difficult to get them at that price'.[31]

The shortage of strawboard reflected the major problem of the war years, securing an adequate supply of paper. Since the quantity of esparto and wood pulp imported had been greatly reduced and paper prices were soaring, the government decided early in 1916 to appoint a Royal Commission on paper. By June 1916 Heinemann had prepared a report on paper prices which claimed that 'an ordinary printing paper which could have been bought for 2½*d*. per lb. in 1915 had gone up to 5*d*. and [there was] some evidence of higher prices being asked'.[32]

The importation of esparto grass and wood pulp was progressively reduced as a consequence of the German submarine campaign (particularly following the adoption of unrestricted submarine warfare from the beginning of February 1917), the failure of the North American harvest in 1916, which led to the diversion of much shipping to transport grain from Australia, and by the need to transport United States forces to Europe following that country's entry into the war. The consequent paper shortage and price increases made 1917 a difficult year for printers. In May, Hughes informed O M Edwards that the price of paper for his children's monthly, *Cymru'r Plant*, had doubled and would soon double again.[33] Further restrictions on the supply of paper meant that 1918 was a period of acute crisis for printers. At the end of 1917 the government had announced that the quantity of paper and raw material for papermaking to be imported in 1918 for trade (rather than government use) was to be reduced from 540 000 tons to 390 000 tons.[34] In February 1918 Hughes warned a customer:

The difficulties are increasing daily – for instance we applied to three of the leading makers for a certain class of paper which a short time since any one of the firms would

> have been only too glad to quote, but this week not one of them could supply it nor could hold out no hope of being able to renew stock.[35]

In July 1918, following a further reduction in paper quotas, Hughes informed another customer that 'Paper is continually advancing in price, & owing to our being restricted by the Regulations of the Paper Commission in our purchases, we have not been able to buy a reserve stock, & consequently have to take our quota month by month at the prices prevailing at the time of delivery'.[36]

Paper rationing and successive price increases forced book publishers to live from hand to mouth; the regime made it very difficult for Welsh weekly newspapers to continue to appear. During the early months of 1918 it was necessary to double the price of *Baner ac Amserau Cymru*, whilst greatly reducing its size. From August 1918 onwards the *Baner* survived from week to week; on 10 August it sent its papermaker the desperate plea 'We are within a week of a paper famine, please send us the news that you have on order at once. We cannot publish our papers after next week unless we get a supply',[37] and on 21 September 'We have only sufficient supply for one week therefore if the paper has not been sent please send a supply at once as we cannot print after next week without it'.[38]

The increase in the newspaper's price, the reduction in its size, and the paying off of local correspondents led to a catastrophic fall in sales from 13 000 per week in 1914 to 6000 by September 1918.[39] An investigation carried out by a member of the paper's staff in 1920 revealed that 'there has been a general decrease throughout the whole of Wales. I also find that there are 90 towns and villages, representing about 1200 copies weekly where the Banner has been discontinued since 1914'.[40] The *Baner* was one of a number of Welsh weeklies permanently crippled by wartime shortages and price increases.

Like many other printers, Hughes attempted to derive some profit from the paper shortage by trading in waste paper. By June 1916 it was beginning to pulp slow-selling books, both its own titles and books it had printed for their authors. T Leyshon Rees, for example, was informed that

> as you do not take copies of [*Meysydd Cenhadol*] off our hands at anything like a reasonable rate, & as the debt is now a very old one, we propose to dispose of the copies remaining on our hands, to the best advantage, in order to reduce our loss on the a/c as much as possible. Waste paper is now in demand and commands a fairly good price, failing disposal of copies in any other way, we shall let them go as wastepaper, unless we receive definite assurance from you, that you will take copies over at a better rate.[41]

Having disposed of its own nineteenth-century records by sending over half a ton of waste ledgers to the North Wales Paper Company at Oakenholt in August 1917,[42] Hughes set about destroying the industrial records of north Wales. In September 1917 it told a baker 'What we want is Old Ledgers & a/c books' for which it would pay 10/- per cwt; old magazines (eg *Strand*) and good clean paper 5/- per cwt; third class, 2/6 per cwt.[43] These prices reflected the government order of May 1917 fixing the maximum prices at which waste paper could be sold.[44] State involvement in regulating the trade in waste paper caused Hughes some uneasiness in April 1918 when the North Wales Paper Co asked whether it held a permit. The firm replied 'We have been disposing of our Waste Paper for very many years and since the outbreak of the War have continued to do so. We have not applied for a permit therefore have none. Your Mr Alexander produced his permit as buyer therefore we took it that everything was in order'.[45] The problem was clearly overcome since in November 1918 Hughes informed an Aberdyfi tailor that it would pay 10/- per cwt for old ledgers forwarded carriage paid to Wrexham.[46] Gee similarly sold paper waste and surplus printed sheets (most of its nineteenth-century backlist) during 1917. On being offered £12 per ton for sheets by J H Leighton of Liverpool, the firm claimed to have heard that £20 was being paid for similar waste by other concerns.[47]

Hughes reacted slowly to wartime inflation but was compelled to impose a 'war charge' of 2*d* per shilling from 8 March 1916 onwards.[48] All the firm's books were made net on 19 October 1916.[49] Prices were further increased in the autumn of 1918; a 6*d* cloth book now cost 9*d*; a 1/- cloth book 1/6; a 1/6 cloth book 2/-, and so on. According to Edward Roberts, its chief clerk and traveller, the firm had been extremely reluctant to increase its prices:

> *Ever since prices began to rise, Messrs Hughes have kept before themselves as their main objective keeping the market in Welsh books alive, and* [preferred] *to suffer themselves rather than run the risk of killing the demand for books by raising prices, but the expense has become too much for them, and there has to be an increase.*[50]

The intensifying shortage of paper and labour during 1917 and 1918 compelled Hughes to turn away a considerable quantity of work. In September 1917, for example, it rejected A P Graves's offer of a revised edition of his translations of Welsh poetry since conditions were 'too unsettled' and (quite truthfully) added 'We have several MSS here which were arranged for before the war'.[51] Even the lucrative business of producing programmes for song festivals had to be curtailed. Here Hughes gave preference to established customers, but even these had to make do with briefer pamphlets than they would have wished. Wartime conditions also reduced the demand for certain types of material, notably schoolbooks, since Welsh local authorities, notoriously reluctant to purchase Welsh readers before the war,[52] further reduced their spending. In January 1919 Edward Roberts told W C Williams that the 'rigid economy of Education Committees' had adversely affected the sale of his book but hoped that the firm would now enjoy 'a good demand to make up for the "lean times" we have had in our schools Dept'.[53] The number of titles published by

Hughes fell from nine in 1914 to two in 1915, seven in 1916, and two a year in 1917, 1918, and 1919.[54] Other publishers similarly curtailed their activities; Gee even maintained that under war conditions its capital could be more profitably employed buying bonds.[55] The total number of Welsh books published each year consequently fell from eighty-three in 1914 to twenty-four in 1918.[56]

Although publishers had anticipated a rapid return to pre-1914 conditions, the immediate post-war period was, if anything, more difficult than the war years. 1919 and 1920 saw a speculative boom as a consequence of the pent-up demand for consumer goods, and the government's loose monetary policy. The Paper Controller issued a report on 'reasonable prices' in December 1918 which showed that an ordinary book-paper which might have cost 5*d* per lb in 1915 now cost 9½*d* to 11*d* per lb.[57] As part of the general rush to dismantle wartime restrictions, paper control was prematurely ended on 30 April 1919. The immediate result was that prices rose so that 'publishers were before long to pay as much as 1*s*.9*d*. per lb. for an inferior substance which they would have rejected at 2½*d*. before the war'.[58] Paper prices then fluctuated violently, a fall in price from 9*d* per lb in January 1921 to 3¾*d* per lb in May 1922 being followed by a sharp increase.[59]

During 1919 rapid demobilization relieved the industry's shortage of skilled labour, but the wage rises of the wage-price spiral of 1919 and 1920 reduced printers to despair. By November 1920 wages stood at almost three times the 1914 rates. As part of the movement towards a national scale in 1919 employers had also conceded a reduction in working hours from fifty-one to forty-eight and a week's paid holiday. The former did not affect Hughes since the firm had been a pioneer in reducing hours, introducing the 48-hour week as early as 1897.[60]

It has been claimed that 'The years 1920 and 1921 were darker years in the history of Welsh publishing than is generally known'. The outlook was such that Messrs. Hughes & Son were on the verge of relinquishing the publishing of Welsh books and turning to English'.[61] In April 1920 Edward Roberts wrote '*We fear that if wages and other costs continue to rise the publishing of Welsh books will come to an end*',[62] and in May he explained that 'a work published now would have to be at least 150% higher in price than pre-war, & the question is, could a sufficiently large sale be got for any book at the enhanced price to make it remunerative'. Since Hughes had deliberately kept down its prices during the war, the contrast would be all the greater. 'It may interest you to know that we have been compelled to allow about 40 of our books to go out of print, not because there was no demand for them, but simply because we could not reprint them even though we have "stereos" of them, to sell at present prices'.[63] There is some evidence that the public did not appreciate the problems confronting publishers and believed that they were profiteering. In November 1921, for example,

Roberts replied to a complaint about the price of *Person Crist* 'It must be borne in mind that these books are bound as required and the copies supplied to you only came out of binders hands a few days before being sent to you. How can we sell at "pre-war price" when the materials and labour involved are at present day rates[?]'[64]

The precarious condition of Welsh-language publishing was widely publicized in March 1921 when Ifan ab Owen Edwards (son of the founder of *Cymru* and himself subsequently the founder of the Welsh League of Youth) launched a St David's day appeal. '*Welsh literature*' he maintained '*is today in distress because its circulation is too small to withstand today's high prices ... The circulation of Welsh books must be increased ... If this is not done, books will no longer be published in the language formerly heard in Wales*'.[65] He therefore appealed to the Welsh to form 'Urdd y Cyni' ('*The League of Adversity*'). Its members would undertake to buy at least one Welsh title a month during 1921. The League gained over a hundred members in its first ten days,[66] and in all 557 had signed the undertaking by April 1922. The effect of the campaign was, at best, limited since many members of Urdd y Cyni would probably have bought Welsh books in any case. By mid-September 1921 insiders considered it to have been a failure. Edward Roberts wrote to Ifan ab Owen Edwards

> I am sorely disappointed to find that your campaign did not meet with a better welcome, and that you have decided to abandon it. I had shared your hope that it wd. be the means of awakening our people and putting new life into the demand for Welsh books. We must not let this discourage us, but try again, & keep plodding away, we know the language and literature are worth fighting for, & must keep plodding away in spite of all seeming failures, and the apathy of so many of our people.[67]

By the end of 1921 changes in the national economy had improved the prospects of Welsh-language publishing. Following the collapse of domestic prices from May 1920 onwards, employers argued that wage increases specifically granted to meet increases in the cost of living should be reduced as the cost of living fell. Despite union resistance (including a national strike in July 1922), members of the Typographical Association were eventually compelled to agree to a staged reduction in wages between 1921 and 1923 totalling 20/-. Even so, as Musson points out, the wage for grade-5 towns of 65/6 in force from May 1923 was still higher than that for May 1919, while the cost of living was considerably lower. Wages then remained stable from 1923 to 1940, a factor of great importance for the survival of Welsh-language publishing in the inter-war period.[68]

Hughes proved to be well-placed to take advantage of the more favourable climate. At the end of 1920 Charles Tudor Hughes and Albert Llewelyn Hughes, who had run the firm since 1886, arranged an amicable take-over by the Oswestry firm of Woodall, Minshall, Thomas & Co Ltd. Both brothers retained a substantial financial interest in the new firm,[69] but the key figure for the next two decades was the new managing director, Rowland Thomas (1887–1959). Although Thomas could neither speak nor read Welsh, he was a zealous supporter of Welsh-language publishing and made full use of able advisers both within the firm and in Welsh scholarly and literary circles.

Under its new management, Hughes embarked in 1922 upon a programme of publishing Welsh books in order to test the market. As Edward Roberts explained

> *This office at present is keenly in favour of publishing new books in order to test the question 'is there sufficient demand for Welsh books to make it worthwhile for author and publisher to produce them'.*[70]

To support the new venture Hughes convened a conference of seven leading Welsh scholars at Wrexham in 1923, who suggested a list of over thirty titles which ought to be published. This was followed by another meeting to prepare lists of Welsh books for teaching Welsh in schools.[71]

Despite the firm's enthusiasm, sales were slow. In December 1923 Roberts told Richard Morgan, one of the firm's authors, that his sales were disappointing:

> *the worst of it is that people buy the books only very slowly, we have not yet sold enough of the three books to pay for the costs of composition, not to mention the cost of the paper and the printing and the binding &c and since we don't have a bottomless purse it's necessary for us to keep an eye on the financial side. It's not a question of profits but of carrying on! and the business can't afford for us to have money standing in many books, without having it returned for three or four years or more. To carry such books we have to turn out books that sell sufficiently quickly for us to have our money returned – i.e. the cost of composition, paper, printing, and binding – within a year or so.*[72]

Long-standing problems, notably the poor distribution system for Welsh books and the inability to sustain authorship as a full-time occupation because of the restricted market for Welsh books remained unresolved. As the challenges of the war and immediate post-war period were overcome, fresh challenges appeared, notably those posed by the advent of new media. Cinema rapidly established itself as a prime leisure activity; as early as 1920 there were 252 venues showing films in Wales.[73] Radio broadcasting in Wales (almost entirely in the English language) began on 13 February 1923 and by 1930, 136 320 licences had been issued.[74]

In the longer term the most serious problems for Welsh-language publishing resulted from the profound economic and social changes of the inter-war years. For industrial Wales, largely dependent upon declining primary industries, the early 1920s marked the beginning of decades of unemployment and out-migration, some 430 000 people – mainly the younger and more enterprising – leaving Wales between 1921 and 1940. Rural Wales also suffered a significant loss of population as wartime prosperity rapidly faded.

Although Hughes was the most important Welsh-language publisher of the inter-war years its financial position was rather precarious. Since the new company had been set up during a period of high interest rates, it found itself saddled with high-coupon preference shares. Interest payments on these were such a heavy drain on finances that no dividends could be paid on the ordinary shares during the inter-war years.[75] In 1923 the firm faced disaster when its cashier absconded, leaving behind a note bearing the message 'By the time you read this I shall be on my way to Canada'.[76] He had defrauded the company of almost £1100. In a dramatic recognition of the non-commercial nature of Welsh-language publishing, the Hughes brothers waived £4000 of the £5000 loan they had made to the company at the time of the takeover.

NOTES

Italicized quotations are the Author's translations from the Welsh.

1. G J Williams, 'Cyfres y Werin', *Y Llenor*, 1 (1922), 71–6 (74).
2. National Library of Wales [hereafter NLW] Gee MSS P 249 (95) D S Davies, Denbigh, to A E Harrison, Cardiff, 26 September 1918.
3. See, for example, Philip Unwin, *The Printing Unwins: a Short History of Unwin Brothers The Gresham Press 1826–1976* (London, 1976), 74–5.
4. Picton Davies, *Atgofion Dyn Papur Newydd* (Liverpool, 1962), 131–2.
5. NLW Hughes a'i Fab 1958 Donation [hereafter Hughes Donation], Letter-book 18 September 1912 to 9 November 1922 (232) Hughes & Son to Tarian Printing & Publishing Co, Aberdare, 26 January 1915.
6. NLW Hughes Donation, Letter-book 18 September 1912 to 9 November 1922 (268[b]) Hughes & Son to Ballantyne Hanson & Co, 26 August 1915.
7. John Child, *Industrial Relations in the British Printing Industry: the Quest for Security* (London, 1967), 224.
8. Arthur L Bowley, *Prices and Wages in the United Kingdom, 1914–1920* (Oxford, 1921), 158–62.
9. Thomas Bassett, *Braslun o Hanes Hughes a'i Fab, Cyhoeddwyr, Wrecsam* (Oswestry, 1946), 39.
10. Bowley, *Prices and Wages*, 162.
11. NLW Hughes Donation, Letter-book 21 March 1917 to 15 August 1918 (99[a]) Hughes & Son to R O Jones, London, 22 June 1917.
12. R J L Kingsford, *The Publishers Association 1896–1946* (Cambridge, 1970), 67.
13. Kingsford, *Publishers Association*, 68.
14. NLW Hughes Donation, Letter-book 18 September 1912 to 9 November 1922 (296) Hughes & Son to Revd D O'Brien Owen, Caernarfon, 5 February 1916.
15. A E Musson, *The Typographical Association: Origins and History up to 1949* (London, 1954), 321.
16. Musson, *Typographical Association*, 322.
17. Musson, *Typographical Association*, 320.

18. NLW Hughes Donation, Letter-book 21 March 1917 to 15 August 1918 (29[a]-30)Hughes & Son to H Haydn Jones, Towyn, 25 April 1917.
19. NLW Hughes Donation, Letter-book 21 March 1917 to 15 August 1918 (112[a]) Hughes & Son to Bertha Charlton, Liverpool, 5 July 1917.
20. NLW Hughes Donation, Letter-book 18 September 1912 to 9 November 1922 (361[b] & 362[b]) Hughes & Son to G Jones Owen, Pentre, 19 September 1917.
21. NLW Hughes Donation, Letter-book 21 March 1917 to 15 August 1918 (175[b]-176[a]) Hughes & Son to R C Morris, Oswestry, 19 September 1917.
22. NLW Hughes Donation, Letter-book 21 March 1917 to 15 August 1918 (446[b]) Hughes & Son to J Hughes, Llandudno Junction, 1 July 1918.
23. NLW Hughes Donation, Letter-book 21 March 1917 to 15 August 1918 (456[a]) Hughes & Son to Thomas Powell, Neath, 3 July 1918.
24. NLW Hughes Donation, Letter-book 21 March 1917 to 15 August 1918 (352[b]) Hughes & Son to E T Davies, Merthyr, 18 April 1918.
25. Kingsford, *Publishers Association*, 57.
26. Kingsford, *Publishers Association*, 57.
27. NLW Hughes Donation, Letter-book 21 March 1917 to 14 August 1918 (4[b]) Hughes & Son to The Arthur Cox Illust Co, Birmingham, 28 March 1917.
28. NLW Hughes Donation, Letter-book 14 August 1918 to 18 July 1919 (77[b]) Edward Roberts pp. Hughes & Son to Revd D Watcyn Owen, Whitchurch, Salop, 17 October 1918.
29. NLW Hughes Donation, Letter-book 18 September 1912 to 9 November 1922 (309[b]) Hughes & Son to T Leyshon Rees, Fishguard, 6 April 1916.
30. NLW Hughes Donation, Letter-book 21 March 1917 to 15 August 1918 (111[b]) Hughes & Son to Revd W Hughes, Colwyn Bay, 5 July 1917.
31. NLW Hughes Donation, Letter-book 21 March 1917 to 15 August 1918 (232[b]) Hughes & Son to D O'Brien Owen, Caernarfon, 17 November 1917.
32. Kingsford, *Publishers Association*, 53.
33. NLW Hughes Donation, Letter-book 21 March 1917-15 August 1918 (48 +[49]) Hughes & Son to O M Edwards, 11 May 1917.
34. Kingsford, *Publishers Association*, 54.
35. NLW Hughes Donation, Letter-book 21 March 1917 to 15 August 1918 (289[b]) Hughes & Son to Thomas Powell, Neath, 8 February 1918.
36. NLW Hughes Donation, Letter-book 21 March 1917 to 15 August 1918 (458[a]) Hughes & Son to R Griffiths, Harlech, 5 July 1918.
37. NLW Gee MSS P 249 (86) D S Davies to The East Lancashire Paper Mill Co Ltd, Radcliffe, 10 August 1918.
38. NLW Gee MSS P 249 (93) D S Davies to The East Lancashire Paper Mill Co Ltd, Radcliffe, 21 September 1918.
39. NLW Gee MSS P 249 (95), D S Davies to A E Harrison, Cardiff, 26 September 1918.
40. NLW MS 12161E, J H Roberts, Denbigh, to A E Harrison, Cardiff, 15 December 1920.
41. NLW Hughes Donation, Letter-book 18 September 1912 to 9 November 1922 (316[b]) Hughes & Son to T Leyshon Rees, 14 June 1916.

42. NLW Hughes Donation, Letter-book 18 September 1912 to 9 November 1922 (354[b]) Hughes & Son to North Wales Paper Co Ltd, Oakenholt, 3 September 1917.
43. NLW Hughes Donation, Letter-book 18 September 1912 to 9 November 1922 (355) Hughes & Son to P H Stones, Baker, Farndon, 6 September 1917.
44. Kingsford, *Publishers Association*, 54.
45. NLW Hughes Donation, Letter-book 18 September 1912 to 9 November 1922 (376[b]) Hughes & Son to The North Wales Paper Co Ltd, Oakenholt, 11 April 1918.
46. NLW Hughes Donation, Letter-book 18 September 1912 to 9 November 1922 (386[a]) Hughes & Son to D Hugh Jones, Aberdyfi, 14 November 1918.
47. NLW Gee MSS P249 (69) D S Davies to J H Leighton & Co, Liverpool, 29 September 1917.
48. NLW Hughes Donation, Letter-book 21 March 1917 to 15 August 1918 (153[a]) Hughes & Son to The Educational Publishing Co, Cardiff, 20 August 1917.
49. NLW Hughes Donation, Letter-book 18 September 1912 to 9 November 1922 (327) Hughes & Son to Hilda M Davies, Machen, 19 October 1916.
50. NLW Hughes Donation, Letter-book 14 August 1918 to 18 July 1919 (two leaves numbered 100 & 99 inserted between fols 43 and 44) Edward Roberts to Sir O M Edwards, 14 September 1918. Their reluctance to increase prices was far from exceptional. Philip Unwin, for example, comments that 'those engaged in such a competitive industry... would have found it difficult to believe that they could possibly raise their prices above the minimum without losing work' (Unwin, *Printing Unwins*, 75).
51. NLW Hughes Donation, Letter-book 21 March 1917 to 15 August 1918 (188[a]) Hughes & Son to A P Graves, 27 September 1917.
52. *Welsh Outlook*, 8 (1921), 27.
53. NLW Hughes Donation, Letter-book 14 August 1918 to 18 July 1919 (158[b]) Edward Roberts for Hughes & Son to W C Williams, Aberdare, 3 January 1919.
54. Bassett, *Braslun o Hanes Hughes*, 46.
55. NLW Gee MSS P 249 (54) D S Davies to the Surveyor of Taxes, Rhyl, 24 February 1917. Fortunately for Gee, it disposed of a Russian Imperial bond shortly before the revolution.
56. W Williams, 'Welsh books', *Welsh Outlook*, 20 (1933), 129–31.
57. Kingsford, *Publishers Association*, 56.
58. Kingsford, *Publishers Association*, 56.
59. Kingsford, *Publishers Association*, 87–8.
60. Bassett, *Braslun o Hanes Hughes*, 40.
61. J T Jones, 'Modern Welsh books from the point of view of the publisher', *Report of the Proceedings of the Eighth Conference of Library Authorities in Wales and Monmouthshire... 1933* (Aberystwyth, 1933), 47–53 (47–8).
62. NLW Hughes Donation, Letter-book 7 April 1920 to 25 August 1924 (5[b]) Hughes & Son to Dr Abel Jones, Cardiff, 19 April 1920.
63. NLW Hughes Donation, Letter-book 7 April 1920 to 25 August 1924 (17) E Roberts, Hughes & Son to Professor William Phillips, Cardiff, 5 May 1920.

64. NLW Hughes Donation, Letter-book 18 September 1912 to 9 November 1922 (458[b]) Hughes & Son to E H Williams, Tranmere, 16 November 1921.

65. 'Apêl ar ddydd gwyl Dewi, 1921', *Cymru*, 60 (1921), 97.

66. 'Urdd y Cyni', *Cymru*, 60 (1921), 145.

67. NLW Hughes Donation, Letter-book 7 April 1920 to 25 August 1924 (147[a]) Edward Roberts for Hughes & Son to Ifan ab Owen Edwards, 13 September 1921.

68. Musson, *Typographical Association*, 342–7.

69. Each held a thousand ordinary shares in the new company and left £5000 on loan to it (Robbie Thomas, *The Advertizer Family: a History of North Wales Newspapers Limited* (Oswestry, [1988]), 27).

70. NLW Hughes Donation, Letter-book 7 April 1920 to 25 August 1924 (317[a]) Edward Roberts for Hughes & Son to Professor Henry Lewis, Swansea, 18 October 1922.

71. Bassett, *Braslun o Hanes Hughes*, 52–3.

72. NLW Hughes Donation, Letter-book 7 April 1920 to 25 August 1924 (428[b]) Edward Roberts to Richard Morgan, Llanarmon, 7 December 1923.

73. David Berry, *Wales and Cinema: the First Hundred Years* (Cardiff, 1994), 82.

74. John Davies, *Broadcasting and the BBC in Wales* (Cardiff, 1994), 1, 82.

75. Thomas, *Advertizer Family*, 27–33.

76. Thomas, *Advertizer Family*, 28.

The Beginnings of the Book Trade in Leicester

JOHN HINKS

WHERE TO BEGIN? How far back in time is it legitimate, or sensible, to go in search of the origins of the book trade? Where to begin in the case of the ancient town of Leicester, which prides itself on having apparently been occupied continuously since some time before the Romans arrived to develop Leicester as a regional capital? I am clear about where I want to end. The Civil War was a watershed in the history of Leicester as well as the nation, and its outbreak in the early 1640s is a reasonable terminal date for this brief survey because it enables me to mention the town's first stationer-booksellers. But I want to go much further back than the seventeenth century – back before the coming of printing to Leicester – right back into the Middle Ages, to see if I can trace the origins of the book trades in the town. I want to try to identify some of the conditions which would later enable the various branches of the book trades to emerge and to thrive in Leicester.

Medieval Leicester was a compact, walled town of three or four thousand people, already with growing extramural suburbs. With its thriving markets and fairs, its several churches, chantries and collegiate foundations, as well as an important Augustinian Abbey, Leicester was a fairly typical English market-town of the middle rank. There must surely be some literate people in the town, acquiring and reading books and other documents throughout the Middle Ages. But they leave very little trace of the books they own and read, and there is no evidence of how or where they obtain their reading-matter. There is some evidence of local literacy levels towards the end of our period. Leicestershire yeomen were 33% literate in the 1590s, increasing to 45% by the 1640s. The county's husbandmen were 13% literate in the 1590s, increasing to 19% by the 1640s. Local labourers were totally illiterate in the 1590s and only 4% literate by the 1640s.[1] These figures are no worse than most of the country and they do point to a steady, if unremarkable, increase in literacy levels in Leicestershire in the half-century before the Civil War.

Some idea of the level of book ownership may be obtained by looking at the proportion of probate inventories that mention books. There is a figure for sixteenth-century Leicestershire of 17%, which compares reasonably well with other areas, but the measure is a crude one and comparisons are unreliable.[2] The inventory of an exceptionally wealthy Leicester man, William Wyggeston, a Merchant of the Staple, who died in 1530/31, lists eleven 'Englissh books prynted' valued at 6*s*.8*d* and one 'masse-booke'.[3] The inventory of a much less wealthy man, Henry Foster, compiled in 1596, includes one solitary book, a Primer, valued at *2d.*[4] Books occasionally appear in wills, though again data can be incomplete and misleading. In 1540, the will of Dr Ralph Burrell, vicar of All Saints, mentions his dictionaries, a Bible and a concordance.[5]

Early evidence of books changing hands – whether by way of trade or otherwise – is always of interest, proving that books were considered as tradable or exchangeable commodities. A 1458 entry in the rental records of the Chantry of Corpus Christi reveals one early sale of books in Leicester:

> Rob. Sysson owes 48*s.*6*d.* of which Will. Blower paid 18*s.*10*d.* for surplices and books sold to him by the said Rob. Sysson.[6]

This is a tantalisingly isolated reference. Nothing further has been traced for Sysson or Blower and it would be unwise to assume from this single record that Robert Sysson was in any sense a bookseller.

Even earlier, in 1300, we find an unusual record of book ownership. One Roger Dun, responsible for 'many larcenies and robberies', escapes from custody in Leicester Castle but is re-apprehended. Among the goods that Dun forfeits are four books valued at 7*d.* The ownership of the books is unclear (they may have been stolen), but this odd snippet of evidence does prove that there were manuscript books in Leicester in 1300.[7] Two of the books taken from Dun were Latin grammars, evidence that books were being used locally for the purpose of learning or teaching Latin. There must have been other schoolbooks in the town from an early date, and in 1545 the Free Grammar School was set up to provide a free education, on sound Protestant lines, for the sons of freemen.

The Abbey of St Mary de Pratis (St Mary's in the Meadows) lay about half a mile outside the town, physically – and perhaps spiritually – rather detached from daily life in Leicester. Nevertheless, for almost four centuries the Abbey interacted with the town in various ways, trading in its markets and providing an education for some of the boys of the town.[8] Within the Augustinian order, Leicester Abbey was of considerable importance and was probably, after Cirencester, the wealthiest Augustinian house in England.[9] There was a notable library and, especially in the fifteenth century, the Abbey achieved some eminence as an educational and literary centre. There was a scriptorium at the Abbey, but it seems to have produced only administrative records and service books; there is no evidence of manuscript illumination at Leicester.[10]

By the standards of its time, the library of Leicester Abbey was both substantial and well-organised, comprising nearly a thousand volumes, arranged in broad subject groupings. The library catalogue survives, and has been published.[11] It reveals a collection strong in the usual areas of theology and philosophy, but also with unexpected strengths in law (both canon and civil), astronomy, and medicine (of which there were over eighty volumes).[12] The catalogue was drawn up in 1492/93 by the precentor, William Charyte, who later became prior. He himself bound at least one book and copied music. He gave a number of books (and astronomical instruments) to the Abbey and was responsible for buying or otherwise procuring thirty-three volumes for the library. The catalogue contains a section listing books which Charyte 'caused to be written'.[13]

One of the Abbey's canons, Henry Knighton, was a noted chronicler. He began writing his Chronicle, in Latin, in 1337 and continued it for almost sixty years. The most recent translator of the Chronicle, Geoffrey Martin, notes that in order to compile it, Knighton required, in addition to his superior's permission and sufficient time for writing and study:

> a variety of physical and intellectual resources: parchment (not fewer than 120 sheepskins), ink, pens, and works of reference, together with stamina, an enquiring mind, and an ear for news. How he came by most of these necessities is a matter for conjecture.[14]

In contrast to Knighton's orthodox religious life, the radical creed of Lollardy was prevalent in Leicestershire. (John Wyclif was rector of Lutterworth.) It is not surprising to find book-trade people among their number, given the Lollard view that the scriptures should be published in the vernacular and distributed widely to ordinary people.

Lollards had to be skilled in covering their tracks, so the few surviving records tend to describe interrogations and prosecutions. A few years after Lollardy first emerged, there was renewed concern about the production and distribution of Lollard literature, and a royal proclamation in 1388 ordered the seizure of Lollard books and tracts in Leicester.[15] The following year Archbishop Courtenay visited Leicester and examined a number of alleged Lollards, including two book-trade people, Michael Scrivener and William Parchmentmaker, and also a blacksmith known as William Smith.[16] Knighton's Chronicle tells the interesting story of Smith at some length.

This humble blacksmith had apparently taught himself to read and write – perhaps with the help of Michael Scrivener and William Parchmentmaker – and in Knighton's words:

> had written out solemn texts of the Gospels in his own language, and others from St Paul's and other epistles, and works of the doctors of the church which, as he confessed, he had laboured over for eight years, and which he was made to surrender to the archbishop.[17]

As if this was not punishment enough, Smith and two other people were given the penance of processing round two churches and the market-place, carrying crucifixes and venerating images as they went. The others, a husband and wife, were illiterate and had to recite the Pater Noster and the Ave Maria, but Smith, being literate, was also made to read aloud the collect and antiphon of St Catherine.[18]

This group of Lollards seems to have remained active for a long time. In 1414, among seven Leicester Lollards sent for 'correction' we find William Mably, 'parchmener', and William Smith – almost certainly the same parchment-maker and smith who had appeared before Archbishop Courtenay twenty-five years earlier.[19] By this time, the area between Leicester and Northampton had become an active centre for the copying of Lollard texts. One copyist was Michael Scrivener, while some texts copied at Braybrooke (near Market Harborough) were distributed in Leicestershire by William Smith.[20] Leicestershire Lollardy, and its book-trade activists, certainly had staying power!

A lot of evidence of early book-trade activity in Leicester is to be found in the Borough Records. It is said that no other English town has such extensive and well-preserved administrative records. The Merchant Guild Rolls, beginning in 1196, are the earliest surviving records of any English town and are 'the oldest series of memoranda now extant made outside the king's court or a monastery'.[21] The Borough authorities themselves made purchases from time to time of books and stationery. The purchase of paper is first noted as early as 1378–79, when 1½*d* was spent on paper, 4*d* on parchment, and 1*s*.6*d* for the making of three charters.[22] The Borough Chamberlains' Accounts are complete from 1555/56, and from 1589 they were kept on both paper, as rough drafts in books, and on parchment rolls, as a fair copy.[23] They contain numerous entries relating to the purchase of parchment and other stationery items.

The Borough sometimes paid for written copies to be made of statutes and other documents. For example in 1550/51, a man called Francis Mose is paid for 'making of tow [two] suplicacions...' and someone, possibly Mose again, is paid the considerable sum of £1.6*s*.4*d* for making 'tow bookes of the holl statutes'.[24] From time to time, the Borough sent a representative to London to search and make copies from the public records held in the Tower of London. In 1553/54, 5*s* is paid to a Mr Heys 'for the serche in his offyce in the tower about the townes bessenes'.[25] When the Borough was granted a new charter in 1599/1600, making a copy of it for the Mayor seems to have been an urgent task, as this entry in the Chamberlains' Account testifies:

> twoe quere of paper to copie our newe charter and other wrytings for Mr Maior to have... woodd and coles for a fyer for them that satt upp to copie oute the said chartre and wrytings... for there paynes 8*s*.[26]

In September 1551, an inventory was made of the Town Plate, Books and Armour, 'to be delyuerd from mayor to mayor for the townes vse...'. The record books described all survive: the 'Locked Book', the 'Hall Books', the 'Great Paper Book' (also known as the 'Register' or the 'Town Book of Acts') and a manuscript collection of statutes.[27]

Leicester may be fortunate in its well-preserved Borough Records but, sadly, the churchwardens' accounts of St Martin's (now the cathedral) were lost in the late nineteenth century, although selective transcripts had been published.[28] They record a number of purchases of books and stationery goods, though it is rare for suppliers to be named.[29] For the annual Assumptiontide procession, parchment was bought to make name-labels for the Apostles; in 1499 this cost *4d.*[30] Parchment would have been bought locally, but for specialist stationery goods they had to go to London, as in 1544 when *4s.8d* is spent on a book for the records. It was a large book, of 773 folio-size paper pages, bound in calf with brass clasps.[31]

In 1548/9, St Martin's complies with the royal injunction to obtain and display a copy of the *Paraphrases* of Erasmus. It must have been a substantial copy as it cost 10*s*. A second copy of the Erasmus is bought for 7*s* in 1552/3, along with 'a boke of the new sarvis [service]' (5*s*), and 'a bocke conserning the rebellys [rebels], w^c was rede in ye churche' (16*d*).[32] There are many further entries in St Martin's accounts for the purchase of books, mostly for liturgical use.[33]

In the accounts of St Martin's we find the earliest references to the Town Library, founded in 1587, one of the first public libraries in England. Decidedly Puritan in ethos, the library was intended primarily for ministers and scholars although the townsmen were permitted free access. The library was run jointly by the Borough and St Martin's church, where it was first housed, until 1632 when the Borough took sole charge and moved the library into improved accommodation in the Guildhall.[34] Many of the books in the Town Library were donations, but some were bought from London: in September 1628 the Borough pays £5 to John Angell, who was both the Town Lecturer [Puritan preacher] and Keeper of the Town Library:

> for his charges going to London for the obtaining of the Bishop's licence for the weekly lecture and buying books for the library.[35]

I hope that these few snippets are beginning to give a picture of an emerging market for books and related goods in Leicester throughout the medieval and early-modern period. I want to turn now to evidence of early book-trade activity in the town. Parchment-making was probably established in Leicester some time before the earliest documentary evidence of the trade appears in the oldest of the Merchant Guild rolls beginning in 1196. The first relevant entry is that of Gervase the Parchmentmaker who is admitted to the Guild in 1199;[36] nothing more is known of Gervase. In 1219, Richard, the prior's son, enters the Guild, and entries for other parchment-makers begin to appear. Robert and Alan, both of Lincoln, enter the Leicester Guild in 1227.[37]

I want to dwell on Robert for a moment, because there are several records of Robert the Parchmentmaker. If they all refer to the same person, he was a well-established tradesman, and an interesting picture begins to emerge of one of Leicester's thirteenth-century book-trade people. Robert the Parchmentmaker is found several times in taxation records: in 1252/53 he pays a total of three shillings in pontage (bridge maintenance tax) and gavelpence (another ancient local tax), and is listed as living near the East Gate.[38] Two sons of Robert the Parchmentmaker enter the Guild: Richard the Courteous (whose trade is not given) in 1257, and William the Parchment-maker in 1260.[39]

Robert is found again in tallage rolls between 1269 and 1271. Two other parchment-makers are listed: Simon, who pays a total of 2*s*, and William [Robert's son?], who pays 3*s*. 6*d*, but Robert pays the much larger sum of £1.8*s*.0*d*, indicative of a man of some substance.[40] This is perhaps borne out by references to Robert's land. By 1270/71, Robert's son Richard seems to have inherited a plot of land owned by his father in Parchment (or Parchment-makers') Lane. A second reference to Robert's land occurs in 1303, when a property in Parchment Lane is described as adjoining 'the land which was Robert the Parchmentmaker's' – even though, according to the earlier record, the land belonged to Robert's son Richard more than thirty years previously.[41] The fact that this piece of land was still known by the name of Robert the Parchmentmaker may give some indication of his standing in the town.

There are references to several more early parchment-makers.[42] One of them, Richard Dickyns, made free in 1593/94, gets into trouble with the law in 1598, when he is imprisoned on a charge of

> flatt felonye for helpinge, eadinge or consentinge to the breakinge of [the] gaol, and lettinge oute of [the] prisoners then therein beinge...[43]

That is the last we hear of Dickyns – there is no record of what became of him and his business after his imprisonment. In 1623/24 Edward Robinson becomes the last parchment-maker to be made free before the Civil War.[44] His son Charles will be apprenticed to him in 1645, taking the trade of parchment-making beyond our present period. In fact, the trade will continue well into the nineteenth century.

Turning to the mainstream book-trades – stationery, bookselling, and binding – we find the first stationer in Leicester recorded in 1577/78, when Godfrey Cowper is admitted to freedom, his trade being 'stasyon'.[45] Like many stationers, he also practised the trade of bookbinder. The only other record we have of Cowper is found in 1584, when a carrier called Green delivers a basket of books to him. They turn out to be Nonconformist tracts, which brings Green and Cowper to the attention of the authorities. Green claimed that he had been given the basket in London to be taken to Leicester for collection by an unidentified person. After some time, when the basket had not been claimed, Green opened it and, seeing that it contained books, took them to Cowper to see if they were meant for him. Cowper realised what they were and apparently had the sense to leave them alone. Green was sent to London to be questioned by the Secretary of State, Sir Francis Walsingham; his fate is not known.[46] Godfrey Cowper seems to have been blameless in this affair, and nothing more is known of his business activities.

Another stationer, John Langford, is admitted to freedom in 1591/92. He also trades as a bookbinder and is paid five shillings in 1595 to bind seven books for the Town Library.[47] Langford dies in 1633, worth only £20.5*s*.0*d* (including the stock of his shop valued at £13.6*s*.8*d*). His probate inventory is of some interest, not least because of its mention of bookbinding equipment, including 'two working presses, one sewing[?] press with other tools' valued at 6*s*.[48] Although John Langford's business was of modest size, his inventory indicates that he was probably still trading when he died. If he was trading continuously between his freedom and his death, then his business lasted more than forty years.

John Allen seems to have been the first bookseller in Leicester to become fairly wealthy. He begins trading as a stationer in the town in July 1629, when he is fined £2 for 'keeping a shop and using his trade one month before he was made free'.[49] He obtains his freedom on 21 August 1629; as a 'stranger' (not a Leicester man) he is required to pay a hefty admission 'fine' of £13.6*s*.8*d*.[50] The Chamberlains' Accounts indicate that the Borough begins to buy books from Allen in 1635/36. In the same year, for some reason, they also buy books from London.[51] Allen was important enough to have a book printed for him: *The Groanes of the Spirit*, by George Foxle, was printed in Oxford by Leonard Lichfield. The imprint states: 'sold by J. Allen, Lecester [sic], 1639' (the year after Allen's death).[52] This seems to be the only extant book printed for a Leicester bookseller before the Civil War.

It is very fortunate that John Allen's probate inventory survives (see next page).[53] Although his books are valued in total and not itemised, the stock and equipment mentioned in the shop yield some useful clues about the nature and scale of Allen's business. The picture that emerges from John Allen's inventory is one of a large and thriving bookshop and binding business. It is clear that John Allen traded as both binder and bookseller but the fact that he left such a large stock of bound books, valued at £124.13*s*.8*d*, suggests that bookselling was the major part of his trade. The inventory also includes unbound books in quires, together with turkey leather and pasteboard, to a value of £33.8*s*.11*d*. This indicates a sizeable quantity of books waiting to be bound. Some of these might have been bespoke binding jobs for

An inventory of the goods and chattels of John Allen of the Boro' of Leicester, the bookseller, taken and apprised this tenth day of October 1638 by John Angell confrater of the new hospital in Leicester and Thomas Horne, chief schoolmaster of the said Borough, and John Angell jnr, gent of the said Boro' viz:

	£	s	d
In primis books in the shoppe bound	124	13	8
Item paper, ink, inkhorns and parchment	9	1	6
Item black boxes [?], pictures, mapps, mouth[?] glue and wax	2	1	6
Item shelves, presses and other things in the shop	10	0	0
Item the binding of 19 books in leather	1	2	0
Item books in the chamber in quires, paste board and turkey leather	33	8	11
Item 3 tables and frames, one tray[?], 1 round table, 6 chairs, 10 stools, one cupboard	3	0	10
Item pewter	1	8	10
Item brass		13	4
Item one trundle[?]-bed and bedding	5	2	0
Item fire-iron, cupboards, tonges, fire-shovell, pott hookes, smoothing-iron and two spitts		7	0
Item one drinking pot, one voyder[?], one grater and one boiling-plate		2	6
Item linens	1	9	4
Item wooden vessels		14	0
Item wood and coals	1	9	8
Item hay	1	10	0
Item earthen vessels and three cushions[?]		4	0
Item the deceased wearing apparell	3	10	0
Item his working tools		10	0
Item things unseen and forgott		2	6
Item his purse		5	0
Sum Total	191	6	7

besides his debts what they are or amount unto be uncertain that as yet could not be truly valued but the administrators do protest not to use any delay in the obtaining of them to be praised and adding them to this inventory

customers, but it seems likely that most of them were going to be bound for sale in Allen's shop.

Comparative data from probate inventories need to be interpreted with some care, but a straight comparison with other seventeenth-century booksellers' inventories indicates that John Allen's stock of books (£124.13*s*.8*d*) was more valuable than most. I am aware of only two inventories listing more highly valued book-stock: John Foster of York (1616) £144.16*s*.4*d*, and Brooke of Coventry (1679) £147.3*s*.10*d*.[54] Most known book-stocks are valued at less than £100, much less in many cases. If we add to Allen's stock of bound books the value of other goods for sale in his shop – unbound books, stationery, pictures etc – we reach a total sum in excess of £170.

It is interesting that John Allen and several other 'strangers' – men who had presumably been apprentices, and perhaps journeymen, in London or elsewhere, then chose Leicester as a suitable place to establish themselves.[55] Their choice may have arisen from family connections or other personal reasons, but it may simply be that Leicester was regarded in the early seventeenth century as a town ripe for book-trade development. Of course, despite the growth of the book trades in Leicester and other provincial towns, London remained by far the most important centre. The archives of the Stationers' Company record no less than sixty-nine apprentices with Leicestershire origins bound between 1605 and 1640.[56]

In conclusion, the picture of the early book trades in Leicester that emerges from extant records is probably incomplete. Even as it stands, though, the picture is one of considerable and quite varied activity. The conditions in the town in the last quarter of the sixteenth century seem to have encouraged the establishment of book-trade businesses on a scale appropriate to the town's size and status. Of particular note is John Allen, who seems to have been a bookseller and binder of some substance. Although he traded in Leicester for a little under ten years, Allen died a moderately wealthy man and may justifiably be singled out as by far the most successful of Leicester's early book-trade practitioners.

ACKNOWLEDGEMENTS

This paper derives from my PhD research – into the Leicester book trades to c1850 – under the supervision of Professor John Feather at Loughborough University. I am pleased to record my appreciation of his expertise and support.

I am also very grateful to Dr Maureen Bell for providing information on booksellers' probate inventories, to Carl Harrison and Robin Jenkins for their patient assistance with the transcription of seemingly illegible sections of various documents in the collections of the Record Office for Leicestershire, Leicester and Rutland, to Aubrey Stevenson, County Local Studies Librarian, for his continuing interest and assistance, and to Terence Cocks, Cathedral Archivist, for information on the lost accounts of St Martin's (see note 28.)

NOTES

The very substantial and reliable published extracts from the Records of the Borough of Leicester (noted below as *Borough Records*) have been a key source for my PhD research and for this paper. They comprise seven volumes, the first four of which relate to the period 1103 to 1688. Volumes 1 to 3, edited by Mary Bateson, were published in 1899, 1901 and 1905. Volume 4, edited by W H Stevenson and J E Stocks, was published in 1923. Important references have been verified by consulting the original Borough Records, in the collection of the Record Office for Leicestershire, Leicester and Rutland [noted below as ROLLR].

TLAHS = *Transactions of the Leicestershire Archaeological and Historical Society.*

1. Keith Wrightson, *English Society 1580–1680* (1982), 190. Wrightson's source for the Leicestershire statistics is the Cambridge Group for the History of Population and Social Structure.
2. David Cressy, *Literacy and the Social Order* (Cambridge, 1980), 48, 211–12.
3. A Hamilton Thompson, *A Calendar of Charters and other Documents belonging to the Hospital of William Wyggeston at Leicester* (Leicester, 1933), 39–46. Includes a transcript of Wyggeston's inventory.
4. *Borough Records, 3, 323.*
5. Florence E Skillington, 'Enclosed in clay: a study in Leicestershire wills', *TLAHS,* 42, (1966–7), 43. Skillington speculates that the dictionaries may be those printed by Pynson and de Worde, bound together, and that the Bible was possibly Coverdale's version.
6. *Borough Records,* 2, 269.
7. *Borough Records,* 1, 363–4.
8. Levi Fox, *Leicester Abbey* (Leicester, 1971), 5. Fox considers the Abbey to have been 'an establishment of great importance in this part of the country' and refers to its roles as 'consumer, producer and middleman seller'. A much more detailed account of the Abbey is: A Hamilton Thompson, *The Abbey of St Mary of the Meadows, Leicester* (Leicester, 1949).
9. Fox, *Leicester Abbey*, 5.
10. Thompson, *Abbey of St Mary,* 218. Teresa Webber, 'Latin devotional texts and the books of the Augustinian canons of Thurgarton Priory and Leicester Abbey in the late Middle Ages', *Books and Collectors 1200–1700: Essays Presented to Andrew Watson,* [ed] James P Carley and Colin G C Tite (London, 1997), 30. Webber notes that fewer than twenty manuscripts produced at Leicester Abbey are known to have survived.
11. The original catalogue is in the Bodleian Library. There are two published editions: Montague Rhodes James, *Catalogue of the Library of Leicester Abbey* [nd] [reprinted from *TLAHS* 19 & 21 (1937 & 1941)] is still of interest, although it has been largely superseded by the transcript, informed by recent research, in Teresa Webber and A G Watson, *The Libraries of the Augustinian Canons* (London, 1998), 109–400.
12. James, *Catalogue*, 16–17.

13. 'Libri quos Frater Willm. Charite scribi fecit', catalogue folio 139 (reproduced as a plate in Thompson, *Abbey of St Mary*).
14. *Knighton's Chronicle: 1337–1396,* edited and translated by G H Martin (1995), Introduction, xxviii–xxx.
15. James Crompton, 'Leicestershire Lollards', *TLAHS* 44 (1968–9), 22; Martin, *Knighton's Chronicle,* 441.
16. Anne Hudson, *Lollards and their Books* (1985), 53; Crompton, 'Leicestershire Lollards', 23. The visitation took place in 1389, not 1392 as stated by Knighton.
17. Martin, *Knighton's Chronicle,* 535.
18. Crompton, 'Leicestershire Lollards', 25.
19. Crompton, 'Leicestershire Lollards', 30.
20. Hudson, *Lollards and their Books,* 183, 189.
21. M T Clanchy, *From Memory to Written Record: England 1066–1307* (2nd ed, Oxford, 1993), 96.
22. *Borough Records, 2, 168–9.*
23. *Borough Records* Introduction to vol 3, lxiv.
24. That is 'two books of the whole statutes', *Borough Records,* 3, 67.
25. *Borough Records*, 3, 79.
26. *Borough Records,* 3, 421.
27. *Borough Records,* 3, 66–7.
28. Very selective transcribed extracts are reproduced in John Nichols, *The History and Antiquities of the County of Leicester* vol 1, part 2, (1815, reprinted 1971), 568–78. A much fuller, though not complete, transcript is: *The Accounts of the Churchwardens of S. Martin's Leicester: 1489–1844,* edited by Thomas North (Leicester, 1884).
29. The extracts given by Nichols include several examples, in addition to those cited here, of purchases of books – mostly service-books, psalters and suchlike – as well as stationery items such as sealing-wax, parchment and paper.
30. Nichols, *History,* 1.2, 569.
31. Nichols, *History,* 1.2, 570n.
32. North, *Accounts*, 39, 45 & 61.
33. North, *Accounts*; references to named suppliers are few – and most are isolated mentions of an otherwise unknown individual.
34. Frank S Herne, *History of the Town Library and Permanent Library* (Leicester, 1891); Phillip G Lindley, *The Town Library of Leicester: a Brief History* (1975).
35. Cecil Deedes, J E Stocks & J L Stocks, *The Old Town Hall Library of Leicester: a Catalogue with Introduction, Glossary...* (Oxford, 1919), ix.
36. *Borough Records,* 1, 73. The entry for Gervase reads 'Geruasius Parcheminer'. I have followed the assumption of Mary Bateson (Introduction to *Borough Records,*1, 16, n10.) that

'parcheminer' and 'percaminer' (and their variants) always denote parchment-makers, while 'parmenter' (and its variants), sometimes interpreted as parchment-maker, more likely denotes a tailor, clothier or worker in leather.

37. *Borough Records,* 1, 25, 30.

38. *Borough Records,* 1, 44.

39. *Borough Records,* 1, 73, 88.

40. *Borough Records,* 1, 128.

41. ROLLR document no 10 D 34/346 records the transfer of the freehold of a plot adjoining 'that of Richard son of Robert le Parcheminer'. The document is transcribed in Thompson, *Calendar of Charters,* 297. *Borough Records,* 1, 87, records a transaction of 12 September 1303 concerning a plot of land in Parchment-makers' Lane ('in vico parcamenorum') adjacent to 'the land which was Robert the Parchmentmaker's'.

42. The Guild Rolls include references to Walter Parchmentmaker ('Walt. Parcheminer'), involved in a plea of debt in 1347, and John of Merston ('Joh. de Merston parcheminer'), admitted to the Guild in 1380 (*Borough Records,* 2, 72 & 196).

43. *Borough Records,* 3, 342.

44. Henry Hartopp [ed], *Register of the Freemen of Leicester, Vol. 1: 1197–1770...* (1927), 114.

45. Hartopp, *Register of Freemen,* 82.

46. James Thompson, *History of Leicester in the Seventeenth Century* (1849), 269–70; *Borough Records,* 3, 206.

47. Hartopp, *Register of Freemen,* 90 (made free as John Lanckford, 'stasion'.); Herne, *History of the Town Library,* 4.

48. ROLLR Probate Inventory 1633/72.

49. *Borough Records,* 4, 252.

50. Hartopp, *Register of Freemen,* 117 (made free as John Allin, 'stationer').

51. *Borough Records,* 4, 291; the books in question were law books. The Borough spent 9*s*.10*d* with Allen and £2.10*s*.5*d* in London.

52. E A Clough [ed], *A Short-title Catalogue Arranged Geographically...* (1969), 86.

53. ROLLR Probate Inventory 1638/290.

54. John Barnard & Maureen Bell, *The Early Seventeenth-Century York Book Trade and John Foster's Inventory of 1616* (Leeds, 1994). Additional data kindly provided by Dr Bell.

55. Other early 'strangers' were Edward Rudde (stationer) 1590/91, Edward Robinson (parchment-maker) 1623/24, and William Ball (stationer) 1639.

56. D F McKenzie, *Stationers' Company Apprentices 1605–1640* (Charlottesville, Virginia, 1961). There is a steady increase in the number of Leicestershire apprentices bound to members of the Stationers' Company during this period: from three in 1605–1609 to eighteen in 1635–1640.

A Moving Market: The Influence of London Books of Street Cries on Provincial Editions to c1830

DAVID HOUNSLOW

TUCKED AWAY on the final leaf, or back cover, of numerous little books for children, printed and published in the provinces around the end of the eighteenth and beginning of the nineteenth centuries, among lists which sometimes appear to be extended advertisements for John Newbery's wares, we find regularly listed, *The Cries of London,* or, *The Moving Market,* or, more simply, *London Cries.* At first glance these publications may seem to be mere reprints, but they are not simple piracies, but rather a *mélange* of material taken from some of the earliest books published in London on the subject and generally shorn of any didactic or admonitory elements found in the original texts. Thus the books tend to be neutral in tone and content, and do not reflect trends in publishing for children found in works issued by London publishers such as John Harris or the Dartons in the first decades of the nineteenth century.

Of course, a few provincial books of cries do not fall into this category, being original in both text and image, or ambitious in production, with Lumsden of Glasgow, for example, publishing a rather grand *New Cries of London*, priced sixpence plain, or one shilling coloured, alongside a cheaper *Moving Market; or, Cries of London.* But in the main, the provincial books we shall look at are unoriginal in content, small in size, relatively cheap, generally well produced, drawing on books published between 1765 and 1800, and probably on sale to the public well into the nineteenth century. They are also the kind of books of entertainment most likely to be available to poorer provincial children and as such deserve attention.

It is easy to understand why children in past times were fascinated by street vendors and why booksellers 'in town and country' issued so many little books of their images and cries throughout the period. For children were, and still are, fascinated by the unusual and bizarre, sensing perhaps respectable society's ambiguous attitude towards people living beyond the pale. London's streets teemed with such individuals: street entertainers, beggars, young and old, black people and men and women disabled by disease or work, with most making a fragile living selling goods of doubtful quality. In addition, many vendors sold food and a few simple toys, fixed points in any child's universe. For youngsters street vendors must have appeared both exciting and exotic, and booksellers were quick to capitalise on this interest.

Some street traders deliberately exploited the situation, either through the clothes they wore, the goods they sold, or the way they cried their wares; and a few became famous, appearing in popular prints and books of the day, eventually finding their way into children's books where their identities were often submerged in the process. Not every well-known vendor made the transition however. The *Blind Pig Pie Man*, the subject of at least two engravings, did not, but *Tiddy Doll* and *The Noted Buckhorse* did, and although both were born in the first half of the eighteenth century, they still appear in the penny booklets published in the first decades of the nineteenth. Street traders featured regularly in other early prints, often as background figures in an urban landscape, but it is with the publication of the series based on the water-colours of the immigrant artist Marcellus Laroon (1649–1702) that the subject really took off.[1] First published in 1687, the prints were regularly updated in matters of detail of dress, with the addition of new figures throughout the eighteenth and the first quarter of the nineteenth centuries; most notably, as far as we are concerned, in the edition published by Robert Sayer (*c*1755), where children's interest in the subject is tacitly acknowledged with the inclusion of a title-page showing children gathered around a raree showman.

At this point we should perhaps consider how vendors and street entertainers were depicted in books, prints and paintings. Given that London's streets were crowded, noisy and dirty places, the absence of rubbish in the pictures is notable, as is the general tidiness of the vendors themselves. Little of the shabbiness of the clothing these people wore is evident, except for the occasional tear or patch. The images are of the respectable and 'deserving poor', who are plump-cheeked and buxom if the vendor is a woman, and sturdy if the vendor is a man. Only with chimney-sweep boys is there evidence of dirt and even then the reality of the deformities and diseases associated with chimney-sweeping is obscured by a layer of soot. In the painter Jonathan Richardson's (*c*1665–1745) words the painter's task was, 'to raise the Character: To divest the unbred person of his rusticity, and give him something at least of a gentleman'. We need only look at Pyne's *Costume of Great Britain,*[2] which contains numbers of street traders, to see the process at work. [3] Whether in conscious imitation or not, we see this repeated in the children's books, rendering them even more suitable for the offspring of the 'middling sort of people'; a notable example is the elegant but sterile *Sam Syntax's Cries of London* published by John Harris in 1820. The texts, particularly in the earliest books, as we shall see, were often another matter.

It is Robert Sayer who introduced *Tiddy Doll* into the 'Laroon' series of prints on which so much was based, but he had already been included in one of the most famous sets of engravings of the eighteenth century, Hogarth's *Industry and Idleness* where he is found selling gingerbread, and having his pocket picked, in*The Idle*

Fig 1: Hogarth's *The Idle Apprentice Executed at Tyburn – Tiddy Doll* righthand bottom corner

Apprentice Executed at Tyburn (Fig 1). William Hone tells us that, 'He affected to dress like a person of rank: white goldlaced suit of clothes, laced ruff shirt, laced hat and feather, white silk stockings, with the addition of a fine white apron'.[4] One of his lengthy patters is recorded in Hone and is a typical piece of eighteenth-century contradictory nonsense which he finished by singing the chorus of a popular ballad, full of 'tiddys', 'diddys' and 'dol-lols'.[5] He certainly cut a dash and it is small wonder that he was remembered for so long.

Although eccentric, *Tiddy Doll* did have a respectable air about him, which is more than can be said for *Buckhorse*. Neither did *Buckhorse* ever make it into Sayer's edition of Laroon, but he was the subject of at least one popular print where he is pictured, ugly as sin, trousers undone, running through the streets with a bundle of switches, known as Jemmy Tartars, under one arm.[6] He was also the subject of a picaresque work, in prose, but similar in content to Richard Brathwait's *Drunken Barnaby's Tour.*[7] Like so many of his brethren, *Buckhorse* made his living in a variety of ways, as a bareknuckle fighter, street entertainer, shoeblack and a vendor of whips to the horse-racing fraternity. But he was still a good enough boxer to be included in Pierce Egan's *Boxiana,*[8] and it is Egan who furnishes the information that *Buckhorse's* mother was a lady of easy virtue and that they were both turned onto the streets by their landlord, a publican, when *Buckhorse* was but a small child.

Most vendors, however, were generally noticed by the wares they sold, rather than for themselves as individuals, and these make up the bulk of the trades depicted in prints and books. Some wares are present throughout the period. Cherries and oysters, for example, regularly featured in popular prints and were carried over into children's books, and traders such as knife-grinders, sweeps and tinkers appeared frequently. Some occupations, however, did not make the transition and the reasons are sometimes all too obvious. A few early eighteenth-century children's books sometimes display a coarse humour, often scatological or sexual, but even one of the earliest publisher of street cries for children shied away from including some of Laroon's subjects. *A London Curtezan*, for example, was not included although *The Sow Gelder*, turned into a children's bogeyman, was. He also included other plates such as *A Summons to Horn* Fair – a notorious annual celebration of cuckoldry and cross-dressing – which do not appear in any of the various editions of Laroon, even though *Horn Fair* itself was the subject of several popular prints (Fig 2).

A New Summons to Horn Fair.

Fig 2: From Ryland's *Cries of London*, vol 1 (reproduced by kind permission of the Bodleian Library – Opie P150)

Edward Ryland's *The Cries of London; or, Child's Moral Instructor: for the use of Schools, Families, Governesses, Tutors, &c.* is probably the first book of cries published specifically for children. It was certainly one of the most influential, and in three volumes, with a total of ninety-two plates, one of the most substantial. Available for certain in 1765, it is mid-century in content and attitude, leaning heavily on the popular culture of the day.[9] Each volume is fronted by a copperplate of a popular actor in one of his best-known comic roles and, apart from Ned Shuter who claimed to be the son of a sedan-chairman and an oysterseller, there seems little reason otherwise to include these people in the books. The inspiration for most plates, however, is immediately obvious. Although generally crude and heavily incised, and with the addition of a city background, many of the illustrations are copied from Sayer's edition of Laroon, including a number of figures such the vendor of 'Singing Glasses', who do not feature in subsequent books of cries either in London or the provinces.

Each plate is accompanied by several verses, with the first usually directly related to the goods on offer and, although the texts are admonitory in tone and aim to teach a moral, they are frequently discursive and reflect anxieties of the day: anti-semitism, contempt for the 'undeserving poor', loose morals, the evils of drink and xenophobia, as in this on the Scots:

Saint Andrew is the saint they own;
In dirt they're mighty rich;
And touch their hand, 'tis ten to one
But that you'll catch the itch.

Not surprisingly, our friend *Buckhorse*, making his probable first appearance in a children's book, also comes in for criticism and is described variously as 'wretched', 'a silly elf', or 'silly fellow'. Elsewhere in the books we find a number of vendors whose images and accompanying verses make appearances in provincial imprints, including *Hot Cross Buns, Shoe Black, Cucumbers, Oysters* and *Yorkshire Muffins*.

Although John Newbery did not publish a set of cries, two of his successors, Thomas Carnan (1770) and Newbery's nephew Francis (?1771/2) did, and both books had a lasting influence. Carnan's is the less elaborate of the two, consisting of twenty-six woodcuts, each with a simple one- or two-line caption below. Here, once more, we meet *Buckhorse*, this time striding, rather than running, from right to left in an upright posture with a bunch of canes under his arm. The infelicities of undone trouser buttons and ugly face have been replaced by neutral features and a neat and tidy apparel and this is how he appears in the later provincial books.

Francis Newbery's book of cries is much more substantial, but is disappointing nonetheless. The cuts in the main are crude copies of Sayer and bear no comparison with later collections. However, the book was imitated and widely used. The text is much better, and I believe this was either prepared in John Newbery's lifetime, or by one of his hacks working for his nephew, for it has the hallmarks of being from his stable, with references to Hoyle and quotations from Pope and the *Bible* in the preface, and a quirky humour in the verses:

Tell me, O Muse, how shall I stick in
A word that aptly rhymes with *Chicken*,
Or in what mode the lines must roll
To tag a couplet with *Fat Fowl*!
And now since half my work's complete,
O Newbery, let thy servant eat!
For gladly now I would be picking,
From old *Parnassus* a nice Chicken;
And if of Claret thou hast none,
Some water send from *Helicon*.

Like Ryland's books, Newbery's cries have it in for some of the vendors. The *Old Cloaths Man* is described as, 'This dirty son of Israel's race...'; the vendor of *Filberts* gives short weight; the *Chair-mender* and his wife are drunks, as are the *Bellows-mender* and the *Wild Fowl Seller,* and the *Tinker* makes more holes than he mends. But others are held as exemplars of acceptable behaviour. The *Broken Bottles*

Man is honest, as is the *Spratseller,* while the *Cooper* is described as being a good workman. Despite its visual shortcomings the book remained in print for many years, being reprinted by John Harris, Elizabeth Newbery's successor, in the first decade of the nineteenth century and the work was plagiarised by Robert Harrild around 1820 and by Edward Billings, Harrild's erstwhile partner, in the 1840s.

Before turning to the provincial editions of street cries, we need to consider one other published in London around 1775 and probably the most attractive in terms of illustration. This is *The Cries of London, for the Instruction of Good Children.* 'Printed and sold by all Booksellers in Town and Country'. The woodblocks were eventually acquired by Philip Norbury of Brentford some time in the first decade of the following century and reissued by him. The pictures derive from the Laroon prints, but are far from being mere copies, although, of course, they could not match the quality of the copper-plate engravers responsible for Laroon. However, the vendors show real character and stand firmly on the page. It is with this book that we see the probable start of practices followed by the provincial publishers, with single verses lifted directly from Ryland, in the process introducing an overall neutral and generally non-judgemental tone, and with the occasional switching of trades (Laroon's *Oysterseller* becomes a *Potatoeseller* for example) and changes in detail in the illustrations. So, *Tiddydoll,* who rests his left hand on his hip in the Sayer print, has his hand in his pocket; the manner in which the *Broomseller* (Fig 3) ties his brooms together differs from that shown in Sayer, and the male *Balladseller* is removed entirely, leaving a single female figure holding a slipsong in her right hand (Fig 4), and it is these small details which regularly appear in the provincial booklets, suggesting that the wood-engravers were not going back to Laroon, but copying the images directly from existing books.

Fig 3: Copy of Laroon's broom-seller from an unknown source

The influence of this particular little book was widespread. Not only was it copied by other publishers of cries, but the images were used in conventional chapbooks by the like of Randall in Stirling (*Hot Cross Buns, Brooms* and the female *Balladseller* for example) and on song sheets published by James Catnach (1792–1841). Catnach it seems acquired blocks from an otherwise unknown book of cries which are close copies of the originals, although with the images reversed. Ballad sheets published by Catnach and others frequently contain pictures which originated in earlier books for children, and at least one other set of cries[10] saw out their days on song sheets published by Thomas Batchelar in the 1820s. Elsewhere chapbook publishers such as Ann Bell in Penrith and Jollie in Carlisle were using cuts based on images which were probably taken from children's books.[11]

Fig 4: Female ballad-seller from a Catnach songsheet

One of the more unusual of the provincial cries is the already mentioned *The Moving Market; or, Cries of London* published by Lumsden in 1815. The book starts conventionally enough, drawing texts from Ryland's and Norbury's books of cries with illustrations copied from both works. However, from page 22 onwards the style of illustration changes markedly (although *Tiddy Doll* still has his hand in his pocket), and the accompanying verses are taken from a contemporary book of cries published in London by J T Ward in 1808, and in numerous other editions throughout the decade and beyond. While other provincial booksellers were probably secure in plagiarising earlier works, Lumsden is the only provincial bookseller to lift material from a book so recently published quite so blatantly, and one has to ask why he felt secure in doing this. The most likely explanations are that Lumsden reprinted parts of Ward's book with the London publisher's permission, or, and this is perhaps more likely, he was merely taking a chance that Ward would never know of his piracy, or, for that matter, even care, and as we have seen, smaller London booksellers certainly had no scruples about lifting material from other publishers' works. Whatever the reason, Lumsden seems to have been alert to publishing trends in the English capital, for his *New Cries of London* (*c*1820), with coloured plates and minimal text, bears a close resemblance to a book of cries published by John Wallis in 1802 and the children's books published by John Marshall in the first two decades of the nineteenth century.

Another thoroughgoing piracy, this time of Francis Newbery's book, is *The Moving Market...* published by Houlston in Wellington some time between 1807 and 1815. Apart from the frontispiece, which is taken from 'the Booksellers/Norbury', and the title, lifted from Mackenzie, there is no attempt to conceal the major source for the work, with the vendors even appearing in the same order as in Newbery's collection. All that is missing are the verses which accompanied the original, and neither does it contain all the vendors, for this is another booklet of thirty-two pages bound within pictorial paper wrappers.

Elsewhere, other booksellers were following the same path. Mary Luckman of Coventry (*fl* 1784–1801), for example, took verses from Ryland, 'the Booksellers/Norbury' and Francis Newbery's books and copied images from all three and other as yet unidentified sources, together with a frontispiece of a city view with what looks suspiciously like a minaret included in the picture. Mrs Luckman's book is otherwise unexceptional, with each vendor portrayed, without a background, within a plain double-ruled border, with the cry at the head of the page and a four-line verse at the bottom.

The city of York provides no less than five (or perhaps even six) examples of books of cries, the best-known being those published by Kendrew. But the Kendrew booklets are not the earliest examples. This honour belongs to Edward Peck who some time between 1795 and 1800 published a small book of cries which is entirely original in its illustration and where even our old friend *Tiddy Doll* is pictured differently. Including the pictorial paper wrappers, there are a total of twenty-five trades present of which several are not usually found in the smaller children's books of cries. So here we find toy swords on offer, *Choice fruit, sir?– A bill of the play?* and *Young lambs …* with a verse not found elsewhere.

It is Kendrew, however, who exploited the situation rather more successfully, for not only did he publish two books of London Cries, but also two *Cries of York, for the Amusement of Young Children*. The two *Cries of London* are the usual mish-mash of sources for both image and text, with the slightly longer edition probably published first. This last includes *A Merry New Song*, sung to the tune of *Sally in our Alley*, lifted from the second volume of Ryland's cries and many of the verses are from the same source, either from Ryland direct, or filtered perhaps through 'the Booksellers/Norbury', although in this instance Kendrew draws on material from all three of Ryland's volumes, whereas others normally do not, suggesting that he had access to a complete set. Nor are the illustrations original. Thomas Hugo in his *Bewick's Woodcuts*[12] illustrates a number of vendors similar to Kendrew's, ascribing them to a book of street cries published by [?Solomon] Hodgson of Newcastle, and he reprints a number of others by the same hand which were not used by the York publisher. From the surviving evidence Hodgson's book seems to have been better executed, but sadly no copy has so far come to light. Kendrew's *Cries of York* was also published in two editions; one of sixteen pages and the other thirty-two, further evidence, if it was needed, of the popularity of the subject. The book is unique too in that one of the woodcuts is signed. There are no initials, but the engraver is probably Michael

William Carrall who was trading from 184 Walmgate, York, in the early 1820s as a bookseller, binder and engraver.[13]

Two other books supposedly published in York are similarly elusive. Hugo in his supplement to *The Bewick Collector* lists a book of cries published by Thomas Wilson in 1812, describing it as '24mo. Pp.31, with frontispiece and twenty-seven cuts' and priced One Penny,[14] suggesting it to be a small booklet with the minimum of text and bound in either Dutch floral paper or pictorial paper wrappers. Evidence of the other is found in Pearson's *Banbury Chapbooks*[15] (Fig 5). Here Pearson illustrates a book of cries based mainly on Thomas Carnan's *London Cries*, ascribing it to Kendrew. The verses accompanying the pictures are certainly those used by Kendrew, but the execution of the cuts is far too crude for it to have been published by either him or Thomas Wilson. Unless a copy of the book turns up, we are unlikely ever to know who produced it or where they worked.

Fig 5: Copy of Carnan's *Noted Buckhorse*, incorrectly ascribed by Pearson to Kendrew's *Cries of London*

Given that the sources for so many provincial books of cries were books published in London, it seems fitting to conclude with a little work published a mere thirty miles from 'The Great Wen', which owes little or nothing to the efforts of the Dartons, the Newberys or John Harris. The book, to give its full title, is *Old English Cries with Attractions to the Notice of Children; in a Set of Pictures Characteristic of the Various Modes Adopted by Itinerant Traders, to Obtain an Honest Living* (*c*1815), and the publisher was one Isaac Marsden of Chelmsford. It is a work inspired more by popular pastimes and the printed ephemera of the day, than by Laroon or his many imitators, and probably drew its inspiration from the game played on Twelfth Night where participants impersonated characters decided on by drawing lots. Many crudely engraved Twelfth-Night sheets were produced for the occasion by the likes of Bowles and Carver, with names such as *Bet Boozer, Roger Mac Rappum* (a night-watchman); *Robert Rope'em* (an onion-seller) and *The Chimney Doctor* (a sweep), and these bear a more than passing resemblance to Marsden's *Dame Fanny Hound* (a cherry-seller) and *Little Tommy Creep* (a chimney-sweep). Despite its rather overblown title, it is an entertaining and unpretentious little book of a mere sixteen pages and serves to remind us that children preferred 'delight' to 'instruction' and that some publishers, at least, knew this.

ACKNOWLEDGEMENT

Practically all the research for this paper was done in the Bodleian Library, particularly among the great collections put together by Francis Douce, John Johnson, and Iona and Peter Opie, and it is Clive Hurst, Head of Special Collections, and his colleagues that I must thank for the unstinting help they have given me. I would like to thank too Andrea Immel, Curator of the Cotsen Children's Library, Princeton, for the information on Mary Luckman, and William K Sessions for additional information on the York printers. But, above all, I must thank my great friend, Barry McKay, for all the help and encouragement he has given me over the years.

A CHECKLIST OF CHILDREN'S BOOKS OF STREET CRIES DISCUSSED IN THE TEXT

The Cries of London; or, the Child's Moral Instructor: for the Use of Schools, Private Families, Governesses, Tutors, &c. Decorated with 32 Copper Plates Elegantly Engraved. [3 Vols] London: Printed and Sold by Edwd. Ryland, Printer at the Old Bailey. [?1765] Bodleian Library, Oxford.

The London Cries, for the Amusement of all Good Children Throughout the World. London: Printed for T. Carnan... 1770. S Roscoe, *John Newbery and his Successors 1740–1814 a Bibliography* (Wormley: Five Owls Press, 1973) J 233(1). Bodleian Library.

The Cries of London, as they are Daily Exhibited in the Streets; with an Epigram in Verse adapted to each. Embellished with Sixty-two Elegant Cuts... London: Printed for E. Newbery... [c1780]. This edition not in Roscoe. For subsequent editions see Marjorie Moon, *John Harris's Books for Youth* (Winchester, St Paul's Bibliographies, 1987), No. 173; Karen F Beall: *Cries and Itinerant Traders* (Hamburg: Hauswedell, 1975), E20 &28. Bodleian Library.

The Cries of London, for the Instruction of Good Children. Decorated with Twenty-four Cuts from Life. London: Printed and Sold by all Booksellers in Town and Country. [c1775] Bodleian Library.

The Cries of London, for the Instruction of Good Children, Decorated with Twenty-four Cuts from Life. Brentford, Printed by P. Norbury, and Sold by all Booksellers in Town and Country. [c1800] Birmingham City Library.

The Merry Merry Cries of London, Designed for the Use of Children, Adorned with Twenty-eight Entire New Cuts. London: Printed and Sold by J. Mackenzie... [c1790] Bodleian Library.

The Cries of London, for the Amusement of all Good Children Throughout the World. Coventry: M. Luckman [Between 1784 and 1797] Cotsen Children's Library, Princeton University.

The Cries of London; or, Picture Exhibition. Newly Collected for the Entertainment of Little Misses and Masters throughout the Kingdom. York: Printed and Sold by E. Peck, Lower-Ousegate. [c1795-1800] Bodleian Library.

The Cries of London, as they are Daily Exhibited in the Streets. With Thirty-two Prints of Living Characters. J. T. Ward... 1808. Bodleian Library.

The Cries of London, for the Instruction and Amusement of Good Children. Decorated with Wood-cuts from Life. York: Printed for J. Kendrew, Colliergate. [nd, but *fl* 1803?- 41] Roger Davis, *Kendrew of York and his Chapbooks for Children* (Wetherby: Elmete Press, 1988), 13; Beall, *Cries*, E64. Bodleian Library.

The Cries of London, for the Amusement and Instruction of Good Children. Decorated with Cuts from Life. York: Printed by J. Kendrew, Colliergate. [nd, but *fl* 1803?-41] Davis, *Kendrew*, 12. Bodleian Library.

The Cries of York, for the Amusement of Young Children. Decorated with Cuts. York: Printed for J. Kendrew. [between 1811 and 1825?] Davis, *Kendrew*,14. Bodleian Library.

The Cries of London for the Amusement of all Good Children .Throughout the World. Taken from Life. York: Printed by Thomas Wilson and son, High Ousegate. 1812. Thomas Hugo, *The Bewick Collector. A Supplement* (London: Reeve, 1868), 4247.

Old English Cries with Attractions to the Notice of Children; in a Set of Pictures Characteristic of the Various Modes Adopted by Itinerant Traders, to Obtain an Honest Living. Chelmsford: Printed and Sold by I[saac]. Marsden. [c.1815] Bodleian Library.

The Moving Market; or, the Cries of London: for the Amusement of all Good Children. Adorned with Cuts. Wellington: Printed by F. Houlston and Son. [Between 1804 and 1816] Bodleian Library.

The Moving Market; or, the Cries of London. For the Amusement of Good Children. Glasgow: Printed by J. Lumsden & Son. 1815. S Roscoe & R A Brimmell, *James Lumsden & Son of Glasgow* (Pinner: Private Libraries Association, 1981), 104. Bodleian Library.

Sam Syntax's Description of the Cries of London, as They are Daily Exhibited in the Streets. With Appropriate Engravings. London: Printed for J. Harris and Son. 1820. Moon, *John Harris,* 766; Beall, *Cries*, E41, describing the second edition. Bodleian Library.

The New Cries of London with Characteristic Engravings. Glasgow, Published by J. Lumsden and Son. [C1820]. Roscoe & Brimmell, *James Lumsden*, 105. Edinburgh: Museum of Childhood.

NOTES

1. S Shesgreen, *The Criers and Hawkers of London* (Aldershot: Scolar Press, 1990).
2. W H Pyne, *The Costume of Great Britain* (London: William Miller, 1804).
3. Harris Myers, *William Henry Pyne and his Microcosm* (Stroud: Alan Sutton, 1996), 5–6.
4. Jenny Uglow, *Hogarth: a Life and a World* (London: Faber, 1977), 158.
5. William Hone, *The Every-day Book: or, the Guide to the Year Relating to Popular Customs* (London, 1825–6), 1, col 575–7.
6. Bodleian Library, Douce Portfolios 139.
7. Richard Brathwait, *Drunken Barnaby's Four Journeys to the North of England* (London, 1638 & later editions).
8. Pierce Egan, *Boxiana, or Sketches of Ancient and Modern Pugilism* (London, [1812]–1821), 1, 35–6.
9. Martin Holmes, 'Samuel Gamidge: bookseller in Worcester', in [ed] Peter Isaac & Barry McKay, *Images & Texts: Their Production and Distrubution in the 18th and 19th Centuries* (Winchester: St Paul's Bibliographies; New Castle, DE: Oak Knoll Press, 1997), 30.
10. *The Merry Merry Cries of London* (London: J Mackenzie, *c*1790)
11. Barry McKay, 'Cumbrian chapbook cuts: some sources and other versions', in [ed] Peter Isaac & Barry McKay, *The Reach of Print: Making, Selling and Using Books* (Winchester: St Paul's Bibliographies; New Castle, DE: Oak Knoll Press, 1998), 79–82.
12. Thomas Hugo, *Bewick's Woodcuts* (London: Reeve, 1870), nos 730–52.
13. British Book Trade Index record 31044.
14. Thomas Hugo, *The Bewick Collector. A Supplement* (London: Reeve, 1868), 4247
15. Edwin Pearson, *Banbury Chapbooks and Nursery Toy Book Literature of the Eighteenth and Nineteenth Centuries* (Reprinted, Welwyn: Seven Dials Press, 1970), 47.

From Scotland to the Strand: The Genesis of Andrew Millar's Bookselling Career

RICHARD B SHER, with HUGH AMORY

IN A LETTER printed in the Edinburgh periodical *The Bee* in June 1791, a writer identified as 'Authenticus' related an anecdote from early in the career of the London bookseller Andrew Millar in order to prove a general point, that 'the proper business of the bookseller is to make money', rather than to uphold high ideals or serve mankind. When Millar was starting out as a bookseller in London, the story goes, he had 'but a scanty stock' and dwindling resources. He was then in the habit of publishing 'good books in philosophy, history and morality, that tended to enlarge the understanding, and improve the heart', but they sold poorly. When his 'stock of cash was nearly exhausted', 'a more worldly friend' advised him to publish a translation of a French pamphlet about a recent scandal involving Father Girard, a Jesuit priest who had raped a girl in his care. 'The scruples of Mr. Andrew began to subside', says Authenticus, and he paid £20 to have the work translated into English. It was hugely successful, earning its publisher 700 guineas (£735) from three editions in the space of just one month. During this period, Millar silently endured harsh criticism from his domineering wife, who disapproved of his actions on moral grounds. One evening, however, he spread his newly acquired coins on the table in a dramatic display, to the astonishment of his wife, who exclaimed: 'Praise be God for such a lucky discovery; could we find twenty such books, our fortune might be made'.[1]

Andrew Millar (1705–1768) was the greatest bookseller in mid-eighteenth-century Britain, and it is therefore not surprising that stories like this one were in circulation nearly a quarter of a century after his death. Millar is justly famous for publishing Henry Fielding's novels, Samuel Johnson's dictionary, and David Hume's philosophical and historical writings, to name only some of his best-known projects. Almost from the time he became an independent bookseller in the Strand in 1728, until his death forty years later, he was a major figure in the London book trade. During the course of his career, Millar associated himself with William Strahan, an ambitious Scottish printer in London, ten years his junior, who would help to move his publishing business forward. Towards the end of his career, he was equally fortunate in his choice of his former apprentice, Thomas Cadell, as his *de facto* business partner and successor. After Millar's retirement and death, Strahan and Cadell, and subsequently their heirs, would continue and expand the publishing empire that Millar had founded.

Millar was celebrated for his generosity towards authors. An obituary in the 7/9 June 1768 number of Strahan's newspaper, the *London Chronicle*, stated that 'he was so liberal an encourager of men of genius, that he has justly been said to have raised the price of literature'. The same phrase was attributed to Samuel Johnson in Boswell's *Life*,[2] and it is likely that the publication of that work on 16 May 1791 provoked Authenticus into publishing his anecdote about Millar in the *Bee* a few weeks later. Elsewhere, Johnson called Millar 'the Maecenas of the age', and Authenticus used the term 'these Maecenases' in referring, ironically, to booksellers like Millar.[3] Yet in paying authors generously, Millar did no harm to himself, and he died an exceedingly wealthy man, with an estate worth £60 000.[4] During his final years, he divided his time among a home at 25 Pall Mall that Robert Adam had designed for him, a country house at Kew Green in Richmond, and extended visits to Bath and other fashionable watering holes.[5]

Considering all this, it is remarkable that so little has been written about Millar's life, particularly the years preceding his emergence as a prominent London bookseller. That he originally came from Scotland is universally acknowledged, but scarcely anything more can be learned from the existing secondary literature. When and where was he born and raised? What was his family background? From whom did he learn the book business? How did he get from Scotland to his own shop in the Strand while still in his early twenties? And how did he make his way once there? Not knowing the answers to any of these questions, John Nichols, in the *Literary Anecdotes* that he penned in the early nineteenth century, conveyed the impression that Millar was entirely self-made, and 'literally the artificer of his own fortune'.[6] It was also said that Millar had taken over the premises of Jacob Tonson's shop opposite Catherine Street in the Strand, known as Shakespeare's Head, and renamed it Buchanan's Head[7] – a story that established continuity with the foremost English bookseller in Augustan London, even as it portrayed Millar as a self-consciously patriotic Scot. Stories like these continue to circulate without supporting evidence,[8] with the result that Millar's parentage, background, and early career remain thoroughly misunderstood.

In fact, a great deal of information is available about Millar's early years, even if the record is rarely as complete as we would like. But it can only be obtained if one begins by looking outside London, in the places where Millar was raised and initially trained. This article will focus on two key figures in that process: his father, Robert Millar, and his master, James M'Euen. Understanding their contributions to the making of Andrew Millar's career will require us to take into account their overlapping Scottish contexts in the greater Glasgow region and in Edinburgh. We shall see that the bookseller Andrew Millar did not appear fully-formed in London, or make his career there out of nothing, but rather sprouted from roots deeply embedded in the highly literate Presbyterian culture of early eighteenth-century Lowland Scotland.

Andrew Millar was born into a distinguished family of Scottish Presbyterian divines. In 1672 Revd Andrew Millar, the bookseller's grandfather, became the minister of the Renfrewshire parish of Neilston, where the bookseller's father, Robert, was born in the same year.[9] These events marked the beginning of a close connection between the Millars and Renfrewshire that spanned the late seventeenth and eighteenth centuries. Lying to the west of Glasgow, Renfrewshire was characterized in this period by two prominent features that it shared with the greater Glasgow area: evangelical Presbyterianism and a fast-growing industrial economy.[10] The latter phenomenon refers not to the explosion of heavy manufacturing and large industrial cities that would occur in the nineteenth century, but rather to a movement characterized by extensive trade via inland canals and overseas shipping routes, thriving cottage industry, relatively rapid but still small-scale urbanization, and an increasing number of textile mills located in rural and small-town settings, using water rather than steam as their chief source of power.

Greenock and Port Glasgow, two bustling Renfrewshire ports near the mouth of the River Clyde, were the primary interfaces between this nascent pattern of industrialization and the Atlantic world. Further inland, the archetypal Renfrewshire industrial town was Paisley, a few miles to the west of Glasgow. Its impressive growth during the eighteenth century was based chiefly on the manufacture of linen, and subsequently silk gauze and cotton, and its name would come to be associated with a distinctive textile design. The labour force in this movement was led by hand-loom weavers, who tended to be proud, independent, and exceedingly pious.

They were also remarkably literate. Glasgow was the regional hub for this movement, and several Glaswegian booksellers and printers, such as John Bryce, made a living producing religious literature for this popular reading audience, mainly by subscription.[11] One subscription publication of particular interest is *The Whole Works of the Reverend Robert Millar, A.M.*, the bookseller's father. It was published in 1789 by Robert Reid of Paisley in eight duodecimo volumes, the last of which bore the names of more than a thousand subscribers, mainly from the working classes in the greater Glasgow area, including more than 350 of the pious weavers who constituted such an important part of that community (approximately a third of them from Paisley itself). The fact that Robert Millar was considered worthy of this edition of his works nearly four decades after his death provides some indication of his lasting reputation among this popular reading audience.

Robert Millar grew up during the Scottish episcopal restoration under Charles II and James II, when Presbyterians were persecuted in ways that would later be depicted by his friend, Revd Robert Wodrow, in *The History of the Sufferings of the Church of Scotland, from the Restauration [sic] to the Revolution* (1721–2), and still later by John Howie in one of John Bryce's most popular subscription publications, *Biographia Scoticana: or a Brief Historical Account of the Lives, Characters, and Memorable Transactions of the Most Eminent Scots Worthies* (1775). The Millar family had experienced these hardships firsthand. In 1662 the Scottish Parliament had deprived Robert's father of his parish living at Dailly, in southern Ayrshire, and he was later admitted to the parish of Neilston under a special indulgence that was withdrawn by the Privy Council in 1684, when he was briefly imprisoned for his faith.[12] The Revolution of 1688–9 led to the reestablishment of Presbyterianism, however, and during the 1690s Robert Millar was able to train for the ministry and earn an MA at the University of Glasgow.[13] In February 1697 he received his licence to preach the gospel from the Presbytery of Paisley, and five months later was ordained as the first minister of Port Glasgow, where he laboured for twelve years without church or manse.[14] In June 1702 he married Elizabeth (d 1759), daughter of the collector and surveyor of customs in Port Glasgow, John Kelso.[15] Elizabeth's mother, Mary Hamilton, was the daughter of another Church of Scotland minister, Revd Archibald Hamilton of Wigtown, and the sister of no fewer than three Church of Scotland ministers in Edinburgh and its suburbs.[16]

Robert and Elizabeth Millar had a large family, consisting of eight sons and daughters who survived childhood. Andrew, the future bookseller, was the eldest. Although he is usually thought to have been born in 1706 or 1707, the Port Glasgow parish register establishes that he was baptized on 16 October 1705 OS, and it seems likely that he was born eight days earlier, on 8 October.[17] On 28 December 1709, shortly after Andrew's fourth birthday, Robert Millar became one of the ministers of the Abbey Kirk in Paisley, where he would remain until his death in 1752.

Robert Millar wrote two big books with long titles, on a single, world-historical theme. The first and more important of them, *The History of the Propagation of Christianity, and Overthrow of Paganism*, was published in Edinburgh in 1723 in two thick octavo volumes.[18] His second book, *The History of the Church under the Old Testament, from the Creation of the World*, appeared in Edinburgh in 1730 in a single folio volume, published by Andrew Millar.[19] Taken together, these works were meant to trace the history of Christianity and Christian conversion among pagans and Jews, respectively, as well as to encourage the continuation and expansion of such missionary activities. As Millar wrote in the Preface to *The History of the Propagation of Christianity*, his ultimate aim was to incite Christians with missionary 'Fervour and Zeal' (ix). That book was separately reprinted twice in London and translated into Dutch, and modern ecclesiastical historians have recognized it as one of the seminal works in the literature of the Scottish missionary movement.[20] It was also reprinted in the eight-volume, Paisley edition of Millar's *Whole Works*, along with *The History of the Church under the Old Testament*. In addition, two brief sections from the latter work appeared separately in Edinburgh in 1782.[21]

Both Millar's books were originally published by subscription, but their subscription lists look nothing like the list appended to the Paisley edition of the *Whole Works*. Whereas the latter is heavily concentrated among working-class subscribers in the west of Scotland, the former contain no working-class subscribers and are more geographically diverse. The list of 460 subscribers prefixed to the first edition of *The History of the Propagation of Christianity* includes the second Duke of Argyll and a number of other nobles, Thomas Blackwell and Gershom Carmichael among several university principals and professors, and large numbers of clergymen and merchants. The bulk of the subscribers are located in Scotland, especially the west, but there are also quite a few English and Irish dissenters – eighteen from Dublin alone, including 'Mr. Francis Hutchison Preacher in Dublin'. Robert Wodrow, who was among the subscribers, sent a copy to Cotton Mather in New England, with a strong recommendation of the author as 'my worthy and learned neighbour, and dear brother', and 'a serious, diligent, and laborious minister', whose 'valuable' book 'will show his acquaintance with learning, in most of its valuable branches'.[22] The list of subscribers to Millar's second book is about a third smaller but at least as distinguished, including the Dukes of Hamilton, Buccleuch, and Queensberry, a half dozen earls (the influential Earl of Ilay among them), several provosts, judges, lawyers, and professors, large numbers of Presbyterian clergymen, and many merchants from the greater Glasgow region, as well as 'Robert Fowlis' (Foulis) in Glasgow, who would later enter the book trade and work closely with Andrew Millar. In sum, the three subscription lists attached to the publications of Robert Millar demonstrate that during the course of the eighteenth century his writings enjoyed widespread support among Presbyterians of every social rank, from dukes to flax-pressers, mainly in the greater Glasgow area but also throughout Scotland and, to a lesser degree, elsewhere.

As the eldest son of such an eminent clergyman and ecclesiastical historian, Andrew Millar might have been expected to attend the University of Glasgow and pursue a career in the ministry himself. Two of his younger brothers travelled down that path: John, who became the minister of Old Kilpatrick (on the north side of the Clyde in Dunbartonshire, roughly midway between Glasgow and Port Glasgow) from 1728 until his early death in 1738, and Henry, who followed in the footsteps of his grandfather as the minister of Neilston (five miles south of Paisley) from 1737 until his death in 1771. In addition, two of Andrew's sisters married Church of Scotland clergymen who served as ministers in Paisley during and after the ministry of Robert

Millar, one (Peter Scott) at the Laigh Kirk from 1740 until his death in 1753, and the other (James Hamilton) as Robert Millar's junior colleague at the Abbey Kirk from 1751, and his successor from 1753 until his death in 1782.[23] Other clerical relations in the west included Robert Miller, minister of Ochiltree in Ayrshire, and his two sons, Robert, minister of St Quivox, Ayrshire (who subscribed to Robert Millar's first book), and John, the minister of Neilston from 1703 until his death in 1732.[24] Thus, the manses of the greater Glasgow region, and especially the Paisley vicinity, were thick with Millars, and it seems likely that Andrew Millar could have filled one of them if he had chosen a career as a clergyman.

There is abundant evidence of close lifelong ties between Millar and his family in Renfrewshire. He continued to visit Paisley and his brother Henry's nearby parish, and his 'fine fortune' is said to have financed a factory that Henry and some partners built in Neilston to make inkle, a kind of linen tape that was used for various purposes, including lace-making.[25] In the summer of 1765 Millar wrote to Cadell from Paisley to say that affairs there had kept him so busy that 'I had no time to think of London or what you are doing'.[26] By this time his father had been dead for thirteen years, and his mother for six, yet Andrew kept up ties with his siblings, and once loaned more than £2000 to his first cousin on his mother's side, Captain John Kelso.[27] It is often noted that his will contained bequests to David Hume and the sons of Henry Fielding, but it left far more to surviving Renfewshire siblings, in-laws, and cousins on both sides of his family.[28] In 1730 Millar had married the daughter of the London printmaker and printseller Andrew Johnston, Jane Johnston (1710-1788), who left small annuities in her will to Captain Kelso's daughter, Mary, and to one of Andrew Millar's grand-nephews.[29] Even Millar's printing associate, William Strahan, regularly visited the Millars in Paisley and Neilston when he was in Scotland, and once described Robert Millar in a letter to London as 'a venerable old man'.[30] In 1767 Andrew Millar erected an expensive monument in Paisley in honour of his parents, including a Latin inscription that called his father 'an exemplary, wise, indefatigable, blameless pastor'.[31]

Considering that this inscription was in Latin, and that Millar used Latin in the titles of book catalogues he later issued in London, it is likely that he attended the grammar school at Paisley while in his early teens. At the age of fourteen or fifteen, however, when Scottish boys bound for the ministry and other professions would be at university, Millar was apprenticed to the Edinburgh bookseller, printer, and auctioneer James M'Euen for a fee of £40.[32] The apprenticeship with M'Euen is noticed in a footnote in Robert Fleming's 1815 biography of the Edinburgh bookseller William Creech, who was the successor of Alexander Kincaid and the protégé of William Strahan: 'James Macewen... a bookseller of considerable note,... had also an establishment in London. Mr William Strahan, Mr Andrew Millar, (both of whom early settled in London,) and Mr [Alexander] Kincaid were his apprentices, a circumstance which no doubt laid the foundation of the intimate connection between these eminent men'.[33]

The earliest known reference to M'Euen dates from December 1713, when he announced a book auction at his home in 'Nitherie's Wynd', Edinburgh.[34] Other Edinburgh addresses can be documented from his imprints, but when Andrew Millar became his apprentice in 1720, M'Euen had been settled for at least four years in a shop and auction house across from the Cross Well on the north side of the High Street, where he remained until 1727.[35] While at that address, he issued at least six auction catalogues, dated between 1719 and 1726.[36] In addition, M'Euen's name appears in dozens of imprints, as publisher, printer, and/or seller, and from 1718 he was the co-founder, with John Mosman and William Brown, and apparently managing partner, of Scotland's first successful newspaper, the *Edinburgh Evening Courant*, which remained under his control until 1732.[37] He also published, in 1720, a collection of local poetry, *The Edinburgh Miscellany*, which was the production of a patriotic Anglo-Scots club called the Athenian Society; it is significant because it contains the first published poetry by two young men who were associated with the Athenian, James Thomson and David Mallet.[38] In these years, M'Euen was as versatile, distinguished, and successful as any figure in the Edinburgh book trade.

The previously quoted passage from Fleming's biography of Creech states that M'Euen maintained an establishment in London, and we shall see that this circumstance would prove to be crucially important for Millar's career. Although there is no firm evidence about M'Euen's London shop until the early 1720s, it is possible that he had prior experience in the metropolis. According to the proposals for the *Edinburgh Evening Courant* that appeared in 1718, that newspaper was being printed 'by one from London, who has had long Experience in that Business, having heretofore written several News-Papers'. We do not know whether the individual in question was M'Euen himself (as W J Couper believed) or, as seems more likely, someone hired by him to serve as editor.[39] We do know that M'Euen was a feisty newspaper publisher, who tangled with the Edinburgh authorities more than once for refusing to print their version of events.[40] The *Courant* was popular with 'all except the violent Jacobites', M'Euen told Revd Robert Wodrow on 17 January 1719, 'who hate it for no other reason but because it is a true and impartial paper'.[41] Others considered it 'decidedly Whig' in outlook, and for this reason it provoked the Tory *Caledonian Mercury* into existence a few years later.

From an examination of his Edinburgh auction catalogues, it is clear that M'Euen catered to the learned in that branch of his business. At least two of the catalogues emphasized the inclusion of some 'curious' editions of the 'classicks'. The titles were in a variety of languages, including large numbers in Latin, and there were many books in expensive quarto and folio formats. The interleaved auctioneer's copy of the catalogue of the library of Sir Alexander Seaton of Pitmedden in the National Library of Scotland, dated 1719, shows M'Euen as a major buyer of such books, along with the Advocates Library, famous antiquaries and scholars of the day such as James Anderson and Thomas Ruddiman, and leading Presbyterian clergymen and academics such as William Hamilton, the Edinburgh divinity professor, and later principal, all of whom will be mentioned again below.[42] This kind of broad-based training in the high end of the book business would have provided Andrew Millar with excellent preparation for his later career as a bookseller in London.

Turning from his auction catalogues to his publications, we get a very different impression of what M'Euen was about. With some exceptions – such as the first volume of Alexander Nisbet's illustrated folio, *A System of Heraldry* (1722), and another folio by George Crawfurd, *The Lives and Characters of the Officers of the Crown, and of the State in Scotland* (1726) – the emphasis was on religious books. Most were sermons and devotional tracts by Church of Scotland ministers, including prominent clerical figures such as Thomas Boston (1677–1732), Walter Douglass (1673–1727), Thomas Halyburton (1674–1712), Peter Rae (1671–1749), John Willison (1680–1750), and William Wishart *primus* (1660–1729). M'Euen made a speciality of publishing substantial collections of communion sermons by such men. In 1721, for example, he published separate volumes titled *Five Sermons Preached before and after the Celebration of the Lord's Supper* by Douglass, Halyburton, and Wishart, and the following year he published a similarly titled collection by Willison, as well as *Twenty Sermons Preached before and after... the Lord's Supper. By Sundry Ministers of the Church of Scotland*, including sermons by Wishart, Douglass, Halyburton, and Willison. In 1720 and 1728, M'Euen was involved with the publication of works by Ralph Erskine (1685–1752), who would later break with the established church in the original secession. Perhaps his largest religious publication was a 614-page octavo edition of Thomas Boston's *Human Nature in Its Four-Fold State* in 1720. He also published a number of individual sermons preached before synods and other official ecclesiastical bodies, which almost certainly would not have been entrusted to a bookseller whose own standing in the Church of Scotland was in doubt.

The polemical religious works with which M'Euen was associated are equally revealing. M'Euen seems to have had a particularly close association with Revd John Willison of Dundee, one of the Church of Scotland's most influential devotional writers and Presbyterian controversialists. The affiliation apparently began in 1714, when M'Euen published Willison's anti-Episcopalian tract, *Letter from a Parochial*

Bishop to a Prelatical Gentleman in Scotland, Concerning the Government of the Church. Two years later he published anonymously a much longer and more important work by Willison, *A Treatise Concerning the Sanctifying of the Lord's Day*, which included a controversial postscript. In 1717 the Scottish Episcopalian minister James Small, believing himself to be a principal target of these works, retaliated with *Some Reflections upon the Preface, and Some Paragraphs of a Book Printed for Mr. James M'Euen at Edinburgh, 1716; called, A Treatise concerning the Sanctifying of the Lord's Day*. M'Euen published another polemical work by Willison in 1719, *An Apology for the Church of Scotland*, which provoked another response by Small in the same year. The next year he published Willison's *Sacramental Catechism*, followed in 1722 by a second edition of Willison's *Treatise Concerning the Sanctifying of the Lord's Day*, which subsequently became a Presbyterian classic, reprinted for decades in Scotland and (in 1788) Philadelphia.

Willison and the other Church of Scotland ministers whose works M'Euen published possessed an evangelical Presbyterian outlook similar to that of Robert Millar. Most were of the same generation, who were raised during the difficult 'killing times' of the 1670s and 1680s and reached maturity just as Presbyterianism was being restored as the established church in Scotland. Like all Scottish Presbyterian clergymen, these men remained firm Whigs and Hanoverians during the first half of the eighteenth century, when Jacobitism was no idle threat. But denominational polemics did not necessarily entail intolerant and narrow-minded attitudes. Robert Millar, for one, was on excellent terms with the Tory, Jacobite, Episcopalian printer Thomas Ruddiman, who was involved with the printing of both his books; Millar referred to him in the Preface to his *History of the Church under the Old Testament* as 'my learned Friend'. M'Euen also rubbed shoulders with Ruddiman at book auctions and did business with him on a regular basis. The subscription lists in Millar's two books were filled with the names of Scottish Presbyterian men of learning, who apparently did not see any incompatibility between Millar's historical researches and his zealous missionary goals. Nor does M'Euen seem to have had any difficulty carrying on a career in the book trade that catered at once to the interests of evangelical Presbyterians, the Latin-reading elite, and the general, newspaper-reading public.

Robert Millar was a member of at least the first two, and possibly all three, of these reading audiences. Although no evidence of direct communication between Millar and M'Euen appears to have survived, we know that they shared a common friend and correspondent in the pious Presbyterian ecclesiastical historian and clergyman Robert Wodrow, and they probably shared a similar evangelical vision as well. In this regard, a passage in the *History of the Propagation of Christianity* may contain an important clue about Robert Millar's decision to send his eldest son into the book trade.

Discussing the global expansion of Europe from 'the fifteenth Century, and downward to the present Time', Millar draws attention to the historical importance of printing. He points out that printing enabled 'books and learning [to] have a more easy passage over the world. It is much cheaper and easier to buy a printed book, than to transcribe a manuscript out of a library'.[43] Indeed, Millar views not only the rise of printing, but also 'the reviving of arts and sciences, knowledge and learning', to which printing was thought to have contributed, in a primarily evangelical context, which holds that these events were 'ordered' by 'Divine Providence' for the purpose of spreading Christianity in the former strongholds of 'Satan's kingdom'.[44] Understanding the power of print in this way, and viewing the whole of human history as a global struggle between the forces of light and darkness, he may well have believed that putting his son into the book trade under the tutelage of a man like M'Euen was a way of preparing him to do the Lord's work.

As a result of his success as a bookseller-publisher, printer, and auctioneer, M'Euen expanded his business. By 1719 he was calling his firm 'James [or J.] M'Euen and Company' in many of his imprints. Around the time Millar joined him as an apprentice, if not earlier, M'Euen opened a shop in Glasgow. By 1722 his imprints sometimes referred to 'his shops in London, Edinburgh and Glasgow', as in the second edition of Willison's *Treatise Concerning the Sanctifying of the Lord's Day*. This degree of expansion in western Scotland and England was unprecedented for an Edinburgh bookseller, and it could only have occurred if supported both by sufficient capital and by competent employees. Among the latter was Alexander Kincaid, who would later occupy M'Euen's well-situated shop at the east end of the Luckenbooths, in the centre of the Edinburgh High Street.[45]

The M'Euen connection is the key to understanding Andrew Millar's emigration to London. M'Euen's London shop was situated at 'Buchanan's Head opposite to St. Clements Church Door in the Strand', as we learn from the title page of *A Catalogue of Curious, Valuable, and Uncommon Books, in Several Faculties and Languages*, issued to announce an auction there on 4 June 1723. Almost two years later, 'James Mac Euen, Bookseller in *London* and *Edinburgh*' printed a 72-page catalogue entitled *Collectio Itineraria: or a Catalogue of Valuable Books, Ancient and Modern, in Sundry Faculties and Languages; Chiefly Collected Out of Private Libraries Both in Scotland and England*, announcing an auction that would begin at Paul's Coffeehouse on 'the 17th of March, 1724–5'. We do not know if Millar was in London this early, but it is certainly possible. In 1727, while still an apprentice, he appeared for M'Euen in a legal case involving the sale of piratical Scottish Bibles in London.[46]

By January 1728, when he was just twenty-two years old, Millar was operating independently at the Buchanan's Head shop formerly owned by M'Euen.[47] M'Euen's bookselling career in Edinburgh continued at least until 1733 or 1734, and we do not know the circumstances surrounding the transfer of his London shop to Millar after the latter's apprenticeship came to an end. No matter how or why this occurred, however, there can be little doubt that Millar was eased into a bookselling career in London through his association with M'Euen, who had already broken the ice by opening and operating a shop in the Strand. Contrary to the standard accounts, it was M'Euen, not Millar, who gave his London shop the name Buchanan's Head. At this time, to name a London shop after George Buchanan – the sixteenth-century Presbyterian humanist, Latinist, historian of Scotland, and republican political theorist – was to make a statement on behalf of religious, intellectual, political, and patriotic attitudes such as those we have been tracing. Millar inherited the name and sign, as he inherited the premises, of his master's London shop, and did so by the beginning of 1728, not in 1729, as most commentators have maintained. When Millar moved in 1742 to a more desirable location opposite Catherine Street in the Strand (which never was the shop of Jacob Tonson[48]), he simply took the name Buchanan's Head along with him.

As a young bookseller in London, Millar published, in 1728 and 1729, lengthy book-sale catalogues of mainly Latin libraries that were much like those which M'Euen had produced a few years earlier, except that Millar preferred to mark discount prices in the front of his books rather than sell them at auction.[49] More generally, Millar relied heavily on books and authors rooted in the community of Scottish Presbyterian clergymen and scholars with whom his father and James M'Euen were associated. On the basis of advertisements in the *Daily Journal* on 18 April 1728 and afterwards, it is clear that Millar's initial stock consisted largely of Edinburgh books that M'Euen himself had advertised in the same newspaper on 4, 7, and 11 November 1727. Examples include Robert Wodrow's *History of the Sufferings of the Church of Scotland*, M'Euen's own edition of Nisbet's *System of Heraldry*, the two-volume folio edition of George Buchanan's *Opera Omnia* that was edited by his father's 'learned friend' Thomas Ruddiman, *The Peerage of Scotland* by George Crawfurd or Crawford (who was the son-in-law of the Edinburgh antiquary James Anderson), and an early edition of *The Tea-Table Miscellany* by 'the famous Allan Ramsay'. Thus, Millar assumed ownership of M'Euen's Scottish stock along with his former master's London shop.

In London, Millar occasionally reissued titles from the stock he inherited from M'Euen with cancel title pages, but he also reprinted some of those titles. A prime example of a book in the latter category is Robert Millar's *History of the Propagation of Christianity, and Overthrow of Paganism*. The second edition of that work was published in London in 1726 in a two-volume octavo edition; 'J. Mac-Euen in the

Strand' was among several booksellers listed in the imprint, and M'Euen advertised it in the London *Daily Journal* on 4 November 1727. Andrew Millar advertised the second edition for sale in the *Daily Journal* on 18 April 1728, and in 1731 he published a third edition of the book, also in octavo format, 'with Additions, Alterations, and a compleat Alphabetical Index', as he put it in an advertisement, and the word '*the*' added before '*Overthrow*' in the title. A different tactic was followed in regard to *Collections Relating to the History of Mary Queen of Scotland*, a four-volume quarto work by the Scottish antiquary James Anderson, whose library Millar would sell off in 1729. Anderson's book originally appeared in Edinburgh in 1727–8 and was among the stock that Millar inherited from M'Euen. A 'second edition' soon appeared under the imprint of Millar and several other London booksellers, though it was actually a reissue of the first edition, with cancel title-pages.[50]

Millar's early career as a bookseller was well grounded in the works of Presbyterian ministers in Scotland, several of whom were connected with M'Euen. Besides the works by Robert Millar and Robert Wodrow mentioned above, the stock he inherited from M'Euen included *A Practical Essay on the Sacrament of Baptism* (Edinburgh, 1724), a M'Euen imprint by another Church of Scotland clergyman of his father's generation, John Warden (1671–1751). In 1733 M'Euen was involved in the Edinburgh publication of *Gospel Ministers Christ's Ambassadors* by Peter Rae, the minister of Kirkconnel in Dumfriesshire. Thirteen years later Millar published the second edition of Rae's *History of the Rebellion [of 1715] Rais'd against His Majesty King George I*, first published in 1718, which was now dedicated to George II. We have seen that William Wishart *primus* was among the Church of Scotland ministers whose sermons were published by M'Euen in Edinburgh. Millar's name appears in the imprints of seven publications of sermons by Wishart's sons, George (1702–85) and William *secundus* (1692?–1753). Like his father, William *secundus* served (from 1737 until his death) as principal of the University of Edinburgh, after pastoral stints in Glasgow in the 1720s and at the Scots Church at Founder's Hall, London, in the 1730s, and he was also among the clergymen who subscribed to Robert Millar's *History of the Church under the Old Testament* in 1730. The Wisharts were also closely tied to Andrew Millar's friend and collaborator, William Strahan, who published some of their sermons and left small annuities to George Wishart's children in his will, as Millar left an annuity to Strahan's son and successor Andrew, his godson.[51]

M'Euen's influence on Millar extended into the literary realm. M'Euen's shop in the Luckenbooths had been owned previously by Allan Ramsay, whose circulating library is believed to have been located in the rooms directly above it.[52] Millar undoubtedly benefited from the ties between Ramsay and his master. M'Euen is listed in the imprint of the third edition of the *Poems* (1723) as that work's Glasgow selling agent, and in the imprint of the second edition of Ramsay's *Gentle Shepherd* (1726) as one of its two selling agents in London. The stock that Millar inherited from M'Euen in January 1728 included Edinburgh editions of Ramsay's *Tea-Table Miscellany* and *Ever-Green*. In 1729 Millar and Thomas Longman co-published the 'fifth edition' of volume two of the *Tea-Table Miscellany* with Ramsay himself and booksellers in Newcastle and Glasgow, and Millar was actively selling various editions of Ramsay's publications in London at this time. A letter from Ramsay to Millar, dated 13 July 1732, empowers Millar to intervene in a prior publishing agreement with M'Euen in regard to his *Poems*, and to publish his *Tea-Table Miscellany* 'in what form you please'.[53] Millar's name would subsequently appear in many other editions of Ramsay's various works.

The poet James Thomson stands out as another literary point of connection. As noted earlier, Thomson's earliest published poetry appeared in the *Edinburgh Miscellany* that M'Euen published in 1720, the year in which Millar began his apprenticeship in Edinburgh. It is very likely that Thomson and Millar first met at that time.[54] Thomson was then a divinity student at the University of Edinburgh, studying under Professor (later Principal) William Hamilton, the mentor of George and William Wishart *secundus*, as well as of another Presbyterian minister of their generation whose works Millar regularly published, Robert Wallace. Hamilton, who was also a subscriber to the first edition of Robert Millar's *History of the Propagation of Christianity*, was the father of the Edinburgh bookseller Gavin Hamilton, with whom Millar and Strahan were sometimes connected; many years later Strahan would refer favourably to William Hamilton's divinity teaching in a letter to David Hume.[55] In London, James Thomson became Andrew Millar's intimate friend, and their circle was composed almost entirely of fellow Anglo-Scots with Presbyterian roots, including Patrick Murdoch, who had been Thomson's classmate in Hamilton's divinity class at Edinburgh and would later edit Thomson's works (and much else) for Millar, and the philosopher George Turnbull, another of Thomson's divinity-school classmates who would later be among Millar's authors.[56] Still another of Thomson's lifelong friends from his Edinburgh days was David Mallet, whose juvenile poetry had appeared in the *Edinburgh Miscellany*, and whose writings Millar would subsequently publish in London. Thomson also became Millar's meal ticket, as he produced a steady stream of popular, profitable poetry that Millar regularly published – and zealously protected against any perceived infringement of copyright.

The Scottish mindset of the young London bookseller emerges clearly from an examination of two of his early advertisements. The first of them, bound at the end of some copies of Millar's 1728 edition of James Thomson's *Spring: A Poem*, lists twenty-eight titles in four pages, under the heading 'Books Printed for and Sold by

Andrew Millar, at Buchanan's Head, over-against St. Clement's Church without Temple-Bar'. No fewer than twenty of these titles were Scottish by author or topic, including works that we have encountered before by James Anderson, George Buchanan, Thomas Ruddiman, Alexander Nisbet, Robert Wodrow, James Thomson, Allan Ramsay, and Robert Millar. The Scottish titles also include both of the previously mentioned books by George Crawfurd, several additional titles by Ruddiman, Thomson, and Ramsay, Daniel Defoe's *History of the Union*, Alexander Malcolm's *Treatise of Musick*, the *Pharmacopoeia* published by the Royal College of Physicians in Edinburgh (presumably the fifth edition of 1725), and Sir George Mackenzie's *Institutes of the Law of Scotland.* Among the few non-Scottish titles named in the advertisement were some books that had been part of M'Euen's stock and two 'second editions' of works by the English Calvinist John Edwards, *The Doctrin* [sic] *of Faith and Justification Set in a True Light* and *Some New Discoveries of the Uncertainty, Deficiency, and Corruptions of Human Knowledge and Learning*, which Millar apparently reissued with cancel title-pages in very small quantities, most likely with the approval of his father and others of his theological outlook. Taken as a whole, this advertisement demonstrates the extent to which, at the beginning of his career as a London bookseller, Millar remained focused mainly on books associated with his father, his former master M'Euen, his friend Thomson, and other Scottish authors.

The second advertisement, 'Books Printed for, and Sold by A. Millar, at Buchanan's Head, over-against St. Clement's Church in the Strand', appears in a pamphlet published in London in 1732, and shows that Millar's focus remained essentially unchanged as many as four years after he became an independent bookseller in London. Seven titles are listed, in the following order: M'Euen's folio edition of Nisbet's *System of Heraldry*; Millar's own folio edition of his father's *History of the Church under the Old Testament*; Millar's third edition of his father's *History of the Propagation of Christianity*, followed by an italicized sentence that reads: 'This Book is recommended by the Bishop of London, in his second Pastoral Letter, pag. 31, as written by a faithful and judicious Hand'; two Scottish books which had been among the stock Millar inherited from M'Euen, both recently reissued in London with cancel title-pages: Alexander Malcolm's *Treatise of Musick* and Sir William Hope's *Vindication of the True Art of Self-Defence*; and two works by James Thomson, *The Seasons* and *The Tragedy of Sophonisba*, each published by Millar in both quarto and octavo editions.

The pamphlet in which this advertisement appears, *A Defence of F. John Baptist Girard, Jesuit,... against the Accusation of Mary Catharine Cadiere. Part I*, is also of interest. Although the imprint reads 'printed and sold by J. Roberts', the presence of this advertisement establishes Millar as the publisher, and confirms his participation in the enormously popular literature on the Father Girard scandal that was cited in Authenticus's letter to the *Bee* in 1791. Millar's deeper involvement may be inferred from the fact that other editions of this pamphlet (including parts II and III) also appeared in London at this time under James Roberts's imprint, as did at least nine editions of abridged English translations of *Factum pour Marie Catherine Cadière contre le père Jean Baptiste Girard.*[57] Other aspects of Authenticus's anecdote also ring true, such as the characterization of the relationship between Millar and his notoriously domineering and acquisitive 'city wife'.[58] Could it be, then, that Millar's involvement in the Father Girard affair in the early 1730s represents the moment when the young Scot confronted the cruel realities of bookselling in London, and made the transition from provincial idealism to a single-minded concern with profit, as Authenticus suggests?

Such an interpretation cannot be sustained. Andrew Millar unquestionably sought to make money in the book business, and it is entirely possible that the pamphlets he published on the Father Girard scandal helped him to acquire capital at a critical moment in the early years of his bookselling career. But making money was not necessarily his only objective, and his career after the Girard scandal was not characterized by a descent into the crudest form of publishing for profit, as Authenticus implies. Instead, Millar frequently found ways to make money by publishing good books while at the same time handsomely compensating their authors. This point was not lost on the editor of the *Bee*, James Anderson (no relation to the early eighteenth-century antiquary of the same name), who responded to Authenticus with an anecdote of his own, concerning Millar's extraordinary generosity towards an unknown author, Richard Burn, from whose publications he ultimately earned thousands of pounds. For Anderson, the moral of the story was that Millar 'never altogether abandoned' the idealistic principles of his youth, 'which many of his profession now laugh at as unfashionable and ridiculous; yet honest Andrew Millar, with all these follies, made more money in the end, than any of his profession I have yet heard of'.[59] Anderson might also have pointed out that the works of at least two of the reputable authors whom Millar published in his early years, James Thomson and Allan Ramsay, seem to have been very profitable, and that this pattern would continue to hold throughout his career, as he published Hume, Johnson, Fielding, and many other distinguished, best-selling authors.[60] Authenticus's naïve belief in the incompatibility of the profit motive and a commitment to high literary standards does not stand up to scrutiny.

Just as Millar was able to balance profit and principle, so too did he find ways to balance his Scottish Presbyterian roots with the broader demands of bookselling and publishing in London. As time passed, he became a fixture in the Strand, and his dogged pursuit of the Scottish book trade for reprinting titles that he believed were his property in perpetuity – in accordance with the metropolitan assumptions of the Stationers' Company – helped to fix his reputation as the defender of the rights of the London booksellers against potential rivals in Scotland. More generally, adapting to the broad interests of the London market, and associating with leading English authors, carried him into a wide range of publishing ventures that contributed to his stature as a British bookseller of the first rank.[61]

At the same time, Millar never gave up his initial connection with Scottish authors and books. Besides the poets James Thomson and Allan Ramsay, he had a hand in the publication and sale of philosophical publications by Andrew Baxter and George Turnbull from the early 1730s to the mid-1740s. During the final two decades of his life, he contributed mightily to the development of the movement now known as the Scottish Enlightenment. A milestone of sorts was the publication in 1755 of the posthumous, two-volume quarto edition of Francis Hutcheson's *System of Moral Philosophy*, printed by Robert and Andrew Foulis in Glasgow for Millar and Thomas Longman in London. Seven years earlier, on 13 July 1748, Millar was made a burgess and guild-brother by the Edinburgh town council,[62] and in the same year he began publishing works by Hume. He subsequently published significant numbers of new scholarly books by Hume and other Scottish authors, including Adam Smith, William Robertson, George Campbell, Alexander Gerard, Adam Ferguson, James Ferguson, Thomas Reid, and Lord Kames, often in collaboration with the Edinburgh firm of another of M'Euen's former apprentices, Alexander Kincaid. Most of these works were secular in nature, although several of their authors were Church of Scotland ministers; when they treated religious topics, they tended to be philosophical and restrained, as in George Campbell's *Dissertation on Miracles* (1762) and Alexander Gerard's *Dissertations on Subjects relating to the Genius and the Evidences of Christianity* (1766). Thus, in helping to launch the mature Scottish Enlightenment, Millar also contributed to the redefinition of enlightened Scottish Presbyterian learning. The dual commitment to Presbyterianism and secular literature and learning that his father, Robert Millar, and his master, James M'Euen, had tried to promote was reaffirmed in a new form, which was generally more moderate and polite, and less evangelical, polemical, and antiquarian. The ability to maintain continuity with his Scottish Presbyterian past, while adapting to the changing nature of Scottish and English authors, books, and markets, is among the characteristics that justify Andrew Millar's reputation as the premier bookseller and publisher of his age.

NOTES

1. 'Anecdotes of Mr. Andrew Millar', *The Bee*, 7 June 1791, 3 (1791), 127–33.

2. James Boswell, *The Life of Samuel Johnson*, [ed] G B Hill, [rev] L F Powell, 6 vol (Oxford, 1934–40), 1, 288.

3. Boswell, *Life*, 1, 287, n 3; 'Anecdotes', 128.
4. *Gazetteer and New Daily Advertiser*, 9 June 1768.
5. Hugh Amory, 'Andrew Millar', forthcoming in the *New Dictionary of National Biography*.
6. John Nichols, *Literary Anecdotes of the Eighteenth Century*, 9 vol (London, 1812–16), 3, 386–9.
7. This story dates at least from Gordon Goodwin's late nineteenth-century sketch of Millar in the *Dictionary of National Biography*.
8. See, for example, Carol Hall, 'Andrew Millar', in *The British Literary Book Trade, 1700–1820*, [ed] James K Bracken & Joel Silver (Detroit, 1995), 184–90.
9. Hew Scott, *Fasti Ecclesiae Scoticanae: The Succession of Ministers in the Church of Scotland*, new edn, 7 vol (Edinburgh, 1915–28).
10. See Richard B Sher, 'Commerce, religion and the Enlightenment in eighteenth-century Glasgow', in *Glasgow Volume I: Beginnings to 1830*, [ed] T M Devine & Gordon Jackson (Manchester & New York, 1995), 312–59.
11. Sher, 'Commerce…', 326–7; Andrew Hook & Richard B Sher [ed], *The Glasgow Enlightenment* (East Linton, 1995); Ned C Landsman, 'Presbyterians and provincial society: the Evangelical Enlightenment in the west of Scotland, 1740–1775', in *Sociability and Society in Eighteenth-Century Scotland*, [ed] John Dwyer & Richard B Sher (Edinburgh, 1993), 194–209.
12. Scott, *Fasti*, 3, 29 & 158.
13. Scott, *Fasti*, 3,166.
14. William Forrest Macarthur, *History of Port Glasgow* (Glasgow, 1932), 211–2.
15. James Paterson, *Histories of the Counties of Ayr and Wigton*, 2 vol (Edinburgh, 1863), 1, 741–3.
16. Scott, *Fasti*, 2, 383; 1, 7, 15 & 46.
17. Old Parish Register, Port Glasgow, examined on microfilm at the Scottish Genealogy Society, Edinburgh. One source of confusion is the inscription on Millar's tombstone in Chelsea, which Nichols reproduced in his *Literary Anecdotes*; it states that Millar was sixty-one years old when he died on 8 June 1768, when in fact he was sixty-two. A second source of confusion is a list of birthdays in one of William Strahan's ledgers (British Library, Add. MS 48803A, fol 103), which shows Millar's birth date as 19 October 1706 (see Hall, 'Andrew Millar', 184). Although Strahan got the year of Millar's birth wrong, he was probably right about the day and the month, once they are converted from new style (19 October) to old style (8 October).
18. The title continues: *Wherein the Christian Religion Is Confirmed, The Rise and Progress of Heathenish Idolatry Is Considered, The Overthrow of Paganism, and the Spreading of Christianity in the Several Ages of the New Testament-Church Is Explained, The Present State of Heathens is Enquired into, and Methods for their Conversion Offered.*
19. The title continues: *with a Particular Account of the State of the Jews, before and after the Babylonian Captivity, and Down to the Present Time: Wherein the Affairs and Learning of Heathen Nations before the Birth of Christ, Are Also Illustrated. To Which Is Subjoined, A Discourse to Promote the Conversion of the Jews to Christianity*. Although the imprint identifies

only the printers, Thomas & Walter Ruddiman, Andrew Millar listed the book in advertisements for his publications.

20. J A De Jong, *As the Waters Cover the Sea: Millennial Expectations in the Rise of Anglo-American Missions 1640–1810* (Kampen, 1970), 113–14 (De Jong's title phrase is taken from Millar); Ronald E Davies, 'Robert Millar – an eighteenth-century Scottish Latourette', *The Evangelical Quarterly* 62 (1990), 143–56; John Foster, 'A Scottish contributor to the missionary awakening: Robert Millar of Paisley', *International Review of Missions*, 37 (1948), 138–45; Arthur Fawcett, *The Cambuslang Revival: The Scottish Evangelical Revival of the Eighteenth Century* (Edinburgh, 1971), 213–15.

21. *The Life and Transactions of Herod the Great* (Edinburgh, 1782) and *The History of the Jews, from the Death of Herod the Great, to the Final Destruction of their City* (Edinburgh, 1782; also Glasgow, 1786).

22. Wodrow to Mather, 29 July 1724, in *The Correspondence of the Rev. Robert Wodrow*, [ed] Thomas M'Crie, 3 vol (Edinburgh, 1843), 3, 154.

23. Scott, *Fasti*, 3, 166, 168, 174 & 354.

24. Scott, *Fasti*, 3, 61, 66, 158.

25. 'Neilston', *New Statistical Account of Scotland*, 15 vol (Edinburgh & London, 1845), 7, 335.

26. Millar to Cadell, 16 July 1765, National Library of Scotland, MS 9819, fol 196–7.

27. National Archives of Scotland, CC 8/8/125/2, fol 423–30.

28. His will is reproduced, along with his wife's, in Vere Langford Oliver, *The History of the Island of Antigua*, 3 vol (London, 1896), 2, 265, because one of his executors was his brother, William, who had been a physician in Antigua.

29. The grand-nephew was Peter Davidson, son of Revd Archibald Davidson, the principal of Glasgow University from 1786, and his wife Grizel, who was the daughter of Revd Peter Scott of Paisley and Millar's sister Anne or Anna (d 1768).

30. Strahan to Richardson, 2 September 1749, in *The Correspondence of Samuel Richardson*, 6 vol (London, 1804), 1, 144. See also Strahan's Scottish travel diaries in the library of the American Philosophical Society, Philadelphia, B/St 83.

31. George Crawfurd & William Semple, *The History of the Shire of Renfrew* (Paisley, 1782), 304.

32. Ian Maxted, *The British Book Trades, 1710–1777* (Exeter, 1983), no 1015.

33. Robert Fleming, 'Account of the life of the late Mr William Creech', in Creech's *Edinburgh Fugitive Pieces* (Edinburgh, 1815), xvi–xvii. On Kincaid's apprenticeship and subsequent career, see Richard B Sher, 'Alexander Kincaid', *New Dictionary of National Biography*, forthcoming. On Strahan's apprenticeship, J A Cochrane, *Dr. Johnson's Printer: The Life of William Strahan* (Cambridge, Mass, 1964), 2, claims that 'by his own account he was apprenticed to John Mosman and William Brown', but the evidence supporting this contention is ambiguous (ibid, 60), and Cochrane appears to be unaware of Fleming's testimony.

34. *A Catalogue of Books, to be Sold by Auction, on Wednesday the 9th Day of December 1713. At Mr. James McEwen's House in the Head of Nitherie's Wynd* [Edinburgh 1713].

35. Scottish Book Trade Index, compiled by John Morris and others, accessible at the website of the National Library of Scotland: www.nls.ac.uk/catframe.htm.

36. The titles follow, along with the date when each auction took place or began: *A Catalogue of Books, in Several Faculties and Languages, Being the Library of Mr Alexander Inglis of Murdistoun* (1 July 1719); *A Catalogue of Curious and Valuable Books, in Several Faculties and Languages, with Curious Editions of the Classicks* (15 February 1722); *A Catalogue of Curious and Valuable Books...* (10 December 1723); *A Catalogue of Curious and Valuable Books... with Some Curious and Ancient Editions of the Classicks... Being an Appendix to a Former Catalogue* (4 February 1724); *A Catalogue of Valuable and Curious Book, in Several Languages and Faculties* (11 May 1725); *A Catalogue of Curious and Valuable Books in Several Languages and Faculties* (18 January 1726). Most of these catalogues were not listed in the *English Short-Title Catalogue* at the time this article went to press, but were examined on microfilm reel Mf. 816 in the National Library of Scotland.

37. W J Couper, *The Edinburgh Periodical Press*, 2 vol (Stirling, 1908), 2, 19–25.

38. Mary Jane Scott, *James Thomson, Anglo-Scot* (Athens, Ga, & London, 1988), 58–60, 316, n 48.

39. Couper, *Edinburgh Press*, 2, 19.

40. Couper, *Edinburgh Press*, 1, 99–100; 2, 23–5; Robert Chambers, *Domestic Annals of Scotland from the Revolution to the Rebellion of 1745*, 3 vol (Edinburgh & London, 1861), 3, 439–40; Robert Wodrow, *Analecta*, 4 vol (Edinburgh, 1843), 3, 213.

41. Quoted in Chambers, *Domestic Annals, 3*, 439.

42. *A Catalogue of Valuable Books, in Several Languages and Faculties... Being the Library which Belong'd to Sir Alexander Seaton of Pitmedden* (Edinburgh, 1719).

43. Robert Millar, *The History of the Propagation of Christianity, and the Overthrow of Paganism*, 3rd edn, 2 vols. (London, 1731), 2, 207 & 227–8.

44. Millar, *Propagation of Christianity*,2, 227; De Jong, *As the Waters Cover the Sea*, 113.

45. *Scots Magazine*, 77 (1815), 687.

46. *Eyre* v. *Baskett* and others, Public Record Office, C 11/2726/37.

47. Millar is listed at that address in the proposals for James Thomson's 'The Four Seasons' that appeared, according to James Sambrook, in various London newspapers in January 1728, as well as in the 1728 edition of Thomson's *Spring: A Poem.* Besides Millar and Thomson himself, the subscription-takers included Allan Ramsay in Edinburgh and two other Anglo-Scottish booksellers in London with whom Millar was closely connected, John Millan (who is believed to have shortened his name from 'McMillan' when he moved from Scotland to London) and George Strahan (who may have been related to William Strahan). See James Thomson, *The Seasons*, [ed] James Sambrook (Oxford, 1981), xliii–xliv

48. Hugh Phillips, *Mid-Georgian London: A Topographical and Social Survey of Central and Western London about 1750* (London, 1964), 170.

49. *Librorum, In Omnibus ferè Facultatibus & Linguis, Catalogus: Being the Libraries of an Eminent Physician, and of a Gentleman of the Inner-Temple, Both Lately Deceased* (advertising a sale at his shop, beginning 16 May 1728) and *Catalogus Librorum Praestantissimorum in omnibus ferè Artibus & Scientiis: or, A Catalogue of the Libraries of the Learned and Judicious James Anderson Esq; Famus Antiquary, and Late Post-Master-General of Scotland; and of a Celebrated Judge and Lawyer in England, Both Lately Deceased* (advertising a sale at his shop on 17 April 1729).

50. I am grateful to Juliet Chadwick of Exeter College Library, Oxford, for this information.

51. Cochrane, *Dr. Johnson's Printer*, 206; Oliver, *History of Antigua*, 2, 265.

52. *Scots Magazine,* 77 (1815), 687; *The Works of Allan Ramsay*, [ed] A M Kinghorn & A Law, 4 vols (Edinburgh, 1970), 4, 28–9. Contrary to popular belief, however, M'Euen probably did not acquire Ramsay's circulating library.

53. *Gentleman's Magazine,* 39 (April 1853), 370.

54. Scott, *James Thomson, Anglo-Scot*, 246.

55. Strahan to Hume, 30 October 1775, National Library of Scotland, MS 23,157, no 66.

56. Scott, *James Thomson, Anglo-Scot*, 46, 245–6. Both Murdoch and Turnbull eventually took orders in the Church of England, which was a strong attraction to assimilation-minded Anglo-Scots of this generation. The complexity of the problem of national identity that they faced is discussed from a literary point of view in Gerard Carruthers, 'James Thomson and eighteenth-century Scottish literary identity', in Richard Terry [ed], *James Thomson: Essays for the Tercentenary* (Liverpool, 2000), 165–90.

57 *The Case of Mrs. Mary Catherine Cadiere, against the Jesuit Father John Baptist Girard* (London: printed for and sold by J. Roberts, and by most booksellers in town and country, 1732). All the editions that appeared with this imprint have the same pagination and are dated 1732. Two other versions of this work are also of interest: an Edinburgh 'tenth edition', with different pagination, 'printed and sold by Allan Ramsay and Gavin Hamilton, 1730', which is presumably an incorrect publication date, and at least a half-dozen London editions of the unabridged work, published under the imprint of J Millan in 1732. Millan is best known for owning and then selling to Millar some of the copyrights of James Thomson's earliest poetic works, which were entered for him in the Stationers' Hall Register in 1726–7 by James Roberts. See Alan Dugald McKillop [ed], *James Thomson (1700–1748): Letters and Documents* (Lawrence, Kan, 1958), 63–4.

58. The reference to Millar's 'city wife' appears in *The Autobiography of Dr. Alexander Carlyle of Inveresk 1722–1805*, [ed] John Hill Burton (London & Edinburgh, 1910; reprint ed Bristol, 1990), 456. Cf Hume's joke about the wealthy Millar having been declared bankrupt as a result of 'the Extravagance of his Wife', in a letter to William Rouet, 6 July [1759], in *The Letters of David Hume*, [ed] J Y T Greig, 2 vols (Oxford, 1932), 1, 310–11. On 13 June 1773 James Beattie remarked in his diary that 'Millar durst not contradict his wife in any thing' (*James Beattie's London Diary 1773*, [ed] Ralph S Walker (Aberdeen, 1946), 53).

59. 'Anecdotes of Mr. Andrew Millar', 131–3.

60. Nearly all the existing secondary literature on Millar deals with these major authors. See Austin Dobson, 'Fielding and Andrew Millar', *The Library*, 3rd ser, 7 (1916), 177–90; Hugh Amory, 'Andrew Millar and the first recension of Fielding's *Works* (1762)', *Transactions of the Cambridge Bibliographical Society*, 8 (1981), 57–78, and '"*De facto* copyright"? Fielding's *Works* in partnership, 1769–1821', *Eighteenth-Century Studies,* 17 (1984), 449–76; Allen Reddick, *The Making of Johnson's Dictionary, 1746–1773* (Cambridge, 1990); Ernest Campbell Mossner, *The Life of David Hume*, 2nd edn (Oxford, 1980).

61. See, for example, Guido Abbattista, 'The business of Paternoster Row: towards a publishing history of the *Universal History* (1736–65)', *Publishing History,* 17 (1985), 5–50.

62. *Roll of Edinburgh Burgesses and Guild-Brethren, 1701–1760*, [ed] Charles B Boog Watson (Edinburgh, 1930), 139.

'What Constitutes the Crime which it is Your Pleasure to Punish so Mercilessly?': Scottish Booksellers' Societies in the Nineteenth Century

IAIN BEAVAN

CONDEMNING the Glasgow Booksellers' Protection Association John Joseph Griffin commented 'The Association is strictly coercive in its character. It deprives every man of his legal right to buy and sell books as he pleases'.[1] He thus encapsulated one side of a highly divisive nineteenth-century debate on the principles and practicalities of maintaining the retail price of printed material.

This paper has two aims: first, to open up a somewhat neglected theme in provincial book-trade studies; second, to consider what we know of Scottish booksellers' protection societies, their common purpose, and effectiveness in the early- to mid-nineteenth century.[2]

In November 1844, the Glasgow publishers and wholesalers, Griffin & Co, were provoked into writing, in scathing terms, to the much larger and influential Edinburgh firm of Oliver & Boyd. Moreover, the correspondence was soon afterwards exploited and published by Griffin as part of their battle against what they saw as a repressive set of attitudes to be found in the trade, and as particularly exhibited by the Edinburgh firm.

The letter acknowledged receipt of a circular from Oliver & Boyd, and grieved that such a firm should treat 'the Glasgow Trade with the insulting contempt which that document manifests'. The fundamental issue was over the right of individual members of the Glasgow trade to determine the prices at which they sold their stock either to other retail booksellers, or to the general public. Griffin was also concerned to challenge the defensibility of Oliver & Boyd's plans to monitor the prices at which the Edinburgh firm's own publications were sold in and around Glasgow.

'You inform us', the letter noted, 'that you have appointed Mr. David Robertson to be a spy, on your behalf, into the manner in which the Glasgow Trade conduct their business... and to give you at all times full information on this matter'. On receipt of the name of a supposed underseller, the Edinburgh firm was (quite correctly) assumed to have been prepared to refuse to transact any business with the named bookseller. In other words, any Glasgow bookseller who refused to acknowledge and obey those trading conventions to which Oliver & Boyd subscribed, faced the prospect of slow commercial extinction.

After further accusations of despotism and of exercising a 'self-appointed office of Censor of the Booksellers of Glasgow', Griffin & Co concluded that 'even the prime movers of the "Glasgow Booksellers' Illegal Conspiracy" would not be so devoid of independence and self-respect as to submit to their "insolent missive" '.[3]

A number of questions immediately arise. What was the 'insolent missive', who was David Robertson, what was the meaning of the reference to the 'Glasgow Booksellers' Illegal Conspiracy', and who were Griffin & Co?

The 'insolent missive' of 8 November 1844 reads straightforwardly enough, and essentially confirms the factual content of Griffin's accusations: Oliver & Boyd were indeed concerned to hear that several Glasgow booksellers had been selling their publications considerably below the stipulated retail price, and, if discovered, they would decline to supply them with any more books. David Robertson, as their agent, had been asked to keep them informed.

David Robertson was a large wholesaler and publisher in Glasgow, and was sufficiently aspiring to have got himself appointed Her Majesty's Bookseller in that city. More significantly, though, he was the wholesale agent for the West of Scotland for Oliver & Boyd's publications. Robertson also organised annually a supplement to Oliver & Boyd's *Edinburgh Almanac*, and loyally stood by that publication against rival productions.[4] Altogether, then, Robertson had secured for himself a steady and seemingly secure, though ultimately dependent, income flow.

What of the 'Glasgow Booksellers' Illegal Conspiracy'? Properly entitled the Glasgow Booksellers' Protection Association, it was formed in 1834 (ten years before Griffin's tirade against Oliver & Boyd), with David Robertson as its first chairman, and its purpose was the same as the association established in London in 1829.[5] In late 1834 a provisional agreement was arrived at by a large number of Glasgow booksellers not to submit to pressure from the public which had been 'led to imagine that they ought to have a discount on all publications', to resist what was seen as unfair competition from within the retail trade itself, and not to offer copyright books for sale at a discount of more than 2*d* in the shilling (early in 1835 modified to 10%). The document made an explicit appeal for support from specialist wholesale houses. But beneath that plea lay an unmistakeable threat, that the retail trade itself would not transact business with any wholesaler that dealt with undersellers. It is however clear that the Glasgow Association had initially attempted a more direct approach, namely that of asking wholesalers and publishers simply not to deal with undersellers in the West of Scotland. W Bounds (probably Secretary of the London Booksellers' Committee) wrote in 1835 to John Reid, his counterpart in Glasgow:

> After the most mature deliberation, that to call on the wholesale houses to decline all dealings with those gentlemen who do not join with you in your measure of protection would rather injure than serve you.

> The Committee have during these deliberations borne in mind the unpleasant collision that would certainly take place between the London and Scotch trade on the very first proceedings of the Glasgow Booksellers against their Opponents with this conviction... they consider it would be the height of impolicy for them to interfere.

Bounds was not, however, unhelpful, and suggested a more effective way for the Glasgow retail trade to achieve its ends, by having its members make themselves known to those London firms that supplied those booksellers 'who take off large discounts to the public', and to decline to place orders with any house that persisted in supplying any of the undersellers.[6]

That one element of internal trade pressure was thenceforth to work back from the point of retail supply is made explicit by one of the resolutions of the Aberdeen Booksellers' Society which stated that 'We further engage, that we will not either... Buy or Sell Copyright Books with any Wholesale House which supplies Copyright Books to Retail Booksellers who refuse to concur with us'.[7]

Why was the Glasgow Association formed in 1834? There appears to be no single cause, though at least one contemporary report had the Scottish retail book trade struggling to come to terms with markedly increased competition, in the form of an influx of cheap magazines sold by 'every man, woman, or child, who should open a booth... with no other knowledge of literature or bookselling than the faculty of distinguishing, by the shape or general appearance, *Chambers' Journal* from the *Penny Magazine*'. It was said that such was the demand that sellers quickly emerged, and the trade 'had the mortification to see that... they had diverted the stream of custom from themselves to a shoal of new rivals, whom they would scarcely acknowledge as booksellers'.[8]

The Glasgow trade was never unanimous in its opinion over the issue of underselling. Two years after the foundation of the Association, David Robertson wrote to George Boyd (of Oliver & Boyd) that he was sending 'a supply of circulars for the Edinburgh trade – containing our agreement & the signatures of those who concur with us – Ogle – Dewar & Griffin stand out and whether we are able to carry through the rule or not – depend on it – these individuals cannot soon stand well with their brethren'.[9] Two individuals in this group are particularly interesting: Dewar was brought to submission by the Glasgow Association, whilst Griffin materially contributed to its temporary abandonment.

John Chapman, London bookseller, publisher, and leading publicist for the undersellers' cause, in his famous pamphlet of 1852, *Cheap Books and How to Get Them*, made a particular point of calling some Glasgow booksellers hypocritical for having acknowledged the retail regulations, only to have circumvented them by routinely adopting the stratagem of lightly defacing a new book, declaring it damaged, thus allowing themselves the liberty of selling it below the stipulated retail levels. But

Chapman (p 31) took comfort by accurately noting that the initial attempt at a Glasgow Association had been abandoned at some time previous to 1852 because it was feared that, if tested in court, it would be construed as an illegal conspiracy.

Griffin's pamphlet of mid-1844, *Is the Glasgow Booksellers' Protection Association a Lawful Association*...? argued its case largely on legal precedents, citing a case proven against five Glasgow cotton spinners for conspiracy. The illegality of the Booksellers' Association, as argued by Griffin, lay not in the Association itself but in its 'force and violence' in coercing individuals to accede to the regulations. Griffin reported in his pamphlet that such coercion had been successfully applied against Charles Dewar of Falkirk who had been discovered selling books, secretly marked so that they could be readily identified, at more than the acceptable level of discount, and future supplies to him had been refused, as a result of the implied threat against wholesalers.[10]

What drove Griffin to publish his pamphlet in 1844? Griffin was aware that Dewar was not the only one to have been adversely affected by pressure exerted by the Glasgow Booksellers' Association. In 1843, Blackwood & Sons, the Edinburgh publishers, had been forced to withdraw from sales arrangements with Alexander Hadden, a Glasgow bookseller, because of the latter's refusal to subscribe to the Glasgow Association's rules. But, more generally, Griffin had come to view the Glasgow Association's rules as positively counterproductive, in actually 'diminishing sales and that in a growing city'.

However, Griffin & Co remained reluctant members of the Association. 'When I was not a member', J J Griffin wrote, 'violent means were taken to force me to become so. I was threatened with loss of custom... the very publishers in London for whom I was agent, were threatened with diminished sale of their books in Glasgow, if I was retained their agent and not induced to become an associate. Therefore I remain with you, an unwilling conspirator'.[11]

The Glasgow Association was sufficiently frightened by Griffin's pamphlet to have decided, in July 1844, to take professional advice, only subsequently to learn, with considerable consternation, that it was indeed considered illegal as constituted and, moreover, that counsel were not prepared 'to suggest any change in its constitution that would render it unobjectionable'. As a result, the Association came to a temporary end one year later.[12] It is worth noting that one serious problem besetting the various protection associations was the contradictory legal advice received, thus giving support to both sides of the argument. In 1797, advice given was that the stance against underselling taken by the Edinburgh Booksellers' Society was legal; in 1844, the Glasgow Association received contrary opinion, yet also had before it the conclusions of learned counsel from some years previously that the London Booksellers' Committee's regulations were within the law.[13]

The Glasgow Association's appeal in late 1834 for cooperation from the trade in Edinburgh and London is a tacit acknowledgement of its interdependence with the major houses in the capital cities, where large-scale wholesalers had evolved during the early decades of the nineteenth century. Such wholesale houses invariably gave their support to the local and metropolitan protection societies.[14] It is important to recognise the close business relationships between some of the protagonists in the underselling controversies in London, with those involved in the debate in Scotland. Amongst the publishing houses that unwaveringly backed the London retail regulations was John Murray, for whom Oliver & Boyd had been sole Scottish agents since 1819. When the hitherto internal trade debate finally became public in 1852 (substantially due to Chapman's campaigning), and subject to an independent committee of enquiry, Murray had sufficient respect for his Scottish agents to write asking if the Edinburgh firm had any suggestions to make which he would be pleased to take on board in discussions in London.[15] Griffin & Co deserve more detailed study, but some rather suggestive features can readily be identified. Particularly over the 1830s and 1840s, Griffin's name is found linked, both in newspaper advertisements and imprints, with Thomas Tegg of London, who is famous, if not notorious, for having made a fortune by buying up bankrupt and remaindered stock, and reissuing it cheaply under a new title-page and imprint. There is an interesting question of perception here: a scavenger to some, Tegg was seen by others, notably William Chambers (of the Edinburgh firm) as enterprising, as having 'the audacity... to disregard the assumed etiquette of the profession' and as having achieved 'two important ends... the shelves of the publishers were relieved of much dead stock, and the public were satisfied'.[16] All three, Griffin of Glasgow, Tegg in London, and Chambers in Edinburgh had distanced themselves from the aims of the various booksellers' protection associations. And one basic point of similarity among all three was (relatively) cheap print: Chambers through their *Edinburgh Journal* and their educational series, and Tegg and Griffin through inexpensive reissues. And it may be no coincidence that the writer, polemicist and publisher John Joseph Griffin had previously worked with Thomas Tegg in London.[17]

The Glasgow Association was revived in August 1851,[18] though it was in a weak position. One month earlier, David Robertson, who had continued to keep Oliver & Boyd in touch with underselling activities in the West of Scotland, wrote:

> I had a complaint today from a bookseller that... McCullochs School books were selling... in our Bazaar at 25 per Cent discount to the public... It is obvious if this is not checked – not one of the trade will keep any stock of these works.

> The name of the person bookseller I won't call him who sold it is Doyle – I do not think it is likely you have an account with him nor perhaps any in our Bazaar – [and] if not – these books must be got from Mullan Belfast &c &c who is destroying the trade in the North of Ireland in Greenock and here.
>
> The other booksellers in the Bazaar are I believe selling books in the same way.[19]

Evidence suggests that within Scotland Oliver & Boyd were amongst the most assiduous publishers and wholesalers in identifying and acting against undersellers. The Glasgow Association looked upon them (and A & C Black) as especially strong allies, though the Edinburgh firm had sometimes to call on local knowledge. In 1836, Oliver & Boyd informed Robertson that they had received an order from R Farie & Co of Glasgow (presumably acting as a wholesaler) for 150 copies of McCulloch's educational works, 'doubtless designed for some recusant... being wanted in qrs'. As Farie's name was absent from the Glasgow Association's list of members, Oliver & Boyd refused to deal with them, 'but before we write them, we would like to hear for whom you think... [the books] are intended'.[20]

Contemporary accounts confirm that booksellers' protection associations were established in many large cities, including Manchester, Birmingham and Bristol, though attempts to establish such an organisation in Liverpool, however, were described as 'hopeless'.[21] Some generalisations about them can safely be made. The basic regulation adopted was that the maximum discount from the announced published retail price of copyright books was to have been 10% – though some societies stipulated that this was permissible only for cash transactions. Rules were also drawn up to cover the sale of books to clergymen, teachers and libraries, and the discounts in these instances varied between 10% and 16%. Regulations were also sometimes laid down for dealings with other members of the trade – printers, stationers and binders.

The first systematic effort in England to introduce these or similar rules seems to have been in 1829, by the London Booksellers' Committee, which occasioned at least one provincial reaction, with the establishment of the Aberdeen Booksellers' Society in 1830, following the encouragement of James Lumsden, the Glasgow stationer and publisher, though, as is already clear, Glasgow itself had to wait until 1834 before such a society was established in the West of Scotland.[22]

The Edinburgh trade had squared up to these issues roughly thirty years earlier.[23] Accusations of underselling medical texts were proved, in 1796, against George Mudie, an Edinburgh publisher and bookseller, at least to the satisfaction of leading members of the Edinburgh Booksellers' Society. And the general terms in which Mudie was attacked reappeared in statements issued by the Edinburgh Society in 1819, and in the London resolutions of 1829.[24] Mudie's actions were seen as damaging the legitimate interests of the trade, and his offering of texts for sale at up to 30%

below published prices was 'an unfair & unjust practice, and highly detrimental to the interest of the fair trader'.[25] Against the weight of the Edinburgh Booksellers' Society (which was then prepared to countenance a discount of 5% for new books for ready money) Mudie finally buckled.

But the hopes of the leading figures of the Edinburgh Booksellers' Society were forlorn. Far from receding, the problem increased. The Society was sufficiently concerned that 'a System of underselling has prevailed for some time in the Book Trade of Edinburgh which has brought discredit on the Profession & threatens the most serious consequences to the regular Trade', to call a meeting on 14 October 1819 to which non-members were also invited. They resolved that there should be a maximum retail discount of 10% on all copyright and undepreciated books, 'on which terms all shall engage to sell without endeavouring to injure one another by making further deductions'. Moreover, 'the Trade in general, with a view to protect themselves, engage to give the Bookseller's discount only to the Regular Booksellers, and the irregular dealer shall uniformly be charged the full retail price, and no Credit given'. In other words, one tactic to try and maintain 'regularity' in transactions, was to face the situation by accepting an increase of an extra 5% on the retail discount of the 1790s, but to impose that limitation as rigorously as possible. The Society, at this October meeting, also reaffirmed the then prevailing economic realities by proposing that 'the principal houses in London be informed of these regulations... with a request that they will cooperate with the Trade in Edinr'. At a meeting a fortnight later, it was announced that the trade in Edinburgh was nigh on unanimous in accepting the terms – all except John Carfrae, bookseller, auctioneer, and minor publisher, against whom sanctions were to be applied. The Edinburgh booksellers might nearly all have given their agreement to the resolutions, but the continuing actions of a sufficient number ruined any chance of their effectiveness. At a further meeting in April 1820, attended by then powerful and influential figures in the Edinburgh trade including Cadell, Constable, Bradfute and Blackwood, the general conclusion was that 'it appeared that these Resolutions had not been generally acted upon in such a manner as to render them efficient, and that it would be better to give them up altogether; it was therefore generally agreed that the Members should now be absolved from their engagements on this subject'.[26]

The 'regular' trade in Edinburgh detected further deterioration. In 1835 an anonymous, though entirely sympathetic, letter was sent to the Society. It reiterated the claim that underselling was 'destroying the respectability as well as ruining the temporal interests' of the trade, and the writer drew up a complex set of regulations designed to counteract what was seen as the 'unprincipled & ruinous way of doing business'. It was clear to the correspondent that conventions were frequently flouted, and an increasing number of circumstances were occurring when potential profit was lost. Secretaries of various societies, clergymen, clerks, shopmen, bookbinders, stationers and their apprentices were all accused of being supplied individually with titles at discount, and then selling them on at below full retail price. A special word of condemnation was reserved for teachers, who 'have contributed more to the present State of the trade than any other person... they have in a great many instances been allowed the trade discount and abused the privileges... by supplying their pupils at cost price for the purpose of inducing Parents to send their Children to the School... it is not proper that they should be... on the same level as a Bookseller, who has a Shop Rent & establishment to Keep up'.[27]

There is no indication that the Edinburgh trade was more effective than in any other part of Britain in controlling underselling. Indeed, in 1850 the Edinburgh Booksellers Association was established as a vehicle to tackle the problem.[28] It appears (like the Glasgow Association) to have been influential enough to get widespread overt compliance, but it must have been sorely irritated by the exposure given to it in 1852 by Chapman, when he claimed that he had been told by an informant in Edinburgh that 'upwards of twenty booksellers, including some of the oldest and most respectable names... were coerced into joining the Association or that they entirely disapprove of the plan'. This was challenged, but Chapman, never scared of a fight, promptly published his information which included a letter from James Nichol, an Edinburgh publisher, who concluded that that 'no such Association could be long lived, from being... impracticable in nature, impolitic in its tendency, and so far as some could judge, illegal'. Nichol, in early 1852, sounded very much like Griffin in 1844.[29] But Nichol's published letter also went to the heart of the controversy, namely that 'it is an unwarrantable interference with the right which every man ought to possess, to conduct his business as he considers best calculated to secure his own interests'.[30] It is evident that such an attitude struck deep at whatever cohesiveness there might have been in the book trade.

The number and variety of new titles, and reprints published annually in the nineteenth century increased markedly from eighteenth-century levels; inexpensive magazines were appearing, print runs increased, the consumer market widened, but so did competition. Greater trade specialisation had evolved, with fewer firms combining the roles of publisher, wholesale agent, and, occasionally, retail bookseller. And whilst it is self-evident that none whose livelihood depended on the sale of the printed word would have wished to have seen a widespread collapse in the trade, particularly in printing and publishing, it is also clear that sufficient booksellers saw themselves as individuals in a highly competitive market, and saw their legitimate interests as not extending beyond that of individual trader, and acted accordingly, so as to cause a highly defensive reaction, with the establishment of protection associations. Much effort in the controversy during the nineteenth century was expended on analysing what could or should be done within the conventional pricing structures, but broader issues often affected the debate.

George Mudie's actions were seen as violating the 'honourable understanding' that existed in the trade, and as being unfair and inequitable; and in 1819, the Edinburgh Booksellers' Society saw underselling as 'irregular' and 'discreditable'. 'Regular' trading thereby consisted in abiding by the rules and conventions. In this context, the notion of fair dealing was applied predominantly, not for the benefit of the purchasing or reading public or of the individual trader, but for the 'regular trade'. But this is the very turning point of the argument, as one of the premises of those booksellers and publishers who advocated that consumer freedom should be the final determinant factor on retail prices, was that any given individual had the qualified right to do what he or she might see fit for the benefit of their business.[31]

Underlying the appeals made by protection associations was the expectation that undersellers would recognise that, by being active members of the book trade, they had accepted those constraints which helped determine the benefits (solvency if not profitability) each individual bookseller might receive. However, the application of the idea of mutual benefit was equated in the minds of some undersellers at least, with combination, coercion, and infringements of rights; and, from their point of view, accusations of fairness (or in this context unfairness) were more validly addressed to the protection associations, who were seen as violating that right of an individual trader to conduct his or her business without undue restraint.[32]

In 1844, Griffin had accepted that a trade association, voluntarily formed, was legal; coercion by that association was however illegal. But by 1852, it was clear that the terms in which the debate had been largely pursued, were widening. The occasional recognition of a legitimate public interest in the 1790s and early decades of the nineteenth century had become a major point of reference. Trading did not take place in a vacuum, and Chapman, again, was acutely aware of this dimension:[33]

> The main question is, whether free trade would or would not injure the retail booksellers. But the public, which preferred cheap bread to continuing the guarantee of protected profits to the farmers, will hardly consider the maintenance of any given number of booksellers an object of even equal importance with that of getting cheap books. Unrestrained competition will accurately determine how many booksellers are needful for the efficient distribution of all the books which are published.

Society's interests were best advanced, in other words, by allowing equal freedom to producers, distributors and buyers of books.

Amongst the letters which Chapman published in 1852 was one from the author and publisher Robert Chambers (of W & R Chambers) who concluded that, if full retail prices continued to be maintained, then the attractiveness of, and opportunities for unparalleled profits, not just on the initial print run of a particular text, but also on its subsequent serial or part publication, would inevitably lead to increasing levels of underselling. Chambers summarised that 'Those who seek to support the [London] Association have a weak cause. The tendency of the age is to unlimited freedom of trade and to small profits, and... the Association is heterodox on both points'.[34] Chambers accurately caught the prevailing commercial attitude. A little later the Committee of Enquiry under Lord Campbell published its deliberations, concluding that the regulations were 'contrary to the freedom which ought to prevail in commercial transactions',[35] and booksellers' protection societies throughout Britain quietly folded. In spite of predictions of the collapse of the retail bookselling sector, Victorian liberal ideology, and the principles of free trade, were about to overwhelm bookselling throughout Britain.

ACKNOWLEDGEMENTS

Acknowledgements are due to the following for permission to quote from their papers, or from material under their curatorship: Pearson Education Limited (Oliver & Boyd papers); the Secretary, Edinburgh Booksellers' Society; National Library of Scotland (NLS); Arts Department, Mitchell Library, Glasgow; Special Collections & Archives, Glasgow University Library. Thanks also to colleagues at the British Library of Political and Economic Science.

NOTES

The records of the Glasgow Booksellers' Protection Association, 1834–1851, in the Arts Department, Mitchell Library, Glasgow, ref 891733, are cited throughout as GPBA.
The Oliver & Boyd papers, deposited in the NLS are cited as Acc 5000.
The records of the Edinburgh Booksellers' Society, likewise deposited in the NLS, are cited as Dep 303.

1. *Is the Glasgow Booksellers' Protection Association a Lawful Association, or is it an Illegal Conspiracy?* (Glasgow: Bell & Bain, printers, [1844]),10.

2. Full recognition is given to the major contributions made by James Barnes's *Free Trade in Books: a Study of the London Book Trade since 1800* (Oxford: Clarendon Press, 1964), and Richard Sher's 'Corporatism and consensus in the late eighteenth-century book trade: the Edinburgh Booksellers' Society in comparative perspective', *Book History*, 1 (1998), 32–93.

3. Letter, Richard Griffin & Co to Oliver & Boyd, 9 November 1844, Acc 5000/202, reprinted in *The Glasgow Booksellers' Conspiracy under a New Cloak* (Glasgow: Bell & Bain, printers, [1844]), [1], which, although anonymously compiled, was undoubtedly the result of John Joseph Griffin's editorship, and was almost certainly planned as a form of supplement to his larger pamphlet, *Is the Glasgow... Association... Lawful?* The numeration of the paragraphs in *The Glasgow Booksellers' Conspiracy* appears to have been intended to follow on

from that in the longer work. The title of this paper is taken from this supplementary publication.

4. See, for example, letter, Adam Black to Robertson, 13 July 1836, Acc 5000/198.

5. Barnes, *Free Trade*, chap 1.

6. Letter, W Bounds, London, to John Reid, 10 October 1835, GBPA.

7. Two printed circulars, 31 December 1834, 15 April 1835 from the Glasgow Booksellers' Protection Association; and one from the Aberdeen Booksellers' Society, Acc 5000/197. The circular of 1834 gave retail prices of some publications then on sale in Glasgow. Volumes of Oliver & Boyd's Edinburgh Cabinet Library were available at *3s.10d* or *4s*. The stipulated retail price was *5s* per volume; and the lowest trade price that Oliver & Boyd allowed was *3s.10d* per copy, though more generous terms were available for bulk orders.

8. 'Johnstone's Edinburgh Magazine: the cheap and dear periodicals', *Tait's Edinburgh Magazine*, 4 (1834), 491.

9. Letter, David Robertson to George Boyd, 29 June 1836, Acc 5000/198.

10. Dewar might have been a persistent offender, and those trading with him found themselves in considerable trouble. On 13 December 1837, Adam Crawford, a Glasgow bookseller, fruitlessly apologised to his local association, 'On reflection I am thoroughly convinced of the error I have committed in supplying Mr Dewar with the books contrary to the regulations of the association'. The next day the Glasgow Association expelled Crawford. For letter and relevant circular see GBPA.

11. *Is the Glasgow... Association... Lawful?*, 3, 11–12, 15–16. Hadden was a worry to Oliver & Boyd. On 3 April 1843, John Boyd, visiting Glasgow, wrote to his brother, Thomas 'Haddin [*sic*] is still standing out, and has no intention of making any apology – D.R. [David Robertson] thinks he must get many of our books clandestinely, and advises us to look sharp after any customer who appears to be ordering an extra No of Stewart's Geogy or McCulloch's Books', Acc 5000/202. The reference is almost certainly to one of the many editions of Alexander Stewart's *Compendium of Modern Geography*; John M McCulloch's educational texts were also published by Oliver & Boyd.

12. Minute of Meeting, 10 July 1845, GBPA.

13. For general background see Robert Bowes, *Booksellers' Associations Past and Present* (Taunton: printed for private circulation, 1905), 1–4. John Blackie jr writing on 5 March 1845 on behalf of the Glasgow Association to James Duncan, legal agent in London, noted, insightfully, 'It is possible that the progress of Free Trade views... may have had something to do with the opinion given by the Scotch lawyers', GBPA. Advice had been received from Thomas Mackenzie and Andrew Rutherfurd, both eminent Scottish judges. See also Sher, 'Corporatism and consensus', esp 68–82.

14. Document, endorsed 'Edinburgh Wholesale Trade 1835' confirms that the leading Edinburgh houses (including Bell & Bradfute, A & C Black, Blackwood, and Oliver & Boyd) agreed to support the emergent Glasgow Association, GBPA.

15. Letter, Robert Cooke (of Murray) to Oliver & Boyd, 29 April 1851, Acc 5000/207.

16. William Chambers, *Memoir of William and Robert Chambers* (Edinburgh: Chambers, [188-]), 144. For a recent assessment of Tegg, see James J Barnes & Patience P Barnes, 'Reassessing the reputation of Thomas Tegg, London publisher, 1776–1846', *Book History*, 3 (2000), 45–60.

17. For John Joseph Griffin, see DNB. See Barnes, *Free Trade*, on the roles of Thomas and William Tegg in the underselling controversy. The views of members of the firm may have modified over time. A letter (possibly disingenuous) of 15 July 1836 suggests Tegg gave support to John Reid, Secretary of the Glasgow Association, and wrote, 'I am not favourable to associations of any kind still I think Mr Griffin should comply with the wishes of his brethren of the trade', GBPA.
18. Printed circular, 29 August 1851, GBPA.
19. This letter of 28 July 1851 (Acc 5000/207) provides an unexpected insight into aspects of nineteenth-century Irish-Scottish book trade relationships.
20. GBPA.
21. John Chapman's comments in *Report of the Proceedings of a Meeting (Consisting Chiefly of Authors)... for the Purpose of Hastening the Removal of the Trade Restrictions on the Commerce of Literature* (London: Chapman, 1852), 19. Also *The Present System of Publishing...* (London: Groombridge, 1844), 25. Chapman exaggerated; the printed *Regulations of the Liverpool Booksellers' Association*, 19 June 1837, were retained by the Glasgow Association, GBPA. Research into such protection societies is problematic. Secretive, defensive, and certainly against the spirit of the age, it was not in their overall interest to publicise their stance, especially not outside the trade itself.
22. I Beavan, 'Notes on Aberdeen booksellers' societies', *Bibliotheck*, 10 (1980–1),158-69.
23. Fully discussed in Sher, 'Corporatism and consensus'.
24. The London (1829) resolutions are cited in Barnes, *Free Trade* , 175–6.
25. Minute of meeting of Edinburgh booksellers, 19 December 1796, Dep 303/23.
26. Minutes of meetings 14, 28 October 1819; 3 April 1820, Dep 303/3.
27. Letter to Samuel Aitken (of Bell & Bradfute, and sometime Secretary to the Edinburgh Society), 19 March 1835, Dep 303/25. The issue of teachers' discounts seems to have been a peculiarly Scottish complication. See also Barnes, *Free Trade*, 56.
28. There is some evidence that a protection society was attempted in Edinburgh before that date. The report of the Committee of the Glasgow Association, 27 June 1839, recorded, 'The Committee have much pleasure in alluding to the formation of similar associations in Edinburgh Paisley & Greenock, which they are happy to think are succeeding well', GBPA.
29. In 1796, George Mudie had suggested that the Edinburgh Society could be adjudged an illegal conspiracy. Unlike Mudie, Griffin had the confidence to publicise the issue, and in terms that were guaranteed to heighten the debate. It is reasonable to assume that Griffin anticipated a significant level of support, particularly outside the trade.
30. *Report of the Proceedings of a Meeting*, 3–4.
31. Qualified, not absolute right. Some activities (eg fraud, corruption) were condemned as prejudicial to society. See J S Mill, *On Liberty* (London: Parker, 1859), 170.
32. For broader theory see John Rawls, 'Justice as fairness', in *Philosophy, Politics and Society* (2nd ser), [ed] Peter Laslett & W G Runciman (Oxford: Blackwell, 1962), 132–57.
33. *Report of the Proceedings of a Meeting*, 18.
34. *Report of the Proceedings of a Meeting*, 12–13.
35. Cited in Barnes, *Free Trade*, 183.

From Curry's to Collins Street, or How a Dubliner Became the 'Melbourne Mudie'

WALLACE KIRSOP

ONE OF THE PARADOXES of the history of books in nineteenth-century Australia is that it is in many ways less easily knowable or discoverable than that of pre-Revolutionary Paris. French official or quasi-official sources – registration, censorship, guild supervision, bankruptcy papers, notarial files – provide records that are hard to match once the Australian colonies escaped from their early penal destiny. The authorities were simply less inclined to note in detail what happened to traders. It is true that until the recent discovery of part of the business archives of the Widow Desaint[1] we had remarkably little information from the inside on how Paris booksellers conducted their dealings with confrères in the capital, in the provinces or abroad. However, apart from the miraculous re-emergence of material relating to E W Cole and his Book Arcade in the 1890s and later,[2] we are equally bereft of reliable evidence about the trade in Melbourne and Sydney prior to Australian Federation in 1901. Hearsay and reminiscences from the first half of the twentieth century have had to replace serious research on most of the major figures in bookselling and publishing after the Gold Rush of the 1850s. Thus the available accounts owe at least as much to piety and to hallowed legends as to exploration of the documents. For this reason alone it is useful to return to a uniquely significant firm and to attempt to sum up what can be uncovered about its operations.

Samuel Mullen (1828–1890) first arrived in Victoria on the *Great Britain* in 1852. After one or two false starts and a further period in London he was firmly established in the Melbourne trade by the middle of 1859.[3] Thirty years later, on 30 September 1889, he retired, selling his business to a consortium that included his brother William and that assumed the style of Melville, Mullen & Slade. What had the founder achieved and in what ways was he representative of a quite special period in the history of bookselling in the nineteenth-century Australian colonies? To say that he was active in both bookselling and publishing, that he conducted what became the leading commercial lending library in Melbourne and therefore – at that time – in Australia as a whole, that he was a visible participant in a range of societies and good works is already to stake out his claim to detailed notice. Yet Mullen can be seen as more important, more significant again despite the patchiness of the documentary record. To do him justice it is appropriate to look in turn at what I have called – with a touch of hyperbole – the 'Golden Age of Australian Bookselling',[4] at his Dublin antecedents, at his first steps in Melbourne and his difficult relationship with George Robertson & Co, at the variety of his bookselling activities, at the grand circulating library that he established in the heart of the fashionable promenade, the Block, in Collins Street, and at his involvement in various forms of publishing. Overall, and giving due attention to the nature of the sources, it is possible to present an image of a dealer working zealously to promote and maintain the Anglo-Australian book-trade connection.

It was fortuitous that the Gold Rush of the 1850s and the consequent enormous expansion of the Australian population coincided with Lord Campbell's determination and the opening of the era of free trade in books that lasted until the Net Book Agreement at the end of the century. The new professionals who arrived as, or along with, gold prospectors were able not only to profit from their Northern Hemisphere training – in Dublin, in the cases of Mullen and Robertson – but also to take advantage of a situation that was potentially favourable to colonial retailers. After the relative anarchy of the period up to 1820, when books were brought in by individual settlers and officials and occasionally traded in the auction marts, and then the uncertainties of the following decades, when speculative consignments from London houses like that of Edward Lumley dumped unwanted remainders in colonies that were starved for literature,[5] it was high time for Australian residents aware of local tastes and needs to take control. By setting up London buying offices from the late 1850s on, various wholesalers, of whom Robertson was the most substantial – over £100 000 of imports by the early 1870s – were able to purchase for cash at the best possible discounts and to sell at prices that eventually came down to London levels despite the problems of distance and transport costs. More than this they were in a position to carry relatively huge stocks of titles – 55 000 in Robertson's Melbourne warehouse for example.[6] Today's equivalent would be a now unthinkable several hundred thousand items. Trade sales, elaborate catalogues, advertising magazines, travellers and branches across the colonies, including New Zealand, brought the benefits of Melbourne's quasi-metropolitan culture – in a city approaching half a million inhabitants by the time of Mullen's retirement – to the whole of Australasia. This easily documentable reality is very different from the miserable picture that a visiting Macmillan chose to send back to London in the early 1880s,[7] thus contributing to the launching of one of the most successful 'Colonial Libraries' and to the concerted reconquest of the Australian market by British publishers in the last two decades of the century. Twentieth-century Australian bookbuyers eventually forgot that their grandparents had enjoyed low prices and the free availability of non-pirated titles from all over the English-speaking world. It goes without saying that Mullen was a major player in this book-rich environment free of the resale price maintenance and territorial copyright provisions of a later time.

The accepted version of Mullen's background and early training in the trade – as found, for instance, in the late John Holroyd's article in the *Australian Dictionary of Biography*[8] – seems to be based on information supplied at the time of the bookseller's two marriages in Melbourne – as a bachelor in 1855 and as a widower in 1870 – and on the reminiscences of Leonard Slade, who served in the firm in its various guises from 1876 to 1939.[9] At the Irish end information is harder to discover, not least because of the destruction of so many birth registrations during the Troubles. Let us accept, then, that Samuel Mullen was born in Dublin on 27 November 1828, the son of George Mullen and his wife Eliza, née Orson. Whether George was a bookseller, as claimed, and not a bookbinder, as Charles Benson's researches indicate, is another question. At all events the young man clearly belonged to a well-known family of binders.[10] The details supplied on education at Nuttgrove College and Trinity College and on an abortive indenture at sixteen to an apothecary are unverified. Similarly one has to take on trust for the moment that he was then apprenticed to the booksellers William Curry, Jun & Co, and that in 1848 he went to work for John W Parker & Son in London.

A possible connection in the Dublin time with George Robertson, who was born three years earlier and who also worked for Curry, is part of the tradition. However, there are problems other than the apparent rift that occurred when Mullen, sent by Robertson to manage his London office in 1857, found himself on arrival supplanted by the older man's brother William. Was the fact that both men arrived in Melbourne on the *Great Britain* planned or a mere coincidence? After all, the celebrated E W Cole, whose meteoric career as the Barnum of the book trade was then more than a decade off, was also a passenger.[11] Mullen allegedly carried a letter of introduction to a squatter and went off to try his luck in the Western District. Robertson settled down immediately as a bookseller in the capital of the colony. Is this surprising when one knows – thanks to Charles Benson and to Dublin directories of 1847 and 1848 – that William and George Robertson were in partnership at 35 Sackville Street as booksellers, publishers, stationers and bookbinders?[12] This detail, missed by Robertson's Australian biographers,[13] helps to explain the decisiveness with which this other Dubliner, born, it is true, in Glasgow, moved to dominate within a few years the wholesale importing business in his new country. Robertson's father was a Congregational minister, and the Nonconformist connection remained important for him. On the other hand Mullen was a practising Anglican to the end of his days. Rumours of rivalry for the hand of a young lady in Ireland are unsubstantiated and hardly fit with Robertson's readiness to employ Mullen as an assistant between 1853 and 1857. Hearsay and reality need to be disentangled in all this. What is certain is that

Mullen and the English publishers who supposedly supported his return to Melbourne had to find another niche for him in the Australian market.

This was not so difficult. Robertson's ambitions were not universal. Circumstances made him the most important publisher by far in nineteenth-century Australia, but there is little evidence that he was consciously building a backlist and following a creative policy like his younger unrelated namesake of Angus & Robertson in Sydney from the mid-1880s.[14] For a period he turned the retail side of his business over to Thomas Harwood, who also started up a circulating library. He does not appear to have wanted to enter into direct competition with Henry Tolman Dwight, who was Melbourne's leading secondhand and antiquarian bookseller from 1859 till his death in 1871.[15] There was, therefore, space for Mullen, who was able to concentrate on a retailing role in the service of the city's more comfortably-off inhabitants.

How, in the absence of business records, do we come to grips with Mullen's day-to-day activities? As always the remarkable newspapers of nineteenth-century Australia come to the rescue. However, we badly need indexes that go beyond the editorial and news columns and grasp the life pulsating in the advertisements. Few of the printed catalogues issued by Mullen appear to have survived, so one can do no more than sampling. However, *S. Mullen's Monthly Circular of Literature, &c.* began its career in January 1884, so that we have for the bookseller's last five years and a half a detailed record of what he was importing, buying locally and, more revealing, pushing to his customers. It is an indispensable source. The successor firm Melville, Mullen & Slade maintained it well into the 1890s, but, regrettably, libraries were less diligent in preserving the later numbers. To this we can add the archives of major customers, notably the Melbourne Public Library, which became the Public Library of Victoria, and is now the State Library of Victoria. All in all one gets a sense of Mullen's preferences and of his *modus operandi*.

The State Library of Victoria's collection of booksellers' catalogues includes some Mullen items from the early and mid-1860s. *Mullen's Monthly Price Current of Books, including a select list of the new publications imported by Samuel Mullen, Bookseller, 55 Collins Street East, Melbourne*, reminds us that his supplies were independent from those available through Robertson's wholesaling operation. The selection was generous, ranging from a new edition of Wilkie Collins's *The Woman in White* for 8/6 through Paul Du Chaillu's *Explorations and Adventures in Equatorial Africa* for 26/-, John Hollingshead's *Ragged London in 1861* for 9/6, *Lillywhite's Guide to Cricketers*, Spring edition 1861 for 2/-, John Selby Watson's *Life of Richard Porson* for 17/6 and T A Trollope's *La Beata* in two volumes for 18/- to Darwin's *Origin of Species*, fifth edition for 16/- and a subscription to 20 monthly numbers of Anthony

Trollope's *Orley Farm* for 25/-. In April 1867 *S. Mullen's Occasional List of New Books and New Editions, in all branches of literature. Also, new supplies of standard books* proposed a new serial: Anthony Trollope's *The Last Chronicle of Barset* in 24 weekly numbers for 16/- 'or by post, 20s'.

The range continued to be wide in the 1880s after the *Monthly Circular* began. Apart from a standard structure adopted in that publication: 'Current Literary Topics' (= discursive news and gossip from local and overseas sources), 'Forthcoming New Books', 'New Australian Publications', display advertisements for selected titles, there were not infrequently special catalogues and lists tipped in. Since similar monthlies were being produced in this expansive and booming decade by other houses, notably George Robertson & Co and Walch in Hobart, it is possible to determine exactly how Mullen defined his own market. Broadly enough, no doubt, but with a certain bias towards the upper end. The presence of works in French is sufficient indication of this. There were far more native speakers of German in nineteenth-century Australia, but French was the foreign language of choice for the educated and the refined.

Mullen's work on behalf of the Melbourne Public Library illustrates quite well his skills in procurement. Surviving vouchers from the 1860s in the Public Record Office of Victoria show that Mullen was one of a number of local suppliers used in this period.[16] By the 1880s he had taken over from H T Dwight as the preferred bookseller for purchases from auctions held in Melbourne, particularly by the specialist firm of Gemmell, Tuckett & Co. In 1884, for example, he acquired for the Library at the major sale of John Macgregor, a former Minister for Mines who had a taste for philosophy and the history of science, lots amounting to £56.19*s*.9*d*, on which he charged commission of £2.15*s*.[17] At the same time he was handling many of the Library's subscriptions to European scientific journals.[18] *S. Mullen's Monthly Circular of Literature, &c* announced the Macgregor sale in its August 1884 number and advised intending purchasers to send their commissions to the Dubliner. A month later a report appeared on the auction and some of its extraordinary realizations, followed by a list of 'Books purchased at the Macgregor Library and other Sales, and offered at Very Reduced Prices', such as the 1876 edition of Dibdin's *Bibliomania* for 12/6.

In his own time and well on into the twentieth century the name of Mullen was attached above all to his circulating library, the 'Melbourne Mudie's'. From the 1860s this department of the business was managed by the Scottish-trained Adam Graham Melville (1842–1921), who became one of the successor partners in 1889.[19] Circulating libraries were no innovation in Melbourne or in the Australian colonies in general, since the earliest examples go back to the 1820s. Some, like the Derwent Circulating Library the Walches took over from S A Tegg in Hobart in 1846, are much better documented, not only through a full printed catalogue but also via a surviving borrowing register from 1846 to the early 1850s.[20] To date I have not seen a consolidated catalogue of Mullen's collection. As for the readers and borrowers one has to rely on later reminiscences of former employees, on travellers' accounts and on occasional press publicity, as in the *Australasian Sketcher* in 1879 or in the *Illustrated London News* a decade later.[21] The consensus is, however, that this was an 'in-

'The Mudie's of Melbourne' – Mullen's shop in Collins Street
(*Illustrated London News*, 19 January 1889)

stitution', like Cole's Book Arcade, and that many thousands of 'Marvellous Melbourne''s literati, leading citizens and solid bourgeois families frequented it.

What did Mullen offer them? Occasional surviving volumes that crop up in the modern Australian secondhand trade, announcements in the *Monthly Circular* and a few discard lists from the 1860s demonstrate that this was much more than an assemblage of recent fiction, something that many of Mullen's earlier competitors had become. *A List of Surplus Copies, withdrawn from Mullen's Library, and offered at very low prices for cash* (undated, but from the early 1860s) covers a wide range of subjects, with an emphasis on history, travel and fiction. The discounted price is contrasted throughout with the 'current retail price for a new copy', for example Peacock's *Gryll Grange* 5/6 instead of 9/-, Haliburton's *The Season Ticket* 3/6 instead of 12/-, Horne's *Australian Facts and Prospects* 2/- instead of 6/-, *Photographs of Paris Life* 3/- instead of 6/-, Redding's *Keeping up Appearances*, 3 volumes, 8/6 instead of 31/6, Urquhart's *The Lebanon*, 2 volumes, 7/6 instead of 31/6, Waterton's

Essays on Natural History, third series, 2/6 instead of 7/6. There may have been last-minute decisions not to include titles in the Library. A February 1864 discount list adds at the end some 'New books reduced in price * * * *The following are uncut and without the Library labels*', among them Borrow's *Wild Wales*, 3 volumes, Churton's *Gongora, with Translations*, 2 volumes, Hearn's *Plutology*, Bentley's *Critica Sacra, Notes on the Greek Testament* and Dante's *Inferno, translated.* Much later, in October 1895, Melville, Mullen & Slade were making available among the periodicals in the reading room the *Deutsche Rundschau*, the *Gartenlaube*, the *Revue de Paris*, the *Revue des Deux Mondes* and *Mind*. By then, of course, the Public Library itself had a lending department with a more than respectable array of titles.

The *Monthly Circular*, through its advertisements and prospectuses, gives us an insight into Mullen's policy as a publisher. This is all the more necessary since we do not yet have a complete list of publications with his imprint, nor do we possess more than a few scraps of archival evidence. Ian Morrison's *The Publishing Industry in Colonial Australia* of 1996,[22] which indexes all the trade personnel mentioned in Ferguson's *Bibliography of Australia*, is a notable advance, but it leaves out of account the works included in Morris Miller's literary bibliography[23] and in Edward Ford's catalogue of Australian medical works.[24] Since Mullen was present to some degree in both these last fields, the picture is therefore somewhat distorted.

Imprints can be a trap in the Australian colonies. Often a supposed publisher is no more than the distributor or wholesaler of local or overseas productions. This has to be the case with the fourth edition, credited to Mullen in 1887, of Alexander Ireland's *The Book-Lover's Enchiridion*, noted as revised and enlarged. There is scope for more research on a phenomenon discussed a few years ago by John Turner in relation to the Tyneside firm of Walter Scott.[25] Experience suggests that Mullen, unlike Robertson and Cole, was not a major participant.

He had a genuine financial involvement in textbooks, as a couple of documents reveal. In the statement of accounts attached to the grant of probate by the Supreme Court of Victoria in 1890 is the indication 'Thos Harlin – Windsor – Author of University Text Book £25:0:0 – owed for compilation of book pub by Mullens', as well as substantial liabilities to the printers Sands & McDougall and the binder Detmold.[26] The Charles Henry Pearson papers in the La Trobe Collection MSS of the State Library of Victoria contain a copy of a memorandum of agreement between Mullen on the one hand and Pearson and Professor H A Strong on the other for the publication in 1876 of an English Grammar. The authors are to receive two-thirds of the profits after Mullen has defrayed the costs and taken 'the usual publishers commission of ten per cent'. 'Professor Strong undertakes that the Grammar shall be placed on the course of the Melbourne University'.[27]

In other areas Mullen's commitment may well have been less. He was involved in the *Victorian Monthly Magazine*, which lasted for two numbers in June–July 1859 and carried early advertisements of additions to his library stock. Much later he published *The Melbourne Review* for its first year in 1876 and then bowed out. Periodicals in colonial Australia generally lost money, but it was left to George Robertson to kill this one in 1885. In 1878 he was the Melbourne distributor of *The Sydney University Magazine: a Literary, Scientific, and Educational Journal.* Some literary works by Brunton Stephens and Edwin Exon[28] are known to have been published by Mullen, but again his involvement was slight overall. The 120 titles recorded by Ian Morrison are often pamphlets deriving from causes and institutions supported by Mullen, for example the Early Closing Association and above all the Church of England. Were these acts of piety or generosity, or was he merely the distributor? In a number of cases where more substantial works were concerned, later editions were published by George Robertson & Co. Yet the opening of a London office in Paternoster Row in the 1880s and its inclusion in the imprint of a book like Henry Britton's *Loloma, or Two Years in Cannibal-land: a story of old Fiji* of 1884 suggests that Mullen had serious publishing ambitions.

Can one sum up his achievement? His premature death – in Oxford Road, Kilburn, in May 1890 – left the purchase of his business incomplete. The probate papers reveal that the successors had been paying off and were to continue to pay off their purchase at the rate of more than £1000 per quarter till the end of 1893. This eventually happened, so that the firm even managed to weather the Victorian crisis of 1892. One of the silent partners, Hermann William Püttmann, was the son of a Forty-Eighter and former associate in Germany of Karl Marx.[29] Above all, it is important to emphasize the point that, within the free trade context, Mullen stood for an orderly and ethical market in the wider British world to which Australia belonged. Concerns about the operations of a 'ring' at Melbourne auctions, about the circulation of American piracies and about the abuses of door-to-door subscription sellers are themes that recur in the *Monthly Circular*. Mullen's presidential address to the first annual meeting of the Booksellers and Stationers' Association of Victoria in the Temperance Hall on 27 March 1879 covers a number of the same questions. This separately published text, preserved in the Petherick Collection of the National Library of Australia, is fair testimony to Mullen's professionalism and to its recognition by other members of the colonial trade.

ACKNOWLEDGEMENTS

I should like to thank a number of individuals and institutions in Melbourne for their help in bringing together the documents needed for a fresh (but by no means exhaustive) look at Samuel Mullen: Des Cowley and Jock Murphy at the State Library of

Victoria; Richard Overell and the Rare Books Section of Monash University Library; the Public Record Office of Victoria; the Registry of Births, Deaths and Marriages. Charles Benson was, on my visit to Trinity College, Dublin, in May 2000, an invaluable guide to the Irish background. Tom Darragh provided, as always, many useful hints for the search. John Holroyd (1911–2000) died a month after the oral presentation in Newcastle upon Tyne and before I could show him a completed reworking of a story he told me many years ago with the advantage of having been trained in the late 1920s by Leonard Slade. His unfailing generosity in passing on information and reminiscences will be missed by all historians of the Australian book trade.

NOTES

1. See Wallace Kirsop, 'Les Archives de la librairie Desaint: un apport capital à l'histoire du livre parisien du XVIIIe siècle', *Revue française d'histoire du livre*, 98–9 (1998), 185–7.

2. The story of how a well-known collector happened in the 1990s on the library and papers of one of Cole's managers in a dumpster at the Melbourne docks belongs to the stranger annals of serendipity.

3. The bookshop is listed in *Sands, Kenny & Cos Commercial and General Melbourne Directory for 1860*, 245a. However, *Bradshaw's Railway and General Guide to Victoria*, 37 (May 1859), 90, carries an advertisement detailing books recently added to 'Mullen's Select Library' at 67 Collins Street East. The City of Melbourne Rate and Valuation Books for 1859 (*Victorian Public Record Series* [hereafter VPRS] 5708/P2, unit 12, and VPRS 3102/P2, unit 9) show Mullen as the occupier of the shop at that address and as the tenant of R F Bickerton. Previously the premises had been briefly used, in 1858, by William Baker, whose main bookselling outlet was nearby in Swanston Street.

4. See Wallace Kirsop, 'Bookselling and publishing in the nineteenth century', in *The Book in Australia: Essays towards a Cultural & Social History*, [ed] D H Borchardt & W Kirsop (Melbourne: Australian Reference Publications in association with the Centre for Bibliographical and Textual Studies, Monash University, 1988), 41.

5. See chapter 3 'Edward Lumley and the consignment trade', in Wallace Kirsop, *Books for Colonial Readers – the Nineteenth-Century Australian Experience* (Melbourne: The Bibliographical Society of Australia and New Zealand, 1995), 39–58, 88–92.

6. See the long letter by Edward Petherick, Robertson's London manager, in *The Bookseller*, 2 June 1874, 465–6.

7. See Simon Nowell-Smith, *International Copyright Law and the Publisher in the Reign of Queen Victoria* (Oxford: Clarendon Press, 1968), 93.

8. Volume 5: *1851–1890 K–Q* (Melbourne: Melbourne University Press, 1974), 309–10.

9. See John Holroyd, 'Leonard Slade, bookseller', *La Trobe Library Journal*, 59 (Autumn 1997), 27, and the reproduction of Sybil Craig's striking pastel portrait of Slade (1859–1954) on the cover of the same number.

10. See Charles Benson, 'Printers and booksellers in Dublin 1800–1850', in *Spreading the Word: the Distribution Networks of Print 1550–1850*, [ed] Robin Myers & Michael Harris (Winchester: St Paul's Bibliographies; Detroit: Omnigraphics Inc, 1990), 47–59, esp 54–5. Significantly, when Mullen remarried on 17 September 1870, he described his father's

profession as 'Bookbinder' in the place of the 'Bookseller' he had used on 6 October 1855. See also the entry on George Mullen, Samuel's grandfather, in M Pollard, *A Dictionary of Members of the Dublin Book Trade 1550–1800* (London: Bibliographical Society, 2000), 421–2.

11. On Cole's spectacular career see Cole Turnley, *Cole of the Book Arcade: a Pictorial Biography of E. W. Cole* (Hawthorn, Victoria: Cole Publications, 1974).

12. *The Dublin Almanac and General Register of Ireland... 1847* (Dublin: Pettigrew & Oulton), 569b, and *The Post Office Dublin City and County Directory for the year 1848*, 775a, 912a.

13. See in particular John Holroyd, *George Robertson of Melbourne 1825–1898 Pioneer Bookseller & Publisher* (Melbourne: Robertson & Mullens, 1968).

14. On the publishing activities of the younger George Robertson (1860–1933) see A W Barker, *Dear Robertson: Letters to an Australian Publisher* (Sydney: Angus & Robertson Publishers, 1982).

15. See Ian F McLaren, *Henry Tolman Dwight: Bookseller and Publisher* (Parkville: The University of Melbourne Library, 1989).

16. VPRS 1072, vols 3 & 4, 1858–1861, 1865–1866.

17. Stock Book of the Melbourne Public Library, 1884, items 5526–5640. An account of the Macgregor collection is forthcoming in the *La Trobe Journal*.

18. The published reports of the Trustees' library committee in the 1880s show Mullen as the Public Library's major local supplier by a substantial margin.

19. See Melville's article 'Thirty years in a Melbourne library' in *Transactions and Proceedings of the Library Association of Australasia at its Second General Meeting, held at Adelaide, October 9th, 10th, 11th, and 12th, 1900* (Adelaide: C E Bristow, Government Printer, 1901), LXVI–LXVII.

20. See chapter IV 'Bookselling in Hobart Town in the 1840s' in W Kirsop, *Books for Colonial Readers*, 59–76, 93–6.

21. *Australasian Sketcher*, 5 July 1879; *Illustrated London News*, 19 January 1889.

22. (Melbourne: Bibliographical Society of Australia and New Zealand).

23. E Morris Miller, *Australian Literature, 1795–1938* (Sydney: Sydney University Press, 1975), 2 vols (1st edition, 1940).

24. Edward Ford, *Bibliography of Australian Medicine, 1790–1900* (Sydney: Sydney University Press, 1976).

25. See John R Turner, 'Title-pages produced by the Walter Scott Publishing Co Ltd', *Studies in Bibliography*, XLIV (1991), 323–31 and 'Variant title-pages in some late nineteenth- and early twentieth-century books', *The Library*, 6th ser, 20 (1998), 34–58.

26. VPRS 00028/P/0002, unit 000291, file 42/999.

27. Stete Library of Victoria: Box 436/5, MS 7168.

28. Exon was clearly a close associate, since he was a witness both to Mullen's second marriage and to his will, of which he was an executor.

29. See the entry on Hermann Püttmann senior in the *Australian Dictionary of Biography*, 5, 461–2.

'Aristotle to a Wery Tall Man': Selling Secondhand Books in Manchester in the 1830s

MICHAEL POWELL & TERRY WYKE

BY THE 1830s the industrial revolution had made Manchester the centre of the world's largest industrial region. Neither was industrialisation over as new technologies - the Liverpool-Manchester Railway opened in 1830 - promised further economic change. Yet not all parts of the economy experienced the dramatic transformation so evident in cotton, engineering and transport. Changes in the retailing trades, including the book trade, although expanding to meet the increased demands that a continuously increasing population generated, were less obvious.[1] Fortunately our ignorance of the Manchester book trade during the industrial revolution has been reduced in recent years, and a clearer picture of those individuals and firms involved in different parts of the trade is emerging.[2] The bookselling trade was expanding, most obviously with the opening of new shops, selling both new and secondhand books, to meet the needs of a growing book-buying public. The opening of commercial libraries was also a response to that reading public.[3] Change was also evident in the passing away of individuals associated with the book trade, the death of William Ford removing from the local trade one of its best known figures.[4] But, detailed evidence on many aspects of the Manchester book trade remains scarce. We know booksellers by name and can identify the location of their premises but meagre evidence exists about their stock, about what they sold and who their customers were. The working-class reformer, Samuel Bamford recalled one Manchester bookshop in the 1790s. For the schoolboy Bamford the titles displayed in the window of George Swindells's bookshop, close to the Collegiate Church, clearly reached parts of the reading palate that a diet of religious works and moral literature had failed to reach.[5]

> In the spacious windows of this shop, which is now 'The Wedding Ring Coffee House', were exhibited numerous songs, ballads, tales, and other publications, with horrid and awful-looking woodcuts at the head; which publications with their cuts, had a strong command on my attention. Every farthing I could scrape together, was now spent in purchasing 'Histories of Jack the Giant Killer', 'Saint George and the Dragon', 'Tom Hickathrift', 'Jack and the Beanstalk', 'History of the Seven Champions', Tale of 'Fair Rosamond', 'History of Friar Bacon', 'Account of the Lancashire Witches', 'The Witches of the Woodlands' and such like romances; whilst my metrical collections embraced but few pieces besides 'Robin Hood's Songs', and 'The Ballad of Chevy Chase'.

Such revealing glimpses of a bookseller's stock are hardly commonplace. Other sources need to be consulted, and, as we have argued elsewhere, auction advertisements in the local press need to be more systematically analysed by historians of the book trade when reconstructing the stock and premises of booksellers.[6] But such sources remain surrogate ones, turned to in the absence of more direct evidence about the business operations of booksellers. Yet, few of the financial accounts kept by those booksellers, large or small, permanent or transient, metropolitan or provincial, trading during the industrial revolution have survived, at least in public archives. This short article provides a provisional analysis of the account book of one Manchester bookseller, James Weatherley. The accounts cover the years 1831–1833, a period in which the town experienced continuing economic change, political tension and social instability.

As the career of James Weatherley suggests, running a secondhand bookselling business required certain skills and some good fortune. By 1830 Weatherley had been active in the book trade in Manchester for some thirteen years. Those years had seen his fortunes oscillate from the relative prosperity of the early 1820s when he had been able to graduate from an open-air stall to a shop in Market Street, to 1826 when he spent two months in prison as a bankrupt. Selling old books appears to have been a precarious business, one of fluctuating revenues and small profits, a business where a single wrong decision or a turndown in trade brought hard times. By 1830 Weatherley was trading from a cellar in St Ann's Square, though the Manchester commercial directory for that year lists him as a dealer in old books with premises at 35 Market Street.[7] At the beginning of that year he took in Nathan Moore, a former bookkeeper, as a partner. Initially there was an increase in business, helped by the capital Moore brought with him, but this did not continue and the partnership ended in the early spring of 1831.[8] Weatherley recommenced selling books from premises in Back King Street with an initial stock numbering some 1300 volumes. But trading from these new premises did not prove as successful as in St Ann's Square, a situation not helped by the depressed state of the cotton trade. Books provided by far the most important part of Weatherley's business though he also sold prints and, very occasionally, musical instruments.[9] The struggle to meet essential bills intensified. An ill-considered decision to purchase books to the value of £22 from a traveller representing one of the London booksellers exacerbated his problems.[10] A crisis in Weatherley's affairs came in spring 1832 when he was compelled to auction his stock to pay off the rent owed to the landlord of the shop. The sale raised £11.12*s.*2*d*, most of the 92 lots being bought by fellow booksellers including Samuel Johnson, Matthew Thackray, William Willis, Abel Heywood and his former partner, Nathan Moore, who was also selling books in Back King Street.[11] The most expensive lot in the sale realised only 8*s*. 6*d* while the majority sold for less than 2*s*. As ever, the misfortune of a competitor remained an opportunity for others in the trade to obtain stock cheaply. The shop's fixtures and some books were sold to a schoolmaster, John Long, who started up his own bookselling business in the vacated premises.[12] It is noteworthy that the auction was not advertised in the local press but announced in the streets by the town bellman, a further reminder that the auctions advertised in the press are a limited sample of such events.[13]

Thus in the early spring of 1832 Weatherley found himself without premises and with little stock. His response was to return to selling books in the street. Less predictable was his decision to sell books in Liverpool rather than in Manchester. Liverpool was not entirely unknown to Weatherley as he had contacts with the town's booksellers. Weatherley set up a stall in Tythebarn Street and his initial sales suggest that his decision to move away from Manchester had been the right one. However, any expectations that Weatherley might have been holding of rebuilding his business were soon halted when the Asiatic cholera, already devastating other urban communities, reached Liverpool. For Weatherley, as for other street traders, the epidemic disrupted trade.[14] Weatherley returned to Manchester only to see the cholera break out there. It was an anxious period but trade had to be recommenced, and by the first week in July, although cholera remained in the town, Weatherley was once again selling books on the streets of Manchester. His stall was on his old selling ground opposite the Exchange known as Pennyless Hill, where his fellow booksellers included Andrew Caffery, Jacob Bamford and James Ferguson.[14] Weatherley continued trading from this site until 1836 when he moved into shop premises in Smithy Door.

ACCOUNT BOOK AND BUSINESS METHODS

Pathetic as the progress of the petty tradesmen might appear, it should not be assumed that Weatherley was without business skills and sense. His *Recollections* indicate that he kept trading accounts, even if they were stored in a somewhat unusual location. When discussing a partnership with Moore, he recalled taking out a 'small account book that I always carried in my hat and showed him exactly how I then stood'.[15] Weatherley's surviving account book – an exercise book (330mm x 210mm) rather than a printed account book – was far too large to file in his hat. It covers the period from February 1831 to December 1833.[16] The detail provided varies considerably. For some weeks only the total income and profit from sales are recorded whilst for other weeks a daily record is provided of the title, selling price and 'profit' of the books sold. The main sequence of the daily accounts run from August 1831 to March 1832. In April 1832, as we have noted, Weatherley's financial difficulties compelled him to sell up and leave his shop in Back King Street. After this date the recording of sales becomes less consistent. The record of his stay in

Liverpool is incomplete but includes some daily sales, which are provided for the first two weeks of trading on his return to Manchester, before being replaced by simple weekly totals. These weekly summaries end abruptly in November 1832. The accounts recommence in November 1833 with a daily record of each book sold during the following seven weeks, before finally ending on Saturday 21 December 1833.

What do these accounts reveal about Weatherley's business methods? His method of recording sales was an elementary one using three columns: one for the author and/or title of the book sold, one for the selling price, and one for the 'profit' made on each sale. The first two columns are the least problematic, although the details provided by Weatherley of author and title of books sold vary considerably. The profit column however, unlike the sale-price column, did not contain a numerical figure but used a series of symbols to represent the profit made. The code was a relatively simple one which began at threepence, increasing at intervals of threepence (Figure 1).

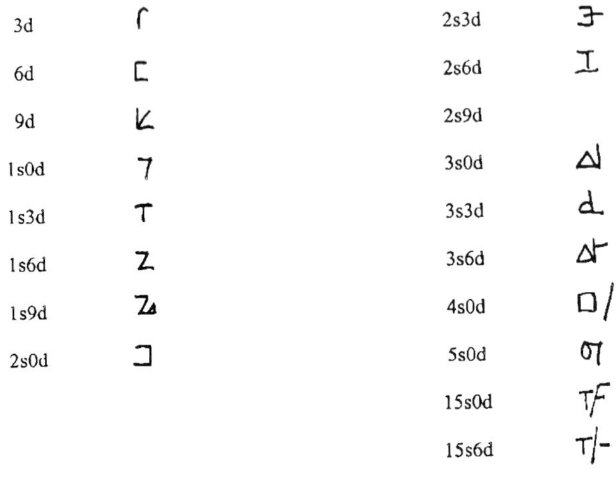

Figure 1: Weatherley's profit code

Significantly, Weatherley calculated his profit on each book in terms of the difference between the purchase price and selling price though precisely how he recalled the price he had paid for each book is unclear, especially as some books would have been purchased as part of a lot at auction or from other booksellers, rather than as single volumes. If he kept a separate stock book it has not survived; neither is there any direct evidence of his marking in code the purchase price in each book. In representing profits in this manner Weatherley appears to have ignored those costs which would have to be taken into account when calculating the true financial position of his business. The absence of information on fixed costs such as rent or an estimate of the value of his stock prevents a more reliable estimate of either his gross or net profits.[17] Limited as these accounts may be for the business historian, they enabled Weatherley to keep track of sales and provide him with what he defined as a weekly record of revenue and profit. For the historian of the book trade they provide, even accepting their limitations, valuable information about the secondhand book trade in Manchester.

SALES REVENUE AND PROFIT

What was Weatherley's turnover and how profitable was his business? Figure 2 provides a graph of the weekly sales revenue and 'profit' between February 1831 and December 1833 for which Weatherley recorded information. Fluctuations in sales

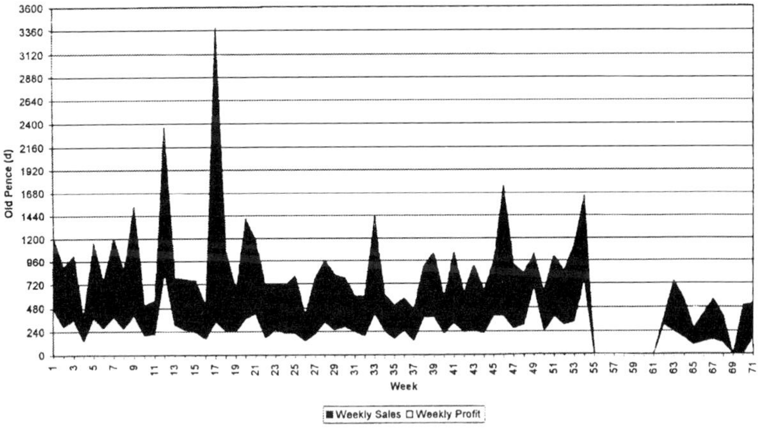

Figure 2: Weatherley's weekly sales/profit 1831–2

revenue, ranging from under £1 in a poor week to over £5 in a good week, characterised the period. The average weekly sales revenue for the 63 weeks for which data are available was £3.13*s*. 0*d*; the average weekly 'profit' was £1.3*s*.9*d*.[18] As we have noted the profit curve does not identify all of the costs that would have to be taken into account for a realistic calculation. Weatherley had other outgoings, not least of which was the money spent in purchasing books to add to the stock. Significantly, for these years, we know that his stock was diminishing: it had numbered 1300 in April 1831 but had fallen to 230 volumes when he recommenced selling on the Manchester streets in the summer of 1832. But even in the absence of such information it is evident that Weatherley's business was not making large profits, and it certainly did not provide Weatherley and his family with a comfortable standard of living. As Mayhew discovered, some twenty years later, in his survey of London street booksellers, the secondhand bookstall provided a precarious living for its owners.[19] Weatherley did make a profit each week but it was often small, and when one takes out necessary living expenses, it left comparatively little to meet business bills or reinvest in stock.

NUMBERS AND PRICES OF BOOKS SOLD

How many books did Weatherley sell? For those weeks for which we have an itemised daily record of sales it is possible to provide an estimate of the numbers of books sold. In the 32 weeks between 25 August 1831 and 30 March 1832, when Weatherley was occupying the shop in Upper King Street, the average number of books sold each week was 51.[20] The accounts are less complete when Weatherley returns to selling in the street though it appears that a smaller number of books was sold each week. In the absence of similar data from other local booksellers it is difficult to assess how representative Weatherley's sales were of the wider secondhand trade. A weekly average of some 50 books might be considered to be a small number, but it is relatively close to Mayhew's findings of a weekly average of 42 volumes sold by London street booksellers.[21] There might have been much browsing and reading at bookstalls, but turning browsers into purchasers appears to have been as frustrating a problem for the nineteenth-century bookseller as for the modern retailer. One intriguing feature of the accounts are the books sold by what Weatherley refers to as a 'knock-out'. The knock-out in the nineteenth-century book trade is generally understood to refer to the collusion between booksellers at auctions which took the form of restrictive bidding, followed by the subsequent sale of lots among members of the ring.[22] Weatherley's use of the term may refer to his selling lots of books outside the shop at times when business was slack and there was a need for cash. The knock-out occurred at least once a month, though not on a particular day of the week, when Weatherley was in shop premises, and produced sums ranging from as little as 1*s*.6*d* to £1.4*s*. None of the books sold in this way is identified, and it may be that Weatherley was attempting to shift stock of little value, appealing to bargain-seeking members of the public who were impressed by quantity rather than quality; Weatherley appeared to regard the revenue from these particular sales as all profit.

Weatherley was not operating at the higher end of the secondhand book trade. The most expensive book he sold during this period was Ireland's *Views on the Thames and on the Medway* which was sold for £1.1*s*.6*d*, realising an exceptional profit of 15*s*.6*d* (Dec 1833). A copy of Blackstone's *Commentaries* for which he charged 15*s*.6*d* produced a simple profit of 5*s* (22 Feb 1832), while other copies sold for 8*s* and 10*s* (18 Apr & 17 May 1832) . But it was rare for Weatherley to sell a book for more than 5*s*, the majority selling for 1s and 2s each. It is equally noteworthy that although he was dealing in cheaper books, he does not record selling any individual book for less than *6d* (a minimum profit of *3d*). If Weatherley had a bargain box of penny and twopenny items, their sale is not evident in these accounts.

SUBJECTS SOLD

What books did Weatherley sell? As we have noted, not every title sold is identified in the accounts – on occasions the sales entry reads simply '7 vols of Novels' or, more usually and even more frustratingly, 'Books' (31 Jan 1832). For the period from August 1831 to March 1832 Weatherley identifies the majority of his sales by a brief title. Although the accounts are reticent on publication details and the condition of volumes, nonetheless, a preliminary analysis of the identifiable titles is revealing.

Religious works formed an important category of the books sold. The most frequently sold book was the Bible; in total, Weatherley sold 32 ranging in price from *6d* to *6s.6d*. Of these all but three – two Welsh Bibles and a Latin Bible – appear to have been in English, and judging from the prices paid, were probably printed no earlier than the late eighteenth century. Prayer books and hymn books also sold well. Wesley's Hymns was a particularly strong seller - some ten copies were definitely sold - and there may have been more as a number of Wesley's publications are not identified in sufficient detail. In contrast only a single copy of Newton's *Olney Hymns* was sold (26 Oct 1831). Devotional works and sermons were also sold including popular works by Richard Baxter (*The Saints' Everlasting Rest*) (22 & 28 Mar 1832), Isaac Watts (*The World to Come*) (10 Sept 1831 & 20 Mar 1832) and Philip Doddridge (*The Rise and Progress of Religion in the Soul*) (16 Nov & 20 Dec 1831, 7 Feb 1832). William Law's influential *A Serious Call to a Devout and Holy Life*, first published in 1729, was another frequently reprinted religious work that passed through Weatherley's hands (26 Aug 1831). The moral works of writers such as Priscilla Wakefield and Hannah More, with their clear guidance on the proper conduct of life, are also to be found in the accounts. Such religious works appear to have been among the easiest to sell, though our ignorance about the provenance of these particular volumes and the small numbers involved, cautions against drawing firm conclusions about the theological inclinations and interests of Weatherley's customers. But they are a reminder of the desire for spiritual guidance and nourishment, and add weight to the view that religious books were among those most commonly found in households of all classes.

Weatherley's accounts also suggest that educational textbooks sold well. Among the regular sellers were primers in grammar, those stepping stones which enabled individuals to secure a firmer foothold on the slopes of literacy. By far the best known of the elementary English grammars were those written by the American-born grammarian, Lindley Murray: eight copies are definitely identifiable amongst the various grammars sold by Weatherley. For generations of students, following its first publication in 1795, Murray became synonymous with the rules of grammar. Such multi-editioned texts varied in price, and one must assume that customers paying 2*s* rather than 6*d* for a copy were buying a more recently published and much less thumbed edition. There was a similar demand for textbooks from those needing to master the basic principles of arithmetic. Here Francis Walkinghame was Murray's counterpart, seven specific sales being recorded. By the 1830s the market for arithmetic primers was an expanding and lucrative one for publishers – other titles sold by Weatherley included those by Thomas Molineux, Thomas Dilworth, Hutton and Fisher – in contrast to earlier generations when students had been left to puzzle over the exercises set by the renowned Cocker.

For those who were pursuing a more extensive education, the accounts indicate that Weatherley sold Latin grammars and dictionaries. One of the most popular of the texts available for students embarking on the mysteries of declensions and conjugations was the *Eton Latin Grammar*, already in its twelfth edition by 1825. For students of Greek there was Richard Valpy's *Elements of Greek Grammar*, which had reached a ninth edition by 1824 (10 Sept 1831 & 1 Mar 1832). Copies of Robert Ainsworth's *Latin Dictionary* also appears to have been good sellers (2*s*.9*d* 5 Mar, & 4*s* 19 Mar 1832). There were also grammars in the living languages French (Chambaud) and German (Wendeburn). Schoolmasters and students were likely to have been among the purchasers of such works, groups who might also have purchased some of the considerable number of classics, including works by Virgil, Plutarch, Xenophon and, above all, Aristotle, identified in Weatherley's accounts.

Science books were also among those sold by Weatherley, while for those individuals less attracted to the ideas of rationality there were books on fortune-telling, in which one's future could be foretold by examining the stars, the hands, or even dregs of coffee (1*s* 19 Sept 1831 & 7 Jan 1832). Books on geography and travel also featured, and included the accounts of voyages of individual explorers including the legendary Captain Cook (3*s* 28 Mar 1832) and Alexis Rochon in Madagascar and the East Indies (1*s*.3*d* 3 Feb 1832). History books also included reasonably well-known titles ranging from the general histories of England by Hume and Goldsmith to biographical studies of Nelson (6*d* 3 Oct 1831) and Napoleon (1*s*.6*d* 10 Dec 1831). A less obvious sale was a History of China (5*s*.6*d* 10 Oct 1831). As might be anticipated in Manchester books concerned with the history of the town, including John Palmer's *History of the Siege of Manchester* (1822), were also sold (1*s* 4 Nov 1831). Of the town's more recent past, the account of the court case challenging Richard Arkwright's patent might not have been technically history but it was already the stuff of history; this volume was sold to James Drew, auctioneer, for 3*s*.6*d* (20 Mar 1832).

Cookery books also featured in Weatherley's accounts though of the six volumes sold only two were identified: Mrs Radcliffe's *Modern System of Domestic Cookery*[23] and Elizabeth Raffald's *Experienced English Housekeeper,* the latter book having well known local connections as the entrepreneurial Mrs Raffald had lived and worked in Manchester.[24] Once again no information is given on publisher, edition, size or binding. Such vade-mecums included advice ranging from making lemon pickle to the management of servants and the treatment of illnesses. Understandably, in a society striving to understand the laws of health, medical books also featured in the list of titles sold by Weatherley. Although Wesley's bestselling *Primitive Physic* was not specifically noted, copies of William Buchan's *Domestic Medicine*, the first of its many editions having been published in 1769, were sold by Weatherley. A number of copies of family herbals, including those by Culpeper and Hill, were also listed (6*d* 23 Sept & 3*s* 4 Oct 1831).

Lighter reading was also sold by Weatherley, though works such as Crébillon's *Edwin and Lucy*, Mrs Sherwood's *Susan Gray and Lucy Clare*, and Sandford and Merton underline the role of fiction in shaping the moral world of the young.[25] Middle-class concerns about the dangers of reading certain types of novels continued to be voiced strongly in the 1830s, and no doubt some of Weatherley's customers would not have approved of those who spent their money on secondhand copies of the *Castle of Otranto* (2 May 1832 & 3 Dec 1833) or even *The Surprising Adventures of Baron Munchausen* (2 Sept 1831). Weatherley also had a steady sale of poetry with Burns being the most popular poet in terms of the numbers of volumes sold.

CUSTOMERS

And what of Weatherley's customers? Frustratingly for the historian, Weatherley recorded the names of purchasers only very occasionally in the accounts or as in the transaction mentioned in the title of this paper – 'Aristotle to a Wery Tall Man' (Figure 3) – the information he provided is sufficiently vague to ensure the customer's anonymity. In some cases the customers were local booksellers such as Willis, Wroe, Bamford, Long and Isherwood, and might have been noted for credit reasons. Other transactions including one with Clough of Liverpool and the books to the value of 5*s*.6*d* sold 'to a bookseller of Oldham'[26] are a reminder that booksellers from other towns visited the Manchester shops and stalls to do business. Some well-known local individuals were among the private customers identified by Weatherley. Two French books sold for 2*s*.6*d* to James Crossley, the Manchester solicitor (5 Dec 1832), suggest that the bookcollecting passion that was to fill his house to bursting point had already begun; a copy of Dibdin's *Typographical Antiquities* was purchased for 10*s* by the Revd William Parr Gresswell, author of the history of the early

Paris book trade (23 Jul 1832); whilst the sale of six volumes of the *Edinburgh Review* to Dalton, may mean that the town's most famous citizen considered it worthwhile to stop and look over Weatherley's stock.[27]

From such broken evidence it is difficult to generalise about the social composition of Weatherley's customers. Some were clearly drawn from the town's fast-growing middle classes, including groups such as the clergy, lawyers and schoolteachers who presumably purchased books to assist them in their work. No doubt some customers belonged to the working classes, though it is difficult to assess how important such booksellers were in helping to spread book-ownership among the poorer sections of the population. The secondhand bookstall, of course, was a familiar landmark in the autobiographies of self-taught working men who stopped there to look, to read and, when they had disposable income, to buy a book to add to their small personal libraries.[28] But by the 1830s publishers had recognised the commercial importance of providing cheap literature for the urban working classes, allowing those who wished to purchase new books the possibility of doing so for a few pence. It is perhaps significant that in Weatherley's accounts there is no direct evidence of his selling those more sensational publications which were finding a large readership among the working classes.[29] Nor does he appear to have sold (or if he did, he did not record the sale) immoral and irreligious publications, works on subjects such as birth control, which worried members of the Manchester Statistical Society when they surveyed the readings habits of local workers in the 1830s.[30] In the context of this unprecedented growth in the publication of cheap literature – penny decents and penny dreadfuls – Weatherley's stock was probably viewed as unappealing and, with the cheapest recorded item being sold for sixpence, well outside most working-class pockets. The book-hungry young Bamfords of the 1830s presumably found their reading matter from other booksellers in the town. But in considering the question of readers it is important to remember that for the majority of Weatherley's customers we have no direct evidence, a silence that needs to be acknowledged and interpreted with care. Thus the absence of references to female customers should not automatically rule out their presence either in Weatherley's shop or at his stall; we should also acknowledge that Weatherley might not have known the names of many of his customers.

CONCLUSION

The limitations of studying a single bookselling business over a relatively short period hardly need emphasising. Yet, brief and uneven as these accounts are, they do allow us to go further into James Wetherley's business than the concise entries in the Manchester commercial directories of 1830 and 1832, which tell us only that he was a seller of old books at 20 St Ann's Square and 6 Back King Street respectively. The first and most obvious point to recognise is that Weatherley's business involved the keeping of accounts, a record of sales which allowed him to calculate his weekly 'profit', even if this did not include all of his costs. Clearly, Weatherley was sufficiently numerate to maintain this record (there are few arithmetical errors in the accounts) and it may be the case that this was not the only account book relating to his business. To what extent other petty tradesmen kept similar accounts is difficult to determine, but it is a reminder that even small retailers required some elementary accounting skills to keep track of stock and sales.

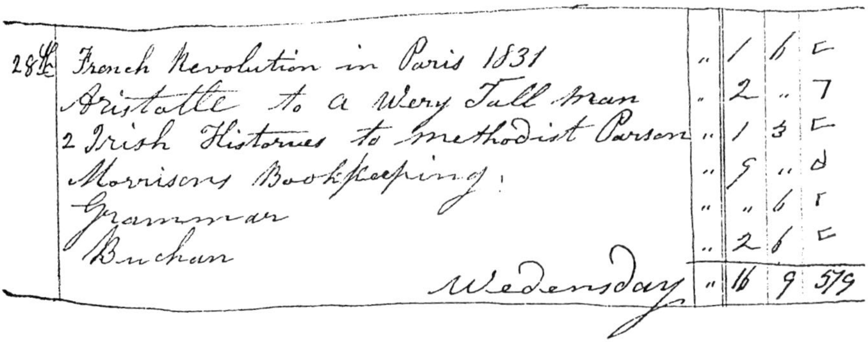

28th French Revolution in Paris 1831	"	1	6	
Aristotle to a Very Tall man	"	2	"	7
2 Irish Histories to methodist Parson	"	1	3	
Morrisons Bookkeeping	"	9	"	
Grammar	"	"	6	
Buchan	"	2	6	
Wedensday	"	16	9	579

Figure 3: Part of Weatherley's accounts for September 1831 (reduced)

Weatherley's accounts provide us with a clearer idea of his turnover and profit, as well as the different types of books sold. Analysing these it appears that Weatherley was operating on the margin of the secondhand book trade, a business characterised by a relatively small turnover of books and cash. Such booksellers might hold on to the dream of a Caxton turning up but the reality was that they were compelled to buy cheap books and to sell them cheaply, books that may have been dirty, torn and generally in a poor condition. It is not clear from whom Weatherley purchased his stock though his financial position meant that he lacked capital to expand.[31] He was no longer in a position to acquire the better lots at auction sales or to join in the 'knock-out' after the sale. Such circumstances left him vulnerable, a vulnerability which helps to explain his dealings with the London bookseller where the appeal of a large line of credit lured him into what turned out to be a blind bargain.

The forced move from shop premises to the street also made making a living more difficult. Bad weather meant fewer customers and increased the risk of damaged stock. Business was also lost because of national events. In these years Weatherley did not trade on the national fast day called to mark the cholera epidemic, and neither was there any business on the day when he 'drew nothing on account of the Public meeting in Castle field on the Reform Bill being cast out of the House of Lords' (12 Oct 1831). Selling books at the lower levels of the trade was a hard and unpredictable way of making a living, circumstances which might have contributed to the drink problem which Weatherley readily acknowledged. 'The brown jug' appears frequently in his recollections and it is not without significance that a ten-shillings beer bill was one of the three items settled with the money from the sale of stock in April 1832. Money spent in the pub could not be used to develop the business.

But Weatherley's years of trading must have provided him with some sense of what books were likely to sell to the type of customers who visited either his shop or stall. Our initial analysis has focused understandably on the books he sold, though a fuller study would need to pay attention to those volumes which did not sell, books which might have been disposed of in the bargain sale or finally sold off as waste paper (26 Mar 1832). Of those books sold by Weatherley that we can identify, a considerable number were widely available titles, volumes that were to remain a feature of the stalls and cheap bookshops throughout the century. Weatherley sold copies of Zimmerman's *Solitude*, Young's *Night Thoughts, The Death of Solitude* and *Paul and Virginia*, all of which, according to one sneering Victorian book-hunter were titles guaranteed to turn up on any cheap bookstall like 'the tax-collector in every-day life, and equally as obnoxious'.[32] But titles dismissed by the more serious book-collector, could be the treasured volumes in the collections built up by other readers. George Eliot includes among the books that Adam Bede read - Taylor's *Holy Living and Dying*, Bailey's *Dictionary* and, even more predictably, *The Pilgrim's Progress* - again all works that passed through Weatherley's hand between 1831 and 1832.[33] It is important for historians of the book trade to remember such bread-and-butter titles kept stock turning over, helping booksellers to make a living. But whilst some of Weatherley's sales might be considered predictable, it is perhaps surprising, at a time when English society was being recast, that there are very few references to titles dealing with contemporary political questions. Manchester's reputation as a centre for radical politics is hardly confirmed in these accounts which identify the sale of a single copy of John Wade's *Black Book* and one work possibly by Tom Paine.[34] Of course, Weatherley might have sold such literature clandestinely, but these accounts provide little direct evidence of the seismic political changes that were happening in Manchester and other industrial towns. It might have been the case that Weatherley was largely uninterested in such issues and publications, preferring instead to buy and sell other types of literature. The accounts, for example, record the sale of some sixty separate pieces of music in these years.

Finally, we should recognise that for all the apparent independence that the life of a petty trader or streetseller offered, these accounts suggest that it was a struggle to obtain a wage much above that received by an ordinary labourer. The 'profits' earned by Weatherley between 1831 and 1833 hardly provided him with a comfortable standard of living. Yet, financially fragile as his business became during these years, it should not be concluded that he was entirely unsuccessful. In a trade where, as we have argued, the turnover of businesses was high, Weatherley continued in business. This was not a bookselling business in which important and profitable volumes passed through his hands, but small as the turnover of stock was, it provided him and his family with a living. These accounts not only allow us to follow these rather ordinary business transactions in some detail, they also stand as evidence of why Weatherley remained a presence in the Manchester book trade.

NOTES

1. D Alexander, *Retailing in the Industrial Revolution* (London, 1970); R Scola, 'Food markets and shops in Manchester 1770–1870', *Journal of Historical Geography*, 1.2 (1975).

2. Brenda Scragg, 'Some sources for Manchester printing in the nineteenth century', in Peter Isaac & Barry McKay [ed], *Images and Texts* (Winchester, 1997), 113–19.

3. G E Maxim, 'Libraries and Reading in the Context of the Economic, Political and Social Changes Taking Place in Manchester and the Neighbouring Towns, 1750–1850' (unpublished MA thesis, University of Sheffield, 1979).

4. Anthony Lister, 'William Ford (1771–1832): the Universal Bookseller', *The Book Collector*, 38.3 (1989), 343–71.

5. Samuel Bamford, *The Autobiography of Samuel Bamford. Volume One. Early Days together with an account of the arrest* (London: F. Cass, 1967; first published 1848–9), 90.

6. Michael Powell & Terry Wyke, 'At the fall of the hammer: auctioning books in Manchester 1700–1850', in Peter Isaac & Barry McKay [ed], *The Human Face of the Book Trade* (Winchester, 1999), 171–89.

7. *Pigot & Sons General Directory for Manchester, Salford &c for 1830* (Manchester, 1830), 295; this highlights the problem of commercial directories as sole sources of information.

8. *Recollections of Manchester and Salford Characters and Anecdotes Relating to Manchester and Lancashire generally from the year 1800 to 1860 by James Weatherley. For nearly half a century a Bookseller. In the locality of the Manchester Exchange*, Chetham Library MS Mun. A.6.30, 63 [hereafter cited as *Recollections*].

9. *Accounts*, 25 January 1832; 18 February 1832, Chetham Library MS Mun A.6.30* [hereafter cited as *Accounts*].

10. *Recollections*, 62.

11. Moore is listed as bookseller at 10 Back King Street in *Pigot's Directory* 1832 & 1836.

12. *Pigot's Directory* (1832) lists John Long as schoolmaster living in Tonge Street, Salford; the 1835 directory identifies him as bookseller in Back King Street, Manchester.

13. *Accounts* record payment of 4*s*.6*d* to 'Bob the Bellman'.

14. *Recollections*, 66.

15. *Recollections*, 62.

16. *Accounts;* hereafter dates in parentheses in the text refer to dated entries in the Accounts.

17. On the calculation of booksellers' accounts see H E Bailey, *The Economics of Bookselling* (London: Hutchinson, 1965), 28–39.

18. Sales revenue based on 63 weeks, profits on 62 weeks.

19. Henry Mayhew, *London Labour and the London Poor* (London: Griffin, Bohn and Co, 1861; reprinted Dover Publications, 1968), 1, 309.

20. In making this estimate we have assumed, for those entries in the accounts where the specific number of books have not been identified, that each book was sold for 1*s*. Thus an entry for 5*s* represents five books. For entries relating to the 'knock out' we have assumed each book was sold for 6*d*. Thus a knock-out sale producing 8*s* represents the sale of 16 books.

21. Mayhew, *London Labour,* 1, 309.

22. 'Auctions and knock-outs', *Chambers's Journal*, 7 December 1895, 777–9.

23. *Accounts*, 29 Aug 1831; it is not possible to say whether this was one of the Manchester editions published by J Gleave in 1823 and 1827.

24. *Accounts*, 1*s* 1 Nov 1831; Roy Shipperbottom, *Elizabeth Raffald: The Experienced English Housekeeper* (Lewes: Southover Press, 1997).

25. Translated from the French, Crébillon's *Edwin and Lucy, or the Happy Orphans* (first published in English in 1759) copy sold 6 Feb 1831; there was an edition published by J. Gleave of Manchester in 1821; *Susan Gray* 9*d* 4 Oct 1831; *Sandford and Merton*, 1*s*.9*d* 17 May 1832.

26. *Accounts,* 10 Feb 1832. There were several of booksellers named Clough active in Liverpool at this period. See Michael Perkin [ed], *The Book Trade in Liverpool 1806–50: a Directory* (Liverpool Bibliographical Society, 1987).

27. *Accounts,* 22 Oct 1831. The *Edinburgh Review* was not recorded in the later nineteenth-century printed catalogues of the Portico Library where Dalton was an honorary member.

28. R D Altick, *The English Common Reader : A Social History of the Mass Reading Public* (Chicago, 1957); D Vincent, *Bread, Knowledge and Freedom : A Study of Nineteenth-Century Working-Class Autobiography* (London, 1981).

29. L James, *Fiction for the Working Man: A Study of the Literature Produced for the Working Classes in Victorian Urban England* (London, 1963).

30. T S Ashton, *Economic and Social Investigations in Manchester, 1833–1933 : A Centenary History of the Manchester Statistical Society* (London, 1934), 18.

31. The same problem faced the secondhand bookseller recalled in 'Bookstalls', *Household Words*, 7.66 (1853), 292.

32. 'Some 'Bookstalling' memories', *Bookworm,* 2 (1889), 3.

33. *Adam Bede,* chapter 19.

34. Pains Tract, *Accounts,* 24 Oct 1831; *Black Book*, *Accounts,* 3*s* 17 Oct 1831. Wade's indictment of 'Old Corruption' was first published in 1820.

New Town, New Newspapers: the Development of the Newspaper Press in Nineteenth-Century Middlesbrough

DIANA DIXON

FOR THE TOWN which gave birth to the first halfpenny daily newspaper in England, newspapers came relatively late to Middlesbrough. It is important to remember that the town itself was a creation of nineteenth-century entrepreneurial enterprise and that it grew out of very modest beginnings. In 1801 it consisted of four houses and twenty-five inhabitants and even by 1831 the census recorded only 154 inhabitants. The change came as a result of a conscious decision by seven Quaker businessmen in Darlington to develop a port further down the river from Stockton on Tees, where the river was difficult to navigate. An extension of the Stockton and Darlington railway was opened in 1830 and staithes for exporting coal were built. From 1830 onwards growth was rapid. In 1839 John Jordison established the first printing business in Middlesbrough in North Street which went on to be a highly successful bookbinders and printers. However, more significant was the arrival in Middlesbrough in 1840 of two ironfounders, Henry Bolchow and John Vaughan. It was their success that transformed this modest port into a thriving metropolis whose population rapidly expanded from 5709 in 1841 to 91 302 in 1901.

The discovery in 1850 of a rich source of ironstone in the Cleveland Hills led to massive expansion of the iron trade, which by 1873 was producing over two million tons of pig-iron annually. The iron trade attracted immigrants from all over Britain and Ireland and brought prosperity to Middlesbrough, with the founding families asserting power in the area.

By 1860 some cultural activity was beginning: the Mechanics' Institute opened in that year, followed by the Middlesbrough Athenaeum in 1863, the Theatre Royal in 1866, and the first free public library in 1870. Unlike many other towns, Middlesbrough had no tradition of a long-standing newspaper press and its inhabitants relied on the newspapers from the surrounding area: the *Newcastle Chronicle,* the *Durham Chronicle,* the *York Herald* and the newly emergent *Darlington and Stockton Times.*

The first newspaper to appear in this rapidly growing town was a monthly broadsheet called the *Middlesbrough Chronicle* in 1853. The Middlesbrough historian, William Lillie, suggested that the so-called taxes on knowledge[1] were to blame for the late appearance of the newspaper press,[2]

> At first glance it seems rather extraordinary that Middlesbrough citizens had to wait for their own newspapers, but the duty on paper did not make for economical printing.

Monthly publications were exempt from the punitive taxes and therefore considerably more lucrative for newspaper printers and proprietors. The *Chronicle*'s printer was Joseph Richardson, formerly a cabinet-maker from nearby Hutton Rudby, who had been apprenticed to a Stokesley printer, Mr Braithwaite. In 1841 Richardson moved to Middlesbrough and set up as a letterpress printer, engraver and lithographer in the premises of his wife's stationer's shop in Commercial St. His work as a jobbing printer involved producing almanacs and tide-tables and he soon became interested in literary endeavours, starting with a monthly periodical entitled *The Literary Pilot* in 1852. He started the *Chronicle* the following year, for which he purchased copy from a London printer, Eglinton, adding his own local information. John Jennings states,[3]

> But it was reserved for Mr Joseph Richardson to give the people something which Middlesbrough could call his own, and accordingly he made arrangements to bring out an insignificant weekly journal which he dubbed The Middlesbrough Chronicle.

This fledgling journal was staunchly radical and aired the many grievances affecting a rapidly growing town. Jennings, a man with considerable experience as a printer in the town, believed that Richardson wrote most of the copy himself, and he suggested the compositor was responsible for the unlikely stories of improbable events in the nearby villages of Stokesley and Hutton Rudby. He also enlisted the services of a Nonconformist minister named Bowen to write regularly. Jennings was of the opinion that the success of the *Chronicle* attracted the envy of a rival printer, Martin, who started a very short-lived magazine, the *Middlesbrough Pilot,* which was not destined for longevity and succumbed within a few months. However, the *Chronicle* became a weekly in 1855 and was re-titled the *Middlesbrough News.* Richardson, therefore, deserves the accolade of 'the father of journalism in Middlesbrough'.[4]

Unfortunately, the earliest issues of the *Middlesbrough News* cannot be traced but at some stage its title changed to the *Middlesbrough Weekly News.* It was founded by Joseph Richardson and printed from the Mechanics' Institute in Durham Street, before moving to larger premises in South St. The paper was purchased in 1863 by liberal Joseph Gould, with printing offices in South St. However, it ceased being liberal in outlook when it was taken over by the conservative Middlesbrough printers, Wilkinson & Burnett. William Wilkinson was sole owner for a short time from March to September 1867. An advertisement in the *Newspaper Press Directory* for 1868 proclaimed the *Middlesbrough Weekly News & Cleveland Advertiser* 'Advocates Constitutional principles and supports Constitutional measures'.

> It is the oldest and leading newspaper published in the extensive and important district of Cleveland. It advocates constitutional principles and is an independent exponent on all questions of the day. It gives the local news of interest throughout the district, the latest markets and a well selected summary of general news.[5]

The paper was printed at the Royal Exchange and remained in the hands of W Wilkinson until 1876 when it was taken over by the Middlesbrough Printing and Publishing Co. Its printer was W Appleyard until its demise in 1884, when it was advertising itself as 'A first class Liberal paper. The oldest established paper in Cleveland'.[6] The final issue of the paper carried an announcement:[7]

> The Publisher of the 'Middlesbrough Weekly News and Cleveland Advertiser' having disposed of the Copyright to the holders of the 'North Eastern Daily Gazette', takes the opportunity of thanking his many friends for the support they have given to the paper during the past twenty nine years. With no 1503 March 28th, the 'News' will cease as a separate publication, and on and after April 5th it will be amalgamated with the 'North Eastern Weekly Gazette'.

Following the repeal of the newspaper taxes in 1855, Middlesbrough saw a number of short-lived titles. The *Middlesbrough Times* was started in September 1860 by another local printer, John Jordison, whose firm was small, with only four employees. The editorial in the first issue declared[8]

> To all those who have watched the rapid progress of Middlesbrough and the great Iron Districts of Cleveland during the past ten years (a progress it is believed unparalleled by any locality in the Kingdom), the want of a newspaper capable of representing the interests and giving expression to the requirements of this vast and important hive of industry must be apparent.

The *Middlesbrough Times* lasted until 1867, having changed its title to the *Middlesbrough and Stockton Gazette* in November 1860. An advertisement in the *Newspaper Press Directory* claimed[9]

> It devotes especial talent to the mining and shipping interest of the neighbourhood, gives the latest commercial political and domestic news, full and accurate reports of public meetings and the principal markets and shipping intelligence, and a weekly report of the iron trade of Cleveland. As a medium for advertisers it is unrivalled, having by far the largest circulation in the district.

Its sister paper was the liberal *Stockton Gazette & Tees-side Advertiser* which was founded by the Unitarian Robert Spears, and first appeared on 30 December 1859.

Despite optimistic puffery for large circulations and well-being for both local newspapers, the reality was slightly different.

> Middlesbrough. A town with competing newspapers, all of which is in a parlous financial state and often fly by night and very short-lived[10]

was the verdict of Hugh Gilzean Reid, a Scottish journalist who came down from Scotland in 1865 with the intention of publishing newspapers in Cleveland.[11]

> Most of all with the knowledge that he could produce a better newspaper than any that existed in the area at the time, he liked his carefully calculated vision for the future, and the role that he could play with his own particular talents in the making of Teesside.[12]

Of Reid's talents there is no doubt. He was born at Cruden, Aberdeenshire, in 1838. He was largely self-educated and planned a career as a Baptist minister. However, while attending lectures at Aberdeen and Edinburgh, he was diverted into a career in journalism, and joined the staff in the Banff office of the *Aberdeen Journal*, before becoming editor of the *Edinburgh Evening News* 1859–62 and the *Peterhead Sentinel.* He established the *Buchan Observer* in January 1863 and remained its owner-editor until 1865, when he cast his predatory eye upon the press of Teesside. He probably purchased the *Stockton Gazette* in 1865 and by 1867 he had also gained possession of the *Middlesbrough Times.* At the time of the purchase the struggling papers had a circulation of only 700 copies a week. His first venture, the *Middlesbrough & Stockton Gazette, and General Advertiser for the North of England*, appeared on 9 January 1867. Initially he published the paper from the offices at 104 High Street, Stockton, and with a staff of four men and two boys and he printed the paper at the Gazette Office, Railway Crossing, Middlesbrough. From these modest beginnings, Reid went on to be an innovator in press history and to develop the successful newspaper that thrives today.

In November 1869 the paper's name was changed to *The Daily Gazette,* selling at ½*d* a copy. It moved to more prestigious premises in Zetland Road, Middlesbrough, in 1871 and adopted steam printing. Reid described the developments[13]

> The spacious offices in Zetland Rd., were erected several years ago and in 1880 was introduced the Marconi Press which is capable of printing and counting the Gazette at the rate of 25,000 copies per hour. The paper is produced by the new process of stereotype plates, and the whole of the appliances are as complete and effective as those in any newspaper office in the country.

The centenary supplement contains an amusing anecdote concerning an occasion when the steam press had failed, and rather than cease production steam rollers were hired to ensure printing continued. Unfortunately the vibrations from the steam rollers caused the beer barrels in the neighbouring Zetland Hotel to release their contents causing a deluge of beer to flood its cellars. Despite this, 64 000 copies of the paper reached the newsagents only one hour later than usual.

In June 1881 its title changed to the *North Eastern Daily Gazette.* Reid retained his interest in the *Gazette* until 1888, but by that time his interests had diversified into the Midlands and Lancashire, especially the *Northern Daily Times* in Blackburn. He briefly represented Aston Manor, Birmingham, as a Liberal MP in 1886 and became President of the Institute of Journalists in 1890. For his services to journalism he was knighted in 1893. A strongly religious man, he developed interests in missionary work in the Belgian Congo and resided for a time in Belgium. He identified himself with social movements for housing improvements and developed interests in the iron and steel industry. He died in Middlesex in November 1911.

The *Gazette* soon developed an ascendancy over other titles and appealed to the populace, acquiring a circulation of 15 000 by the end of the first week. By 1884 this had increased to 20 268 copies a day, showing an increase of over 5632 copies daily from the previous year.[14] In 1881 Reid published a pamphlet celebrating Middlesbrough's jubilee in which he discussed the role of the press:[15]

> The Newspaper Press has played no unimportant part in the progress of Middlesbrough; and it might be stated that the *North Eastern Daily Gazette* was the first daily newspaper in the North Riding, Yorkshire and South Durham; that it was the first to apply steam power to printing in the district; and that it has a larger circulation (with one exception) than any of the daily newspapers published between Leeds and Glasgow.

It should be noted that Reid failed to identify any rival publications existing in Middlesbrough at the time. His rival newspaper proprietor, the printer Burnett, also produced a booklet which was far more generous to his competitors:[16]

> In the literature of the press Middlesbrough is represented by two daily papers The Daily Exchange and the North Eastern Daily Gazette which also print weekly editions, and one weekly, The Middlesbrough News.

The weekly edition of the paper entitled the *North Eastern Weekly Gazette* appeared to have a lightness of tone lacking in its sister paper:[17]

> It gives special attention by gossipy notes and full reports to the requirements of the Tees-side Boroughs. It contains serial stories, complete tales, literary selections and a mass of interesting information not usually found in a weekly paper.

There is no doubt that the *North Eastern Daily Gazette* was extremely successful. An advertisement in the *Newspaper Press Directory* for 1894 justifiably claimed[17]

> The progress of the North Eastern Daily Gazette is unparalleled in the history of journalism in the North of England. The paper permeates the thickly-populated district within a fifty mile radius of Middlesbrough.

It went on to say that the paper is[17]

> thoroughly liberal in politics; possesses an able literary staff; and devotes special attention to the industrial and commercial affairs of the North of England. The North Eastern Daily Gazette is one of the freshest news-sheets in the provinces.

Writing about the reading habits of the working class in Middlesbrough in 1908, Florence Bell, wife of a local industrialist, noted[18]

> The reading that comes under the hand of the workman consists chiefly of the newspapers hawked about the streets, and those supplied by the small composite shops found in the poorer quarters… Of these, some read only a daily paper, the favourite being a local halfpenny evening paper, which seems to be in the hands of every man

> and woman, and almost every child. It contains a summary of general news, a serial story, a good deal of sporting information, also gossip and commercial news.

The *Gazette* was not without competition. The Middlesbrough printers, Burnett & Hood, had started a newspaper entitled the *Middlesbrough Exchange & North Ormesby News* on 8 January 1869. William Hall Burnett, of Smeaton Street, North Ormesby and George Hood of Milton Street, North Acklam, were jobbing printers and stationers with premises in Albert Place, Middlesbrough. Their newspaper carried advertisements for the books they published including *Bates's Guide to Redcar and Saltburn-by-the-sea,* sermons, translations of books from the Norwegian, and the St Paul's North Acklam, Middlesbrough, Parish Magazine. Additionally they sold albums, hymn books, stationery and operated a subscription library and bookshop, all of which they advertised on the front page of the *Middlesbrough Exchange.* The proprietor of the *Middlesbrough Weekly News,* the liberal Joseph Gould, became involved in its publication, but he relinquished his interest in 1874.The paper was anxious to proclaim its social superiority in a notice to advertisers:[19]

> Those advertisers who wish to reach a better class of advertiser will find the Exchange a capital medium. The Exchange now circulates amongst nearly all the clergy and gentry of the locality as well as having a considerable local sale.

It also advertised itself in the *Newspaper Press Directory*:[20]

> The Middlesbrough Exchange is an organ of independent principles, and circulates largely in Middlesbrough and its environs. It contains the fullest reports of local events, excludes all objectionable matter, and commands the most respectable circulation.

The *Exchange* was conservative in tone and not destined for great longevity. Although it started as a weekly, retailing at 1*d,* later it became a daily. A sister paper, the *Guisborough Exchange,* was produced between 1871 and 1875, and William Hall Burnett assumed sole control of the paper until 29 August 1887 when he went bankrupt. Burnett also published the *South Bank News*: *Grangetown, Eston & Normanby Chronicle* which lasted from the end of 1883 to 27 June 1887, the *Cleveland News* from 1884 to 1887, and a satirical weekly entitled *The Dominie: a Local Serio-comic Journal* which ran from 15 May 1875 to 4 November 1876. Jennings described it as 'a weekly budget of satirical prose and rhyme' containing a lithographic cartoon of a local personality in every issue.[21] It was jointly edited by Tom North and Angus Macpherson, who had regularly contributed columns in the *Middlesbrough Exchange* under the pseudonym of 'The dominie' . Earlier Macpherson, who was Secretary of the North Riding Infirmary, had jointly edited with Mrs Hjerled *A Cleveland Literary Annual* in 1873.

In common with most other towns in England, Middlesbrough had its share of short-lived newspapers. Of these, the liberal weekly *Cleveland Journal*, a liberal paper, founded in October 1872 by G F Bates, appears to have disappeared without trace, although the *Newspaper Press Directory* listed it in 1874 claiming it[22]

> Advocates the interests of commerce, manufactures and agriculture; is attached to the Church of England. Devotes great care to the details of every occurrence of interest, publishing ample reports of the meetings held in the district, and gives the latest and home news.

Another short-lived title was the *Middlesbrough and Stockton Evening Telegraph* which first appeared on Tuesday 15 June 1897.

> To please the public is a task that prevents many difficulties. If we have overcome them in any degree in launching the 'Evening Telegraph', we hope to enjoy a meed of approbation... The world of news in all its labyrinthine paths has been ransacked for the best that the enterprise of modern journalism could create. The public will judge of the result and we are content to await the verdict.[23]

The proprietor, Henry Foote Patterson, managed to keep the struggling paper going until April 1900 when it succumbed. Its politics were Unionist and

> It has a special circulation amongst the ironmasters, shipbuilders, shipowners and the chemical, salt, timber, coal mining, ironstone mining, and agricultural interests in the neighbourhood.[24]

Another daily, the *Middlesbrough Morning Mail*, replaced it in 1900 but it, too, only lasted for a few months. There was also a single-sheet *Middlesbrough & Stockton Sporting Telegraph* which was Conservative and established in 1897 and lasted until November 1899. Its chairman was local iron magnate, Sir Hugh Bell. An attempt was made to revive it in 1900 under the title of the *Sporting Telegraph*, but this was unsuccessful. With its importance as a port, there was a need for a record of daily shipping movements and this was met by the *Tees Daily Shipping List* (1887–1916). It is also worth mentioning a monthly magazine the *Middlesbrough Temperance Visitor & Monthly* (1870) which was freely circulated, and

> It is to be hoped it will not injure its elder brother the Daily Gazette to which it bears no small resemblance, as indeed, is not surprising, considering that the imprint bears the same paternity.[25]

The *Temperance Visitor* lasted until 1883 and was considerably more successful than Reid's other venture into monthly publishing. This, the *People's Paper*, only appeared once in December 1871 and its diet of 'random notes, gossip from Paris, police news, serial fiction' failed to attract subscribers. Another more successful venture, *Tweddell's Middlesbrough Miscellany of Literature and Amusements* by the Stokesley publisher, Tweddell, was considerably more attractive. Tweddell appears to have had a low opinion of the citizens of Middlesbrough, prefacing the first issue with the statement[26]

> to be honest we do not consider literary taste a distinguishing characteristic of the people of Middlesbrough.

Nevertheless, they bought his magazine, as at least eighteen issues of the annual are known to have been published.

Jordison's *Northern Review* lasted from October 1886 to August 1894, and claimed to include 'Literature of an interesting, humourous [*sic*] and instructive kind';[27] Jennings regarded it highly,

> With the exception of The Dominie' it is perhaps the best and most promising of any of the publications I have encountered.[28]

Jennings lamented that Middlesbrough was unable to maintain a flourishing local periodical press:

> All these ambitious sheets of literary enterprise have either fallen asleep of themselves or merited the fate of extinction from nameless causes.[28]

The press of Middlesbrough reflected the ethos of the town it served. Just as its growth and prosperity was the result of entrepreneurial vision, so, too, was its successful newspaper. The arrival of Hugh Gilzean Reid in 1865 elevated its newspaper press from mediocrity. Ambitious and committed, Reid was innovative, risking a halfpenny daily earlier than anyone else, and adopting the latest printing technology. His labours bore fruit. Rivals were short-lived and unable to meet the competition. Unlike so many provincial evening newspapers, the *Gazette* began the twentieth century in a strong position and survives into the twenty-first as the *Evening Gazette.*

NOTES

1. Stamp Duty was repealed in 1855, Advertisement Duty in1853 and Paper Duty in 1861. Collectively they were generally referred to as taxes on knowledge and their repeal resulted in a great expansion in the provincial press and the rise of the penny newspaper.

2. William Lillie, *History of Middlesbrough: an Illustration of the Evolution of British Industry.* (Middlesbrough: County Borough of Middlesbrough, 1968), 213.

3. John Jennings, 'The early press of Middlesbrough: a brief sketch', compiled *c* 1890–1894, 2. Handwritten manuscript in Middlesbrough Central Library. This throws interesting light on Middlesbrough's newspaper history. Jennings had been a compositor at Burnett & Hood and other printers, and so had personal insight into the printing industry in the town. It remains the principal source of information on early Middlesbrough newspapers.

4. Jennings, 'Early press', 6.

5. *Newspaper Press Directory* 1868, 158.

6. *Newspaper Press Directory* 1884, 215.

7. *Middlesbrough Weekly News & Cleveland Advertiser,* 28 March 1884, 4.

8. 'Prospectus', *Middlesbrough Times,* September 1860, 1.

9. *Newspaper Press Directory* 1868, 158.
10. Quoted in *Evening Gazette Centenary Supplement*, 10 November 1969, 2.
11. Considering his eminence, there is a paucity of reliable information about Reid's early newspaper career. KJ [James Fowler Kellas Johnstone], 'Local bibliography', *Scottish Notes and Queries,* X (November 1896), 87, lists his newpaper proprietorships and editorships.
12. *Evening Gazette Centenary Supplement*, 3.
13. Hugh Gilzean Reid, *Middlesbrough and its Jubilee.* (Middlesbrough: Gazette Printing Office, 1881),10.
14. *Newspaper Press Directory* 1884, 217. The notice stated that the circulation figures had been substantiated by an accountant.
15. Reid, *Jubilee,* 10.
16. A Macpherson, *Middlesbrough and District: being Notes, Historical, Industrial, Scientific.* (Middlesbrough: W H Burnett, 1881), 46.
17. *Newspaper Press Directory* 1894, 129.
18. Lady Bell, *At the Works.* 2nd edn (London: T Nelson, 1911), 205–6.
19. *Middlesbrough Exchange & North Ormesby News,*17 December 1869, 1.
20. *Newspaper Press Directory* 1874, 180.
21. Jennings, 'Early press', 6.
22. *Newpaper Press Directory*, 1874, 76.
23. 'Editorial', *Middlesbrough & Stockton Evening Telegraph,*15 June 1897, 2.
24. *Newspaper Press Directory* 1899, 303.
25. 'The Dominie', *Middlesbrough Exchange & North Ormesby News,*31 December 1869, 2.
26. 'Preface', *Tweddell's Middlesbrough Miscellany of Literature & Amusements,* 1 (1871), 1.
27. 'Opening remarks', *Northern Review* 1 (1), 2 October 1886, 7.
28. Jennings, 'Early press', 8.

MIDDLESBROUGH NEWSPAPERS TO 1900

Cleveland Journal and South Durham Advertiser Feb–Oct 1873

Daily Gazette for Middlesbrough, Stockton & District Oct 1869–Jun 1881 then *North Eastern Daily Gazette* 1881–1940 then *Evening Gazette* 1940–

Evening Echo 8 Mar 1884

Middlesbrough & Stockton Evening Telegraph Jun 1897–Jul 1900

Middlesbrough & Stockton Sporting Telegraph Jun 1897–Nov 1899

Middlesbrough Chronicle 1853-55 then *Middlesbrough Weekly News & Cleveland Advertiser* 1855–1884

Middlesbrough Exchange & North Ormesby News 1869–1873 then *Daily Exchange* May 1874–Oct 1887

Middlesbrough Weekly Exchange c 1869–Oct 1887

Middlesbrough Gazette Jul–Aug 1869 then *Middlesbrough & Stockton Gazette* 1869–Jul 1876 then *Weekly Gazette* Aug 1876– May 1883 then *North Eastern Weekly Gazette* May 1883–Oct 1895 then *Northern Weekly Gazette* Oct 1895–Feb 1939

Middlesbrough Morning Mail c April–Oct 1900

Middlesbrough Temperance Visitor 1870–1883

Middlesbrough Times Sept–Nov 1860 then *Middlesbrough & Stockton Gazette* to 1867

South Bank News 1883– Jun 1887

The Troubled History of a Welsh Newspaper Publishing Company: the North Wales Constitutional Newspaper Company Limited, 1869–1878

LISA PETERS

ALTHOUGH IT IS DIFFICULT to demonstrate a strong correlation between a favourable press and electoral success, politicians have traditionally striven to influence the content of newspapers.[1] The abolition of stamp duty in 1855 led to a reduction in the price of newspapers, which, in turn, led to an increase in the number of newspapers and the number of readers. Consequently such political controls as stamp duty and covert subsidies were no longer viable and new forms had to be devised. From the mid-nineteenth century if a political party wished to ensure itself of a newspaper's support it either established its own newspaper or bought an already existing one and converted it to its own views. This method of securing a newspaper's support had been used prior to 1855 but took on a new urgency as newspaper circulation rose and the electorate expanded. The Liberals were especially fortunate in that they possessed far more extensive support amongst the provincial press than the Conservative party. Concern over this lack of provincial newspaper support was reflected at the first conference of the National Union of Conservative and Constitutional Associations in November 1867 when one of the stated aims of the Association was 'to increase and multiply the influence of the Conservative press throughout the United Kingdom'.[2] Later historians of the political press such as Koss have commented that Conservative Central Office had very little money for the establishment of Conservative newspapers outside London and relied upon provincial supporters to establish such newspapers,[3] thus leaving then to bear the financial burdens, and the frequent financial losses. This was true of the *Wrexham Guardian* and especially its owners, the North Wales Constitutional Press Company Limited.

The *Wrexham Guardian*, first published in September 1869, was founded in response to the Conservative defeat in the 1868 general election. Nationally the Conservatives lost the general election to Gladstone and the Liberal party, and within Wales, for the first time, the Liberals won more seats than the Conservatives, with twenty-three seats to the Conservatives' ten. With the possible exception of Merthyr Tydfil, where the Nonconformist Henry Richard headed the poll for the Liberals and Gladstone's future Home Secretary, H A Bruce, lost his seat, the most important victory for Welsh Liberalism was in Denbighshire. In the Denbigh Boroughs, whose electorate had risen by nearly 200% as a result of the 1867 Reform Act, the sitting

Conservative MP, Townshend Mainwaring, was defeated by a young, Radical, pro-disestablishment lawyer, Watkin Williams. In the two-member county seat, the sitting Conservative MP, Sir Watkin Williams Wynn, was returned at the head of the poll, but the second seat was taken by another Radical Liberal lawyer, George Osborne Morgan, ahead of the sitting Whig MP, Col Biddulph, the Lord-Lieutenant of Denbighshire.[4] Since the Liberals now held four of the five parliamentary seats in northeast Wales, local Conservatives decided to bolster their party's ailing fortunes by establishing a Conservative newspaper 'to battle, to some extent, with the many Liberal organs in that part of the Principality'.[5]

Although the *Wrexham Guardian* is an example of the establishment of a newspaper by a political party, its actual origins are somewhat unclear. According to its first issue it was printed and published by the owner of the Conservative *Chester Courant*, James Ramsden. He continued to do so for a year, before being replaced by John Vaughan, who printed and published the newspaper for the North Wales Constitutional Press Company Limited. However, according to a circular of 1878,[5] the newspaper was established by the North Wales Constitutional Press Company Limited. Since the company was not incorporated under the Companies Act until 1 July 1870, this suggests either that the company's connection with the newspaper was hidden until after it officially came into existence, or that the newspaper was established by a third party, possibly Ramsden, and then sold to the company.

The *Guardian* openly proclaimed itself to be the 'recognised organ of the constitutional party in North Wales'. It claimed to contain detailed local news reports, agricultural and mining news, market reports, and a summary of national news, and maintained that it circulated amongst 'the nobility, clergy, gentry, professional and trading classes throughout the Principality',[6] the latter statement probably being a considerable exaggeration. In the following year, 1871, possibly in response to disappointing circulation figures, it was less keen to trumpet its link with the Conservative party, stating that it was now 'the organ of the Liberal-Conservatives, but in all matters takes a thoroughly independent course'.[7]

There were early signs that the newspaper and the company were not to be as successful as its founders wished. The initial capital consisted of three thousand one-pound shares, yet fewer than two thousand of them had been sold by March 1871, to fifty-nine people, most of whom resided in the two Welsh border counties of Denbighshire and Flintshire. The occupational breakdown of the shareholders can be seen in Table 1.

The largest group of shareholders, described as 'gentlemen of no occupation', included some of the largest landowners in north Wales. The remainder of the shareholders were drawn from the educated middle classes and professions, and included

Table 1
Occupations of Shareholders of North Wales Constitutional Press Company (1871)[8]

Occupation	Number of Shareholders
None	27
Legal	7
Religious	5
Medical	4
Alcohol-trade	4
Army	3
Miller	2
Auctioneer	1
Member of Parliament	1
Baronet	1
Colliery Proprietor	1
Land Agent	1
Coachbuilder	1
Retail	1

doctors, ministers of religion, and officers in the armed forces. The twelve company directors, listed in Table 2, included some of the most influential figures in north Wales. Sir Watkin Williams Wynn Bt was the largest landowner in Wales, with over 145 700 acres,[9] and was the Conservative MP for Denbighshire, a seat which his family had held since the early eighteenth century. Thomas Lloyd FitzHugh owned 3725 acres,[10] Edmund Peel over 8400 acres,[11] and the Hon George Thomas Kenyon unsuccessfully fought the Denbigh Boroughs in 1874 and 1880 before winning the seat in 1884. William Trevor Parkins was the Chancellor of the Diocese of St Asaph from 1891 to 1908 and a member of Denbighshire County Council from 1889 to 1899, and both Thomas Rowland and Peter Walker were Conservative Mayors of Wrexham, the latter being the brother of Sir Andrew Barclay Walker, the Mayor of Liverpool in 1873–74 and 1876–77. The company's secretary from 1873, Evan Morris, was the first man to be elected Mayor of Wrexham from outside the Council and was knighted by Queen Victoria in 1889.

Since archival information relating to the *Wrexham Guardian* and the North Wales Constitutional Press Company is scanty, the newspapers themselves are the

Table 2
The First Twelve Directors and their Shareholdings[12]

Director	Shareholdings	Occupation
Sir Watkin Williams Wynn, Bart	600	Baronet
The Hon. George Thomas Kenyon	30	None
Thomas Lloyd FitzHugh	100	None
Thomas Taylor Griffith	50	Doctor
Thomas Irven	20	None
Edmund Peel	150	None
William Trevor Parkins	30	Barrister
Thomas Rowland	20	None
Charles Townshend	20	Land Agent
W. Maysmor Williams	30	Tobacconist
Peter Walker	60	Brewer
Edward Williams	30	Doctor

main source of information, supported by company records at the Public Record Office.[13] In addition the Flintshire Record Office possesses, amongst the Gredlington papers, a small collection of letters and documents relating to the newspaper primarily letters written to Kenyon.[14] Unfortunately these letters cluster around the years 1874, 1876, and 1878, and therefore do not offer a complete account of the early history of the newspaper, and its controlling company. Since they all relate to problems in the company's affairs, it is difficult to ascertain whether such problems constantly existed throughout the newspaper's life, or whether Kenyon and the other directors corresponded only when the newspaper was in financial difficulties.

In 1873, less than three years after incorporation under the Companies Act, the North Wales Constitutional Press Company was declared bankrupt.[15] Despite this, in July it secured a loan of £1000 and the Annual General Meeting passed a special resolution to increase the company's capital to £8000 by issuing an extra five thousand shares.[16] However, by December 1876 none of these additional shares had been purchased which suggests that they were not sufficiently attractive to either new or existing investors. Some conclusions as to the financial state of the company and newspaper can be drawn from the company's accounts of October–December 1873[17] and January–March 1874,[18] the only sets to have survived. The newspaper's circulation was approximately 1900 a week (October–December 1873), which was over 3000 less than that of its Liberal rival, the *Wrexham Advertiser*,[19] although that newspaper's figures are based upon those submitted to *Mitchell's Press Directory*, and therefore may not be accurate. The advertising revenue, a key factor in a newspaper's success, varied greatly from over £38 in November to only £12.4*s*. 1*d* in December, the November total being bolstered by parliamentary advertising, mainly relating to railway projects. Both sets of figures make reference to an 'allowance' of over £535 and £630 respectively. This appears to have been a regular political subsidy that the newspaper was receiving to ensure its continued survival.

Despite the decision to increase the company's capital, it remained in financial difficulties. A letter from Parkins to Kenyon, in April 1874, refers to the *Guardian* as being in an 'extremely critical' state. The company was £1830 in debt to the bank, yet the company itself was owed some £900 in outstanding debts, which implies poor credit control. In addition, a Mr Shipps,[20] to whom either the newspaper or the plant, or possibly both, was leased, wished to withdraw from the enterprise unless he was given some assistance, presumably financial.[21] Attempts to save the newspaper were not greatly aided by the decision of the company's main shareholder, Sir Watkin, to give only £200 towards the company's debts, in addition to a subsidy of £100 a year for the newspaper, and that only on condition that he approved a plan for the future financial management of the newspaper.[22] The problems were, in fact, so great that the company directors recognised that the newspaper would not break even.[23]

At least two plans were suggested to improve company finances, but neither came to fruition. The first plan, advocated by Parkins, involved a subsidy of £600 for the newspaper, a subscription to reduce the debt to approximately £800, and for Kenyon to pay the remainder which would be treated as a loan by him to the company. The only alternative, Parkins suggested, was for Kenyon[24] to ask the directors to give him the newspaper and for him to sell it.[25] An alternative plan was advocated by Morris, who feared that Kenyon would sell the plant and 'drop the paper'. He suggested that Kenyon should collect as much money as possible by subscription to pay off the debt; if the company failed to meet the balance, then it was to assign all property to Kenyon and wind itself up. Kenyon would then assign a half-share in the newspaper to Sir Watkin for £500. Morris offered to manage the newspaper himself for a guarantee of £400 per annum for two years, and stated that he would pay any excess himself, if he could have half of the profits when the newspaper became profitable.[26] However Sir Watkin was unwilling to accept this scheme.[27] It is significant that both schemes involved the continued use of a large subsidy.

With the rejection of both these plans, the company's financial problems became increasingly serious. In a final attempt to stay afloat, the company attempted to assign its property to Kenyon in lieu of a debt of £1000, but, according to legal opinion, such a course of action was not possible because Kenyon was a director.[28] Instead William Lee Brookes, Kenyon's election agent, loaned the company £1000 and in default stood to gain all of the machinery and the plant.[29] The exact role of Brookes in the company and the newspaper is unclear. He was not a shareholder, but might have been channelling Kenyon's money into the company, so as to enable the newspaper to survive until the next general election, when its support would be important for Kenyon's campaign. This suggestion is supported by evidence that Brookes had loaned the company £1000 a year earlier, which was later repaid by Kenyon.[30] Financial problems continued until the end of 1874, as the company was involved in a dispute with its accountant, whose bill they were reluctant to pay, unless offered a substantial discount. There is no evidence that the company applied to Conservative Central Office for financial assistance, possibly because it believed that no help would be forthcoming.

In the absence of further correspondence for 1874 it can be presumed that enough of the company's debts were paid to ensure the *Guardian*'s survival. A letter from Morris in August 1875 referred to a satisfactory arrangement having been made to enable the *Guardian* to continue but gave no further details.[31] However, the company continued to be beset by financial difficulties. In June 1876 Sir Watkin refused to guarantee the debt to the bank and consequently the bank refused to advance more funds.[32] Kenyon admitted 'I am quite come to the end of my tether in subscribing to those things. I must positively incur no more risks', although he added, 'I am at present pretty well secured as the paper is mortgaged to me I think'.[33] Morris again suggested a proposal to save the newspaper, namely, that Sir Watkin should guarantee £500, or pay £400 subscription for the current and last year and guarantee £300.[34] It is not known whether this suggestion was accepted, although Sir Watkin did pay a £200 subscription shortly after the proposal was made.[35]

There is no further information relating to the company until January 1878 when Sir Watkin and Kenyon sent a printed circular to local Conservatives informing them of the newspaper's financial difficulties. They admitted that 'the paper has only managed to exist for the last nine years by the liberality of a very few Conservatives. Since 1874 it has been supported entirely by Sir Watkin Williams Wynn, Bart. and the Hon. George Kenyon', who had paid £2870 and £600 respectively.[36] Support was also received from Edmund Peel (£170), Thomas Lloyd FitzHugh (£125), Peter Walker (£400), Lord Penrhyn (£350), Robert Bamford Hesketh (£100), and Lord Edmund Hill-Trevor[37] (£100). The company owed £1500 to the bank; in addition £500 was needed as capital, together with an annual subsidy of £300 to cover losses. The circular urged readers to subscribe towards reducing the debt and to offer an annual subsidy, reminding them that Wales lacked Conservative newspapers in comparison with Liberal ones, and that if the *Guardian* were to cease, Conservatism in Wales and Conservative seats in Wales would be the losers.[38] Unfortunately for the Conservatives, the Denbigh Boroughs Liberal MP, Watkin Williams, managed to acquire a copy of this circular and, no doubt, seeking revenge for many insults in the *Guardian*'s editorials, passed it on to the *Advertiser*. The *Guardian*'s rival not only published it, but also purposefully pointed out that it survived by virtue of its commercial success and not by subsidies from the Liberal party and calculated that the *Guardian* had received a subsidy of around £9000, equivalent to £1000 a year.[39]

The circular apparently failed to produce the desired financial support. When Brookes requested the repayment of his loan in 1878, the company was unable to pay and consequently he took control of the company's possessions and machinery. In July he sold the plant, machinery, goodwill, and copyright of the newspaper at a loss to Morris for £600 and assigned the business to him.[40] In August this was sold on to Frederick Edward Roe, a newspaper owner from Dover for £600, payable in six annual instalments commencing in 1880.[41] The debt to the bank was over £1600 but Roe had been promised a subsidy of £450 a year for three years.[42] The company was wound up in November.[43]

The failure of the *Wrexham Guardian* and of the North Wales Constitutional Press Company Limited did not mean the end of Conservative newspaper publishing in Wrexham. The newspaper's new owner relaunched it in 1879 as the *North Wales Guardian* and it continued under this title until 1925, when it became the *Wrexham & North Wales Guardian*, finally ceasing publication in 1954. Under its new owner the newspaper became so successful commercially that as early as December 1879 Roe could write to the editor of the *Carnarvon & Denbigh Herald*, forcefully refuting that newspaper's allegations that the *Guardian* received a subsidy.[44] It is more difficult to measure the newspaper's success in its role as a promoter of the Conservative cause in north Wales. The Conservatives failed to win the Denbigh Boroughs seat in either the 1874 or 1880 general election, although the Liberal majority was small in both elections; thirty in 1874 and fifteen in 1880. However the founders of the newspaper clearly felt that a party newspaper was an important factor in local success at election times, and this might have encouraged those with political ambitions to donate large sums of money to the enterprise.

NOTES

1. For a detailed discussion of political attempts to control the press in the early nineteenth century see A Aspinall, *Politics and the Press c. 1780–1850* (London, 1949).

2. National Union Minutes, 12 November 1867, quoted in Stephen Koss, *The Rise and Fall of the Political Press in Britain*, 2 vols (London, 1981-84), 1, 184.

3. Koss, *Political Press,* 1, 178.

4. For a detailed discussion of the 1868 general election in the Denbigh Boroughs and Denbighshire see Jane Morgan, 'Denbighshire's *Annus Mirabilis*: the borough and county elections of 1868', *Welsh History Review,* 7 (1974), 63–87.

5. Printed circular, 24 January 1878 from George Thomas Kenyon & Sir Watkin Williams Wynn (Hawarden, Flintshire Record Office [henceforth FRO] D/KT/22).

6. Charles Mitchell, *The Newspaper Press Directory and Advertisers' Guide* (London, 1870), 177.

7. Mitchell, *Press Directory* (1871),102.

8. Wrexham Guardian Shareholders, 17 March 1871 (PRO BT31/1552/4989).

9. John Bateman, *The Great Landowners of Great Britain and Ireland*, 4th edn reprinted, introduction by David Spring (Leicester, 1971), 491.

10. Bateman, *Great Landowners*, 165.

11. Bateman, *Great Landowners*, 354.

12. North Wales Constitutional Press Company Limited, Articles of Association (PRO BT31/1552/4989).

13. PRO BT31/1552/4989.

14. FRO D/KT/22.

15. Aled Gruffydd Jones, *Press, Politics and Society : a History of Journalism in Wales* (Cardiff, 1993), 126.

16. Special Resolution of the North Wales Constitutional Press Company Limited, 3 September 1873 (PRO BT31/1552/4989).

17. Dr Granville in a/c with the Constitutional Association (the *Wrexham Guardian*), from 13 October to December 1873 (FRO D/KT/22).

18. Dr Granville in a/c with the North Wales Constitutional Association, from 1 January to 28 March 1874 (FRO D/KT/22).

19. Mitchell, *Press Directory* (1874), 199.

20. The letter is unclear as to Shipps's relationship with either the company or the newspaper, as he is mentioned only in this one letter.

21. Letter, W T Parkins to G T Kenyon, 20 April 1874 (FRO D/KT/22).

22. Letter, O S Wynne to W T Parkins, 9 May 1874 (FRO D/KT/22).

23. Letter, W T Parkins to unknown correspondent, 23 May 1874 (FRO D/KT/22).

24. A letter from W T Parkins to G T Kenyon, 20 April 1874 (FRO D/KT/22), seems to suggest that Kenyon had guaranteed a bank loan to the company.

25. Letter, W T Parkins to unknown correspondent, 27 May 1874 (FRO D/KT/22).

26. Letter, E Morris to J Jones, 29 May 1874 (FRO D/KT/22).

27. Letter, E Morris to unknown correspondent, 11 June 1874 (FRO D/KT/22).

28. Legal document, *ex parte* The North Wales Constitutional Press Company Limited, 16 July 1874 (FRO D/KT/22).
29. Legal document, North Wales Constitutional Press Company Ltd and William Lee Brookes, 30 July 1874 (FRO D/KT/22).
30. Deed of indenture between George Thomas Kenyon and William Lee Brookes, 12 August 1874 (FRO D/KT/22).
31. Printed letter, E Morris to the North Wales Constitutional Press Company Limited, 17 August 1875 (FRO D/KT/22).
32. Letter, E Morris to G T Kenyon, 19 June 1876 (FRO D/KT/22).
33. Letter, G T Kenyon to W L Brookes, 20 June 1876 (FRO D/KT/22).
34. Letter, E Morris to O S Wynne, 21 June 1876 (FRO D/KT/22).
35. Letter, E Morris to W L Brookes, 27 June 1876 (FRO D/KT/22).
36. Other evidence suggests that Kenyon gave at least £1000 to the company.
37. Conservative MP.
38. Printed circular, 24 January 1878 from G T Kenyon and Sir W Williams Wynn (FRO D/KT/22).
39, *Wrexham Advertiser*, 25 May 1878, 4.
40. Legal document, W L Brookes, Esq and The North Wales Constitutional Press Company Limited to Evan Morris, Esq, 30 July 1878 (FRO D/KT/22).
41. 19 August 1878 (FRO D/KT/22).
42. There is no mention of where or whom the subsidy was from.
43. Liquidators' Return of Final Winding-up Meeting of the North Wales Constitutional Press Company Ltd, 4 December 1878 (PRO BT31/1552/4989).
44. 'The "Guardian" and its contemporaries', *North Wales Guardian*, 27 December 1879, 5. This statement refutes earlier evidence.

John Atkinson's 'Lottery' Book of 1809: John Locke's Theory of Education Comes to Workington.

BARRY McKAY

I BELIEVE IT IS NOT UNREASONABLE to say that many a piece of research into print history started with the purchase of an interesting book in an antiquarian bookshop. This paper will, I hope, be no exception to that statement.

A year or so ago I bought, in a Cumbrian bookshop, a copy of the third edition of *Tables of Exchange* (London, 1803). It was at one time in the possession of one John Atkinson of Workington, and both he and the volume itself will receive further attention in this paper.

Many who have studied children's books or chapbooks will have noticed that occasionally they include in their imprints phrases such as 'where may be had patters, histories, lotteries' and so forth, or similar variations on the theme. Again many, like myself, may have assumed that the lotteries referred to were the legitimate gaming of purchasing a ticket in the hope of winning a substantial cash prize. After all a number of provincial booksellers of the late-eighteenth and early-nineteenth century were also lottery agents. We who accepted unquestionably this interpretation of the word were wrong in that assumption, for the lottery referred to in such instances was a children's game which had grown out of a method of teaching children to read.

The game of lottery as played with the volume under examination was quite simple. Small printed images were cut from a larger sheet, produced specifically for the purpose, and placed intermittently between the leaves of a book. The book was then closed and children would gamble by sliding a pin between the leaves and opening the book at that point. If an image was between the leaves thus selected the child 'won' the picture, if not then the pin was forfeit.

What we have in this childhood entertainment is a combination of three elements incorporating (at least in some degree) the casting of lots, the use of a pin, and the winning of a prize. It is worth bearing in mind that children as a group tend to be amongst the most conservative elements of society, who through many of their games have long been the zealous guardians of part of popular or folk-culture tradition. It is surely not difficult to accept that they would have continued to be amused by this harmless pastime through several generations. Furthermore when considering a society where graphic images were less common than they are today, it is not too difficult to imagine the delight and pleasure these small images would have given.

The casting of lots to arrive at a decision by some form of divination free of human bias has a long history. The *Oxford English Dictionary* records that a lot was

> (... usually a piece of wood) used in a widely diffused ancient method of deciding disputes, dividing plunder or property, selecting persons for an office or duty, etc., by an appeal to chance or the divine agency supposed to be concerned in the results of chance. The 'lots' each bearing the special mark of one of the competitors, were placed in a receptacle (in Homeric Greek a helmet); according to Greek procedure the vessel was shaken, the winning lot being that which fell out first; in Scandinavia the winning lot was drawn out by an uninterested party.

There is also a long tradition of casting lots to arrive at decisions in England. In the sixteenth century the Chapter of Wells Cathedral cast lots to apportion patronage, while in early seventeenth-century Reading on each Good Friday three maidservants cast lots for money left by a benefactor.[1] Such use of lots was not invariably for a beneficial purpose. Furthermore the casting of lots to select from a group of condemned men those to face execution was a feature of military discipline employed during the Civil War, and at other periods, when lucky tickets were sometimes labelled 'life given by God'.[2]

Until the early seventeenth century decision-making by the casting of lots was not unacceptable providing it was not used in a trivial manner. It was, as William Perkins wrote, 'an act of religion in which we refer unto God the determination of things of moment that can no other way be determined'.[3] While in 1577 John Northbrooke warned that 'Whosoeuer vseth this chaunce of lottes in ydle and trifling things taketh the name and prouidence of God in vaine'.[4]

The role of the humble pin in this 'chaunce of lottes' is not to be lightly dismissed, for this common and now everyday item carries elements of superstition and was believed to have the property of conveying good luck. The mere act of finding a pin, and in particular a bent one, was in itself lucky. The Opies record a rhyme on the subject, collected in Newbridge in the 1950s:

> See a pin and pick it up
> All the day you'll have good luck.
> See a pin and let it lay
> Bad luck you'll have all that day.

While in Alton a more imperious version ran:

> Pin, pin, bring me luck,
> Because I stop to pick you up.[5]

Although both these rhymes were collected in the twentieth century the former was recorded in the nineteenth.[6] Furthermore although such phrases as 'not worth a pin' imply something of little value this was not always the case. Brewer informs us that 'at one time pins were a great expense, and in 14th and 15th century wills there are often special bequests for the express purpose of buying pins',[7] while a child of early twentieth-century Birmingham wondered if 'pins were in short supply or were expensive to buy'.[8] Even until comparatively recently pins were certainly of some 'value'. In the East End of London as late as the 1950s it was not unknown for tailors to give a packet of pins in lieu of a farthing or other small amounts of change. They would also accept pins in payment for a small piece of cloth 'purchased' from them to effect repairs on items of worn clothing.[9] Indeed one wonders if when women earned 'pin money' were they sometimes literally paid pins?

How then, and perhaps more importantly why, did these superstitious elements, appeals to divinely inspired choice, and small images combine to be both an element in the teaching of children to read, and provide them with an amusing pastime? And what is their place as an element of print-culture history?

I think it is self-evident that the primary skill of reading is the ability to recognize the individual letters of the alphabet. Reading is perhaps an easier skill to acquire than writing and certainly is a prerequisite of the latter. However command of the former skill is extremely difficult to quantify. Until quite recently most if not all statistical evidence for literacy was based upon whether or not marriage registers were signed, or merely marked with a cross. But what does the presence of a signature 'prove'? Nothing more than that the signatory could write their name. It does not offer proof of literacy; any more than does the lack of a signature 'prove' illiteracy. It would be quite possible for someone who can read – at least in some measure – not to have the manipulative skill of writing, or, if it is a rarely used skill, not to be bothered with the chore of laboriously writing one's name. It has also been suggested to me that a gallant and literate partner marrying an illiterate spouse, might prefer not to shame them by signing their name on the marriage register when the other was unable to do so, and therefore contented themselves with merely making their mark.

What therefore do we mean by literate, and perhaps more to the point, what did the term mean in an earlier time? John Clare noted that both his parents were 'illiterate to the last degree, my mother knew not a single letter... my father could read a little in the Bible, or Testament, and was very fond of the superstitious tales that are hawked about the streets for a penny'.[10] I suggest that the sheer volume of cheap print, chapbooks, sheet ballads, almanacs, last speeches and suchlike street literature, or even the growing number of advertising posters, notices and announcements that began to proliferate on the walls of provincial towns from the middle decades of the eighteenth century onwards, offers evidence – moot evidence perhaps but evidence nonetheless – for a far higher level of reading ability than is often assumed to have been the case. Indeed chapmen (perhaps the major suppliers of cheap print to the contemporary mass market) in some areas were required to prove their own literacy.

Chapmen's societies existed in Fife and Stirling in the late seventeenth century and amongst their rules was the requirement that all members should have a Bible and be able to read it.[11]

If therefore we can accept the premise that a significant proportion of the population across a broad spectrum of society could read, at least to some degree, what methods were employed to assist them in the acquisition of the relevant skill?

John Locke wrote that

> Children may be cozened into a knowledge of the letters, be taught to read without perceiving it to be anything but sport, and play themselves into that which others are whipped for. Children should not have anything like work or serious laid on them; neither their minds nor bodies will bear it... I have therefore thought that if *playthings* were fitted to this purpose, as they are usually to none, contrivances might be made *to teach children to read* whilst they thought they were only playing. (Author's italics)[12]

Locke then goes on to suggest the manufacture of a ball 'like that of the Royal Oak Lottery', unfortunately without giving any indication as to what that was. It was presumably so well-known as to need no explanation, but unfortunately no account of this game – presuming of course that is was a game – appears to have survived. The ball should be made

> With thirty-two sides, or rather of twenty-four or twenty-five sides; and upon several of those sides pasted on an A, upon several others B, on others C, and on others D. I would have you begin with these four letters, or perhaps only two at first; and when he is perfect in them, then add another; and so on till each side having one letter, there be on it the whole alphabet. This I would have others play with before him, it being as good a sort of play to lay a stake as to who shall throw an A or B, as who upon dice shall throw six or seven. This being a play amongst you, tempt him not to it lest you make it business, for I would not have him understand it is anything but a play of older people, and I doubt but he will take to it of himself.[13]

Locke is here suggesting the subtle ploy of excluding the child from taking part in the game and by so doing making it more attractive. Elsewhere Locke warns parents of the dangers of games of cards or dice, yet here he is equating, in some measure, a method of learning by gaming. He goes so far as to suggests the laying of stakes 'as to who shall throw an A or B'. Elsewhere Locke, again equating this 'ABC dice' with the Royal Oak, suggests that the participants might 'play for cherries or apples, etc'.[14]

Locke's *Some Thoughts Concerning Education* was published in 1693 so it is obvious that the Royal Oak Lottery was well-known at that time and it may perhaps be allowable to presume that it was a game of chance played essentially for amusement and is here being converted into a teaching aid.

However the concept of using of dice or similar objects of play as an aid to learning the alphabet predates Locke by a century. In 1594 Hugh Plat suggested

A ready way for children to learn their A.B.C.

Cause 4 large dice of bone or wood to be made, and upon every square, one of the small letters of the cross row to be graven, but in some much bigger shape, and the child using to play much with them, and being always told what letter chanceth, will soon gain his Alphabet, as it were by the way of sport or pastime. I have heard of a pair of cards, whereon most of the principall Grammer rules have been printed, and the School-Master hath found good sport thereat with his schollars.[15]

In the British Museum Department of Prints and Drawings is an eighteenth-century engraved sheet carrying fifty images of figures which appear to be drawn from classical and other mythology. When 'made up' the sheet takes the form of a six-sided dice with nine images on each of five faces and an open 'cross' on the sixth. Thus the object when constructed resembles a basket more than a dice. Is it connected to the Royal Oak Lottery, does one place lots inside it, perhaps small images, and shake them out as part of some game?[16]

In a catalogue of prints issued in 1731 John Bowles advertised 'Lotteries, one hundred different sorts, many of them new designs, and very prettily graved: they are small prints of Men, Women, Fish, Flowers, &c. and are chiefly intended for children to play with, and are printed on half a sheet of Fool's-Cap Paper'.[17] In 1775 Sayer & Bennett also advertised lottery sheets in their catalogue though now 'Five hundred different sorts' were offered, described as 'new designs well engraved'.[18] Apart from the five-fold increase in the number of lottery sheets available from one publisher to the next, it is interesting to note that despite these two printsellers' catalogues being issued half a century apart, both seem to feel the need to describe lottery sheets as being 'chiefly intended for children to play with'.

In 1784 E Tringham of London issued an etched lottery sheet showing thirty-two street traders with their cries. In relation to David Hounslow's paper above it is interesting to observe the fascination which these street traders and the images of them held for the contemporary juvenile mind. Obviously the interest extended from their publication in book form to making them available in sheet form for use in playing the lottery game. It is further worthwhile noting that several traders discussed by David Hounslow are represented on this sheet. The 'Tiddy Dol Man' is here (though shown as 'Doll diddy dall' a reference perhaps to his cry) and the cuckold announcing Horn Fair. Historians of book-trade images may care to note that the Mercury Woman is also shown crying the 'Evening Post,' whilst of relevance to the present paper a pin-seller offers her wares at '12 a penny'.[19]

Many of the catchpenny prints issued by Bowles & Carver in the 1780s and 1790s appear to be lottery sheets. Some of them are of Twelfth-Night characters and perhaps the selection of the role to be assumed on that day's festivities was made by the casting of lots. Others show street traders, characters from the entertaining-history genre of chapbooks: Robin Hood, Jack of Newbury, Mother Bunch, &c, while others, with more and smaller images to the sheet, contain miscellaneous images perhaps intended as aids to the teaching of reading.[20]

George Cruikshank also etched lottery sheets. One, *A Pretty Little Lottery for Children* printed and sold by I M Langham, of Holborn,[21] consists of an etched plate with a large central image of three boys playing rounders, or a similar bat and ball game, surrounded by thirty-six miscellaneous uncaptioned images.[22]

I suspect that many of these lottery sheets, particularly those captioned, were intended as overt teaching materials, while those with uncaptioned images could, either by accident or design, have served the same purpose, consistent perhaps with the object-teaching method of Comenius. This was almost certainly the case with a sheet-print issued by William Darton in about 1825 and entitled *Children's Pictures to Amuse and Instruct*, which has the further distinction of being hand-coloured.[23]

There is a hand-coloured German example in the British Museum of anthropormorphic characters playing a variety of musical instruments.[24] In the same collection are three Spanish examples, each carrying forty-eight images which seem to form part of a narrative sequence and are numbered sequentially.[25] Another Spanish example is in the British Museum, in this instance with no sequential numbering but with numbers which may have some 'value' in the playing of a game. This sheet, which is entitled *Nueva Loteria Para Niños*, carries the following instructions at the tail of the sheet

> Cut out the 48 cards on this sheet and roll them up. Put them in a hat or bag. Make a remainder pile or whatever is wanted for the game, in equal amounts for each player. Each player in turn takes one card out of the bag: if it is a winning card the player takes however many cards from the remainder of the pack as appears on the sign on the winning card. If 'death' is taken the player loses as many cards as there are in the remainder pile; if 'fortune' is taken out the whole of the remainder of the pile is won and the game is finished and therefore starts again.[26]

Presumably, therefore, these Spanish lottery sheets are intended for use as a card game rather than that the images should be cut up and used in the pin-picking game. Perhaps this is a Spanish version of the card game 'lottery' of which Lydia Bennett was so fond, it being 'a nice noisey game… [of which she was]… too eager in making bets and examining after prizes...[and]... talked incessantly of lottery tickets, of the fish she had lost and the fish she had won'.[27]

A suite of four lottery sheets pasted into a guard-book in the Jackson Collection of Cumbria County Library (Carlisle) have a large central image surrounded by a number of smaller, captioned images (Fig 1 *opposite* reproduced by kind permission of Cumbria County Library). These are each printed in a different single colour, and in one instance the sheet consists of two groups of images, each with a larger central

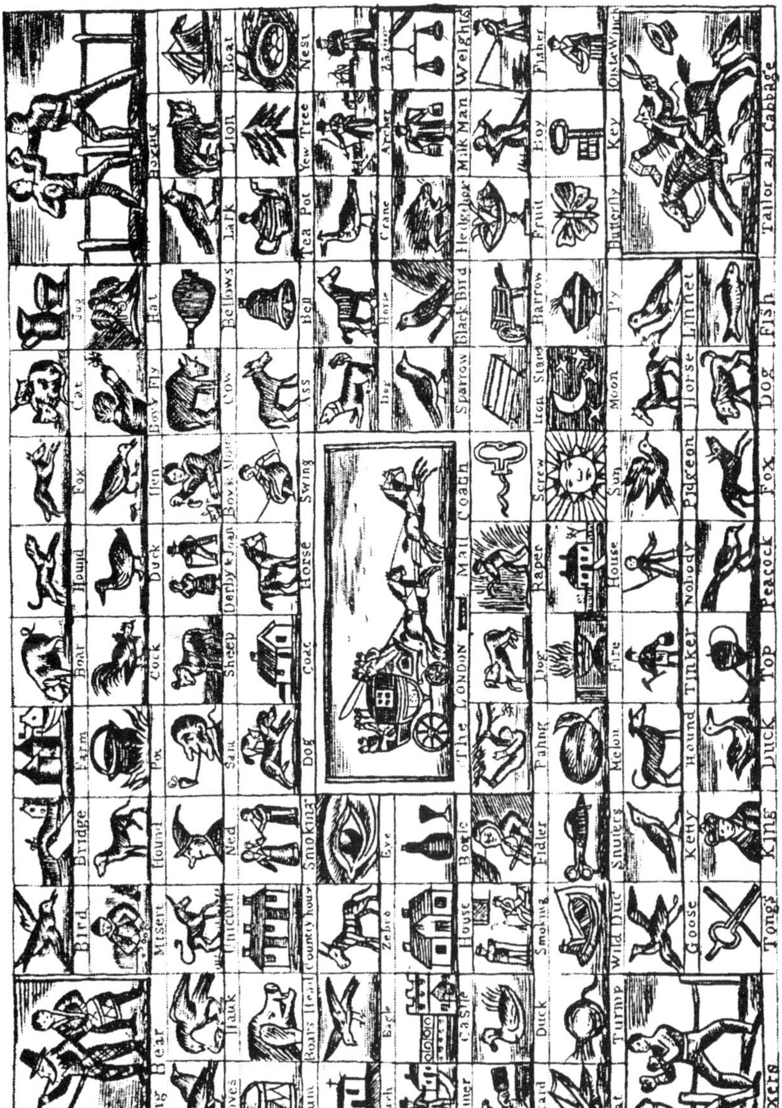
Dancing Bear
Bird
Bridge
Farm
Boar
Hound
Fox
Cat
Kite
Doves
Hauk
Misert
Unicorn
Hound
Ned
Pox
Sam
Cock
Sheep
Duck
Darby & Joan
Hen
Cow
Hat
Bellows
Lark
Lion
Boat
Hand
Drum
Boar's Head
Country house
Smoking
Dog
Horse
Swing
Bell
Tea Pot
Yew Tree
Nest
Parot
Church
Eagle
Zebro
Eye
Crane
Archer
Nest
Farmer
Castle
House
Botle
The LONDON Mail Coach
Sparrow
Black Bird
Hedgehog
Milk Man
Weights
Shaving
Drunkard
Duck
Smoking
Fidler
Dog
Raper
Screw
Iron Stand
Barrow
Fruit
Boy
Fisher
Rabit
Boat
Turnip
Wild Duc
Snuffers
Melon
Fire
House
Sun
Moon
Py
Butterfly
Key
Goose
Hound
Tinker
Nobody
Pigeon
Horse
Linnet
Boxers
Tongs
King
Duck
Top
Peacock
Fox
Dog
Fish

image, separated by a small amount of space between the adjacent borders. Although the full sheet can be said to form an homogenous whole, it would seem that it was also designed to be split down the middle, perhaps for sale in two halves in a manner similar to double slip songs where the sheet could be sold complete or divided for sale as separate items. Unfortunately no imprints are present on these examples, so accurate dating is impossible, although they have the appearance of belonging to the early part of the nineteenth century. Furthermore, the somewhat crude execution of the images is matched by some of the spelling of the captions.[28] They were given to the antiquarian R S Ferguson by the Wigton bookseller Thomas McMechan (*fl* 1857–95) who wrote in a covering letter

> I enclose you a few small matters of what were called 'Lottery' Pictures, once largely sold amongst the children, who cut them and put them into small books, into which other pictures [were] put in. Prick. And if the page contained a picture, the pricker-in got it – if no it was a loss of a pin which was in that day, [of] some value… the quaint pictures may amuse you as showing what pleased a former generation in youth.

Another example of this sort of divisible sheet, though in this instance in four parts and printed by R Harrild of London, is in the John Johnson Collection at the Bodleian Library, Oxford.[29] While another example in the same collection is in six parts and may have been also have been intended to form part of a battledore.

William Davison of Alnwick also produced quite a substantial number of lottery sheets. These were printed 'eight-up' on large sheets. Of those few I have been able to examine three carry six or eight smaller images set between ruled lines and within an ornamental border. Many of the individual images have been identified by Peter Isaac as being made up from blocks which appeared in *Davison's New Specimen of Cast-Metal Ornaments and Wood Types*.[30]

Advertisements for lottery sheets continued to appear for many years. *Old Moore's Almanac* for 1854 carried an advertisement for a 'List of Children's Books, &c., Printed & Published by A. Ryle & Co, Monmouth Court, Bloomsbury, London', which includes 'School Books, Penny and Half-penny Song Books, Valentines, Christmas Pieces, Twelfth-night Characters, Scripture Sheets, Ballads, Hymns, Lotteries, Scraps, Theatrical Characters, Toy Cards, &c'. The *Prize Book* of around 1859 offered a similar selection of material from Ryle's successor William Fortey. In the 1860s or 1870s William Walker & Sons of Otley also advertised their toy books 'printed in oil-colours', lottery sheets, and 'moral and religious tracts for hawkers'. It would seem that by the mid-nineteenth century lottery sheets had moved away from being concerned with amusement and instruction into the realm of entertaining playthings.[31]

Thus far I have been concerned with lotteries in sheet form and offered essentially as graphic images, though doubtless with some education or improving end in mind even if only covertly. But the 'lottery' also appeared in book form.

In 1756 John Newbery advertised *The Little Lottery-Book for Children*. The sixth edition of 1767, the earliest surviving example, is a small volume of thirty-two leaves, published 'bound and gilt' at three pence (the Bodleian copy is in floral 'Dutch-gilt' boards).[32] In issuing this book, which in all fairness is perhaps more of a plaything than a volume for recreational or educational reading, Newbery has obviously been inspired by Locke's teachings. He writes that 'the Business of this little book... [is] to fix the Minds of Children 'till they have acquired a proper knowledge of the Letters and Figures'. Newbery directs that

> As soon as the Child can speak, let him stick a Pin through the Side of the Leaf where the Pictures are, at the Letter on the other Side, which you would teach him; and thus let him do till he has by many Trials run the Pin through the Letter, turning the Leaf every Time he sticks the Pin through, by which means the Mind of the Child will be fixed so long upon the Letter, that he will have a perfect Idea of it, and not be liable to mistake in for any other. When this is done, you may shew him the Picture opposite the Letter, and make him read the name of it; which you will find divided, if it be a Word of two or more Syllables.[33]

Thus having pricked his pin and turned the page the child would see a letter presented in both capitals and lowercase and in roman and italic founts, together with numerals in both roman and arabic forms. On the opposite page were small cuts of suitably captioned images. Thus Newbery, guided surely by Locke's principle, believed the process of looking at the letters and pictures, and reading the captions, would instil the alphabet into the child's mind.

Newbery was not alone in employing this method of using a book and pins as both plaything and teaching aid. Similar productions were issued by William Charnley in Newcastle in 1771, P Norbury in Brentford in about 1800 and Macdonald & Son in London in 1813.[34] Pins and books were also used to test a scholar's ability at spelling. The Irish novelist William Carleton recalled that it was his schoolmaster's practice at the end of each day to gather together

> All the boys capable of spelling... Each boy put down a pin, which the master placed in the spelling book, and then all took their places – forming a circle that almost went round the whole school. The head of the class was called the King – the second Queen – and the third Prince. In that class I held the first place, nor do I recollect that I was ever dethroned. I went home every day with the coat sleeve of my left arm shining with the signals of my triumph.[35]

Newbery's pedagogical publications also included cards. Whilst these were not playing cards in the sense of gaming it seems quite obvious that a clear distinction could be made between (as it were) the medium and the message. In 1744 he advertised as 'newly invented for the Use of CHILDREN' 'A Sett of Fifty Six Squares, with CUTS, and DIRECTIONS for playing with them'.[36] 'Master Michael Angelo' in Thomas Carnan's edition of *Juvenile Sports* of 1773 was probably describing something similar when he recalled his father bringing 'home with him a set of square cards', carrying letters of the alphabet in roman and italic, numerals and 'a great number of moral sentiments'.[37] These cards were perhaps not dissimilar to the 'flash-cards' which enjoyed something of a vogue in teaching circles a few years ago.

The use of pins and books was not only useful as a method of encouraging children to learn to read. A not dissimilar process could also be applied to instilling good behaviour. In 1744 Newbery had produced the first edition of *A Little Pretty Pocket-Book* which was offered for sale at six-pence, or at eight-pence with a ball or pincushion. In the text Newbery explains the purpose of the ball and pincushion:

> I Have also sent you a Ball, the one Side of which is *Red*, and the other *Black*, and with it *ten Pins*; and I must insist upon making this Bargain, that your Nurse may hang up the *Ball* by the String to it, and for every good Action you do a *Pin* shall be stuck on the *Red Side*, and for every bad Action a *Pin* shall be stuck on the *Black Side*. And when by doing good and pretty Things you have got all the *ten Pins* on the *red Side*, then I'll send you a *Penny*, and so I will as often as all the *Pins* shall be fairly got on that Side. But if ever the *pins* be all found on the *Black Side* of the *Ball*, then I'll send a *Rod*, and you shall be whipt as often as they are found there. (Author's italics)[38]

Newbery then offers the same instructions for girls, only they shall have a pincushion rather than a ball.

A similar method was also used to instil religious principles. One informant tells me that as a child at Sunday School she would be asked to match a picture to a biblical quotation in order to obtain the picture.[39] While in the 1950s Mrs Johnston of Barrow-in-Furness purchased from a stationer in the town a 'blessings box' manufactured by Pickering & Inglis. The ornately shaped box is covered with repeat-pattern decorated paper, the lid being lined with gold paper. Within is a compartment containing 145 small pieces of paper rolled into tight cylinders (perhaps a very few may have been subsequently lost). The box originally came with a pair of small tweezers which were used to extract the papers which, when unrolled, revealed a biblical quotation. Perhaps one took one out each morning in order to obtain the day's improving thought. I have not unrolled and read them all, so I do not know if an appropriate quotation from *Proverbs* 'The lot is cast into the lap' is included in the collection.[40]

However pins and books in combination did not always meet with approval. About 1803 Newbery's successor, John Harris, issued an edition of *The Fortune-Teller: by which Young Gentlemen and Ladies may easily Fortel a Variety of*

Important Events, that will Happen both to Themselves, and their Acquaintance, a title which had first appeared in the 1770s published by Carnan. The author – identified only as 'Doctor Hurlothrumbo, Chief Magician and Astrologer to the King of the Cuckoos' – offered the following instructions to 'constantly tell the fortunes of those who apply':

> Cover [the 'curious magical table'] entirely with a piece of paper, and then stick a pin through it, and observing upon which of the squares the point of it stands, the letter in that square will direct you to one of the verses in the following alphabetical collection which will infallibly tell you what your fortune will be, if you answer to the character specified.

Wilson, Spence & Mawman in York had produced a similar work entitled *Mother Shipton's Legacy: or, a Favourite Fortune Book* in 1797, which contained the same instructions and which attracted the ire of Mrs Trimmer. She wrote 'It is sufficient, we should suppose, to read the title of this Book, to convince any person, of common understanding, that it is totally unfit for Children'.[41]

Despite Mrs Trimmer's strictures the use of a pin and fortune book for foretelling the future remained in vogue, at least in rural areas, for many years, for as Clare writes

> And oft, God rest her, in the fortune-book
> Which we at hay-time in our pockets took,
> Our pins in blindfold on the wheel we stuck,
> When hers would always prick the worst of luck
> For try, poor thing, as often as she might,
> Her point would always on the blank alight.[42]

What then of the 'lottery' book of John Atkinson of Workington? The owner of this book would seem to be a mariner and shipowner born in Workington in 1780, the son of another mariner of the same name. Jollie's *Directory* of 1811 describes him as a master and shipowner, while Parson & White in 1829 and Mannix & Whellan in 1847 record him as a shipowner, of Finkle Street, Workington.[43]

He was, I suspect, a book collector rather than a mere occasional buyer of books, and base that assumption on the fact that three books have come to light which carry his bookplate. The earliest of these is an attractive Irish binding of a *Book of Common Prayer* printed in Dublin in 1785. It was perhaps purchased by John Atkinson senior, as it carries his signature, dated 3 September 1785, on the recto of the rear free endleaf. The volume also carries the bookplate of 'our' John Atkinson and his signature, dated 1 January 1820, on the verso of the front free and title page.

Another book carrying the same bookplate is another *Book of Common Prayer*, an Oxford edition of 1826. Atkinson's signature, dated 1832, is at both the head and tail of a leaf of 'Prayers for the Lord Lieutenant of Ireland' which is laid down on the front pastedown (which perhaps explains why the bookplate is on the rear pastedown).

The presence of this leaf suggests that the book was purchased in Ireland and probably in Dublin. That a West Cumbrian mariner should be buying books in Ireland is not in itself remarkable. A great deal of trade, particularly the carrying of coal, took place between the Cumbrian ports and Dublin, and Atkinson was perhaps a frequent visitor to that city.

It is however the third book in this small hoard which should now command attention: *Tables of Exchange. In two parts. Part first. English Money Exchanged in to Irish, for any Number of Pounds, Shillings and Pence... Part second. Irish Money Exchanged into English...* Third edition, London: printed by J. Galton, Eastcheap, for R. Dutton, 45, Gracechurch-street; W.J. & J. Richardson, & Vernor and Hood. 1803.

The front and rear free endleaves carry the inscription: 'John Atkinson Workington June 27th 1809', with his bookplate on the front pastedown. A small piece has been cut from the tail-fore corner of the front free endleaf but leaving the following inscription:

> [missing] [h]ere Acknowledg'd merits Reign Praise to [J's?] Impertinent; and Censure Vain.
>
> Sept r 12 at Sea 1809
>
> Nymph of the grot these Sacred Springs I keep
> And to the Murmar [*sic*] of these Waters Slip
> Ah Spare my Slumbers, gently tread the Cave
> And Drink In Silance [*sic*], or in Silance leave.[*sic*]
>
> By John Atkinson

Closer examination of the volume revealed that within the pages of the book were found three small printed images. Further minute examination revealed a number of small holes in the fore-edge margin of several leaves and a cut in one leaf. Michael Sadleir once wrote that 'In nature the bird who gets up earliest catches the most worms; but in book-collecting the prizes fall to the birds who know worms when they see them'. While I do not claim a high rating on the Sadleirian scale of worm-recognition I realised that I had, albeit unwittingly, caught one, for what I had purchased in the Cumbrian bookshop was a 'lottery book'.

Pin holes can be found in the fore-margin of B2, H3, H6, N4 and T5, whilst in the centre of I1 is a V-shaped cut which has a certain clinical neatness about it consistent perhaps with the damage caused by a sharp pin being dragged through the paper. If this assumption is correct then the player narrowly missed securing a prize, for between the adjacent leaves is a small woodcut image of a ship with a touch of hand colour added (Fig 2 *opposite*). Two other images, both with touches of colour, are also to be found in the volume: a derrick between G5 & 6, and a grindstone between L2 & 3.

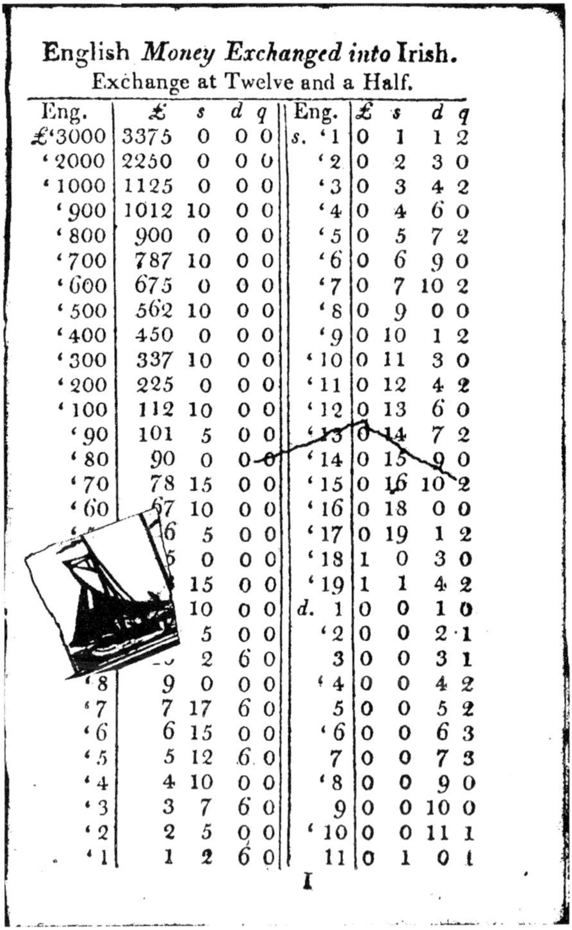

English *Money Exchanged into* Irish.

Exchange at Twelve and a Half.

Eng.	£	s	d	q	Eng.	£	s	d	q
£'3000	3375	0	0	0	s. '1	0	1	1	2
'2000	2250	0	0	0	'2	0	2	3	0
'1000	1125	0	0	0	'3	0	3	4	2
'900	1012	10	0	0	'4	0	4	6	0
'800	900	0	0	0	'5	0	5	7	2
'700	787	10	0	0	'6	0	6	9	0
'600	675	0	0	0	'7	0	7	10	2
'500	562	10	0	0	'8	0	9	0	0
'400	450	0	0	0	'9	0	10	1	2
'300	337	10	0	0	'10	0	11	3	0
'200	225	0	0	0	'11	0	12	4	2
'100	112	10	0	0	'12	0	13	6	0
'90	101	5	0	0	'13	0	14	7	2
'80	90	0	0	0	'14	0	15	9	0
'70	78	15	0	0	'15	0	16	10	2
'60	67	10	0	0	'16	0	18	0	0
[illegible]	[illegible]6	5	0	0	'17	0	19	1	2
[illegible]	[illegible]5	0	0	0	'18	1	0	3	0
[illegible]	[illegible]	15	0	0	'19	1	1	4	2
[illegible]	[illegible]	10	0	0	d. 1	0	0	1	0
[illegible]	[illegible]	5	0	0	'2	0	0	2	1
[illegible]	[illegible]	2	6	0	3	0	0	3	1
'8	9	0	0	0	'4	0	0	4	2
'7	7	17	6	0	5	0	0	5	2
'6	6	15	0	0	'6	0	0	6	3
'5	5	12	6	0	7	0	0	7	3
'4	4	10	0	0	'8	0	0	9	0
'3	3	7	6	0	9	0	0	10	0
'2	2	5	0	0	'10	0	0	11	1
'1	1	2	6	0	11	0	1	0	1

I

Page from John Atkinson's 'lottery' book
the v-shaped tear has been 'enhanced' to make it more obvious

Is this 'artefact' (I submit it can no longer be viewed as merely a book) a most tenuous link between one of the great thinkers of English education and a small shipping port on the north-west coast of England? Was it used to amuse John Atkinson's shipmates on their voyages across the Irish Sea (the book is after all a useful manual for a trader), or was it used to amuse and instruct his children? That I fear is a secret which time is unlikely to vouchsafe to us.

This volume is far from being a unique example of a 'lottery book', though such survivals (or perhaps I should more cautiously say recorded and recognized survivals) are far from common. The great Gummuchian catalogue records an edition of the *Cries of London* of *c*1815 and states that it had 'a few plates slightly pin-pricked by a child'. Furthermore Peter Opie owned a copy of Charles Hoole, *Cato's Distichs Concerning Manners* (1712) which had been converted into a lottery book by one Ambros Walton, an early owner, who annotated the margins of several leaves with the names of occupations such as hatter, bucher [*sic*], goldsmith, and mountebank.[44] Perhaps both are instances of the use of books for fortune-telling.

The game of lottery was not lost before the twentieth century, for as Mrs Valente, born in Deritend, Birmingham in 1919 recalled:

> We used to devise a lot of our own games. I remember we used to cut out pictures from papers or comics (there were none of the nice magazines like there are today). We would put these pictures between the pages of a book and then we did a strange thing, of which I have never been able to find the origin. Our playmates would bring a pin, a straight one, and put it between the pages and then whatever picture was in that page, they could have it and we kept the pins and gave them to our mothers... we used to call this game Pin a Pick.[45]

Nor is this the only childhood recollection we have. The Montgomerie's *Scottish Nursery Rhymes* records a verse on the game:

> Dab a pin in my lottery book,
> Dab one, dab twa,
> Dab all your pins awa![46]

In the Bibliographical Notes and Queries section of *The Book Collector* in the mid-1950s, Sidney Roscoe asked if anyone could 'explain the connotation of the word "lottery" as used in a number of Titles of 18th- and 19th-century children's (and other) books?' I cannot claim to have arrived at the definitive answer to Roscoe's query as this paper contains more or less the sum of what I have been able to glean about lotteries. Their role as both an amusing children's game and as a teaching aid, and indeed their place in print history in general, is however obviously worthy of further investigation.

POSTSCRIPT

Since writing this paper Sheila O'Connell has brought to my attention the existence of a painting entitled *A School for Boys and Girls* by Jan Steen (*fl* 1625/6–79) which, in one corner, clearly shows a group of four pupils. One of the central pair of the group is holding a closed book, another is placing a pin into the volume from the head edge. A third member of this group watches closely (and wears a hornbook, suspended on a cord from her waist), while a fourth kneels on the floor to place a picture (perhaps one won) into a box.

ACKNOWLEDGEMENTS

For their advice and information in the preparation of this paper, I am deeply grateful to Sheila O'Connell, of the British Museum, Department of Prints and Drawings, Peter Isaac, Walter Johnston, John Morris, Graham Taylor, and David Hounslow, and especially to the latter for sharing with me his knowledge of the riches of the Opie Collection and the particular significance of several items therein.

Jan Steen *A School for Boys and Girls* (detail)
Reproduced by kind permission of the National Gallery of Scotland.

NOTES

1. Keith Thomas, *Religion and the Decline of Magic: Studies in Popular Beliefs in Sixteenth- and Seventeenth-century England* (London, new impression, 1977), 140.

2. B Whitelock, *Memorials* (Oxford, 1853), iii, 20, quoted in Thomas, *Religion*, 141.

3. Thomas, *Religion*, 142.

4. John Northbrooke, *A Treatise Wherein Dicing, Dauncing, etc. are Reproved* (London, 1843), 139.

5. Iona & Peter Opie, *The Lore and Language of Schoolchildren* (London, 1980), 224.

6. J O Halliwell, *Nursery Rhymes of England* (London, 1842), 98, quoted in Opie, *Lore and Language*.

7. [Ebenezer Cobham Brewer (original compiler)] *Brewer's Dictionary of Phrase & Fable*, 10th ed (London, 1968), 705.

8. G K Nelson, *Seen and Not Heard: Memories of Childhood in the Early 20th Century* (Stroud, 1993), 70.

9 I am grateful to Graham Taylor for this information.

10. Edmund Blunden, *Sketches in the Life of John Clare* (London, 1931), 46.

11. I am grateful to John Morris for this information.

12. John Locke, *Some Thoughts Concerning Education and of the Conduct of Understanding*, [ed] Ruth W Grant & Nathan Tarcov (Indianapolis, 1996), 114–15.

13. Locke, *Some Thoughts*, 115.

14. Locke, *Some Thoughts*, 116.

15. Hugh Plat, *Jewell House of Art and Nature: Conteining Diuers Rare and Profitable Inuentions* (London: printed by Peter Short… and are to be solde in Paules Chirchyard [by W. Ponsonby], 1594). This quotation taken from the 1653 edition as quoted in Andrew W Tuer, *History of the Horn Book* (Reprinted New York, 1979), 63.

16. British Museum, Dept of Prints & Drawings [hereafter BM P&D], 1868-8-22-7105.

17. *A Catalogue of Maps, Prints, Copy-Books, &c. from off Copper-Plates* (Printed for John Bowles, at Mercers-Hall in Cheapside, London, 1731), 44.

18. Sayer & Bennett's *Enlarged Catalogue of New and Valuable Prints* (London, No 53, in Fleet-Street, 1775), 150.

19. BM P&D, 1878.7.12.432. E Tringham, print-seller & publisher of 36 Hosier Lane, West Smithfield, London, *fl* 1784–6. (British Book Trade Index [hereafter BBTI] 21388). However an engraver named Tringham (forename unrecorded) was trading at 104 Newgate Street, London in 1794 (BBTI 55870)

20. See for instance Bowles & Carver, *Old English Cuts and Illustrations* (New York, 1970) particularly 25, 55, 141 & 144. However it should be borne in mind that, as I am reminded by Sheila O'Connell, many of the Bowles & Carver plates were passed down from earlier Bowleses and so could date back to the first half of the eighteenth century.

21. John Mackey Langham, printer, stationer, engraver, bookseller, printseller & publisher of 3 Red Lion Street, Holborn, London, *fl* 1820–39 (BBTI 26778).

22. BM P&D, Roy XVIIIc Misc 1869.10.9.34, see also George William Reid, *A Descriptive Catalogue of the Works of George Cruikshank* (London, 1871), etchings 3(1), and also (2)

which describe another engraving as 'sixteen small subjects on a sheet, illustrating various trades'.
23. Linda David, *Children's Books Published by William Darton and His Sons*, Catalogue of an Exhibition at the Lilly Library (Bloomington, 1992), 41 & 72.
24. BM P&D, 1997 2-23-2.
25. BM P&D, *La Feria de Sevilla, Semana Santa en Sevilla, & La Vida de San Isidro Labrador* 1995-9-30, 79–81.
26. I am grateful to Lady Melissa Levy for her translation.
27. Jane Austen, *Pride and Prejudice.*
28. Cumbria County Library, Carlisle, M176, f25.
29. Bodleian Library, Oxford, John Johnson Collection of Printed Ephemera, 'Trade in Prints'. Robert Harrild, printer, bookseller, publisher, paper merchant, printers' broker and printing-material repository. *fl* 1802–52, listed at 20 Great Cheapside 1809–21; BBTI 10245 (William B Todd, *A Directory of Printers and Others in Allied Trades; London and Vicinity 1800–1840* (London, 1972), 90).
30. I am grateful to Peter Isaac for drawing these sheets to my notice. For a facsimile of the rare Davison specimen book see Peter Isaac, *William Davison's New Specimen of Cast-Metal Ornaments and Wood Types Introduced with an Account of his Activities as Pharmacist and Printer in Alnwick, 1780–1858* (London, 1990).
31. *Old Moore's Prophetic and Weather Almanack for the Year of Redemption 1854*, title verso. *The Prize Book* (Printed and Published by W Fortey, Printer, Monmouth Court, [1859]), rear cover. I am grateful to Mavis Eggle for bringing these advertisements to my notice. *The Cries of London (Walker's Toy-Books)* (London & Otley, nd but 1860–75), see also Bodleian Library Opie PP422 & 423 for a resetting of this advertisement in a reworking of the same title.
32. *A Little Lottery-Book for Children: Containing a New Method of Playing them into a Knowledge of Letters, Figures, &c.* (S Roscoe, *John Newbery and His Successors 1740–1814: a Bibliography* (Wormley, 1973), J223 & plate 9).
33. *Little Lottery Book*, 6th ed (1767), 5–7.
34. *A New Lottery Book of Birds and Beasts, for Children to Learn their Letters by as soon as they can Speak*, (Newcastle: Printed by T. Saint for W. Charnley, 1771); *A Pretty Lottery Book for Children: Containing a New Method of Playing them into a Knowledge of the Letters, Figures, &c.* (Brentford: Printed by & for P. Norbury, and sold by all booksellers in town and country. Price Two-pence); *The Lady-Bird's Lottery; or, the Fly's Alphabet. By Queen Mab* (Printed by MacDonald & Son, Cloth Fair, West Smithfield, 1813).
35. Gillian Avery, *The Echoing Green: Memories of Regency and Victorian Youth* (London, 1974), 56.
36. *The Penny London Morning Advertiser* 21 March 1744 & thereafter, quoted in Samuel F Pickering, *John Locke and Children's Books in Eighteenth-Century England* (Knoxville,1981), 75.
37. Pickering *John Locke*, 76.
38. *A Little Pretty Pocket Book* (London, John Newbery, c1744, and later editions), 8th ed (1767) 15 (Roscoe, *Newbery*, J225).

39. I am grateful to Peter Isaac for passing this information on to me.

40. I grateful to Walter Johnston for bringing this to my notice, and even more grateful for his presenting this 'blessings box' as a gift.

41. Mrs Trimmer, *The Guardian of Education* (London,1802), 1, 430.

42. John Clare, *The Cross Roads: or, the Haymaker's Story*.

43. *Jollie's Cumberland Guide & Directory* (Carlisle, 1811); William Parson & William White, *History, Directory, and Gazetteer, of the Counties of Cumberland and Westmorland* (Leeds, 1829), Mannix & Whellan, *History, Gazetteer, and Directory of Cumberland* (Beverley, 1847).

44. H Charles Hoole, *1. Cato's Distichs Concerning Manners. 2. Excellent Sayings of the Seven Wise Men of Greece* (London: printed by J. Wilde, for the Company of Stationers, 1712), Bodleian Library Opie B167. I am grateful to David Hounslow for drawing this volume to my attention.

45. Nelson, *Seen and Not Heard*, 70.

46. Nora & William Montgomerie, *Scottish Nursery Rhymes* (third impression, London, 1975), 68. The authors do not record the source of this rhyme, or note from whence they collected it, nor indeed is it included in the second impression of 1946.

Splendide mendax: *Publishing* Landscape Illustrations of the Bible

PETER ISAAC

HORACE'S COMMENDATION of Hypermestra, *Splendide mendax*,[1] was applied to J M W Turner by his friend George Jones RA, and happily accepted by the artist as describing his 'poetic' approach to landscape painting.[2] On the other hand, as we shall see in this brief history of the publication of *Landscape Illustrations of the Bible*, Charles Barry, architect of the Palace of Westminster, recognized the *splendide* but carped about the *mendax*.

The *Landscape Illustrations* is usually mentioned in discussions of Turner's oeuvre,[3] which normally ignore other aspects of its commissioning and production that are of interest to us as 'bookmen'. I must look at two related matters in its publishing history: the 'mechanics' of publication, including the publishers and engravers, and how the principal artists got on with one another and with the engravers.

JOHN MURRAY II AND BOOKS WITH PLATES

When John Murray II bought 50 Albemarle Street from William Miller in June 1812, he took over several books of hand-coloured stippled engravings or aquatints of the dress and manners of the peoples of a number of nations in folio or large quarto; Murray issued some later editions in octavo, books in which the plates were the essence, each plate being accompanied by no more than two pages of text, sometimes in French as well as English.

From about 1811 Murray was publishing books of topographical prints, being responsible for the first eleven parts of *Picturesque Views on the Southern Coast of England* (*c*1811–1825).[4] Although these 'coffee-table books' were never more than a minor element of Murray's publishing, they are important to us today in that the publisher recruited Turner and a small group of artists to prepare watercolours for the chosen engravers to work from. Another was James Hakewill's *Picturesque Tour of Italy, from Drawings made in 1816–1817*, a folio originally issued in parts 1818-1820. Turner usually made extensive sketching tours to fulfil such commissions, which was not possible for the *Italy* or the *Bible Illustrations*; this was true for the other artists working on the latter publication, and was not regarded as strange.[5]

Murray had expected the engravers to work directly from Hakewill's sketches, and was understandably furious when Hakewill commissioned drawings from eight artists including Turner, and told the author that 'it is not my intention to give out any other drawings to the engraver except those of Mr. Turner'.[6] Indeed, Turner's is the only artist's name other than Hakewill's to appear on the plates.[7] The *Tour of Italy* has been mentioned because it is possible that it was this experience that reconciled Murray to the use of well-known artists to mediate between sketches made on the spot and the final published engravings, so essential for the *Bible Illustrations*, and so caused him to recruit the group of artists and engravers already mentioned.

GENESIS OF THE *BIBLE ILLUSTRATIONS*

The illustrations for Hakewill's *Tour of Italy* were engraved on copper, so that the size of the edition was relatively limited[8] – and each part, containing five or six engravings, cost 30*s*. The use of steel engraving for book illustration from around 1820 permitted larger editions, at a much lower cost. Murray had started issuing multi-volume editions of Byron's *Works* in 1817, and the popularity of these works, especially after Byron's death, doubtless suggested to the engravers, William and Edward Finden, the probable profitability of an enlarged illustrated edition.

The Findens had successfully issued in 1832, with the publisher Charles Tilt, *Landscape Illustrations of the Waverley Novels, with descriptions of the views*, and this, no doubt, led them to put about a Byron proposal,[9] because Murray wrote to Edward Finden, on 19 November 1831, strongly objecting to their 'intention of publishing against my will a series of illustrations to my Edition of Lord Byron's Works', indicating 'the absolute impossibility of my sanctioning it'.[10] In spite of this seemingly implacable resolve Murray issued, in 1831–3, an edition, with some illustrations, of Byron's *Works* in seventeen monthly volumes.[11] William and Edward Finden were the engravers responsible for these illustrations, and Turner had provided drawings for some of the plates.[12] Murray, in partnership with the Findens and with the bookseller Charles Tilt, issued these and additional engravings in twenty-four parts, under the title *Finden's Landscape Illustrations to Mr. Murray's First Complete and Uniform Edition of the Life and Works of Lord Byron*. Brief letterpress descriptions by William Brockedon were later issued in three parts to be bound up with the engravings. Of the 124 engravings Turner contributed twenty-six designs.[13] This was a runaway success, and Murray published at least two similar works: the *Bible Illustrations*, the subject of this talk, and, in 1835, *Graphic Illustrations of the Life and Times of Samuel Johnson Ll.D.* He also intended to issue, with the same artists and engravers, illustrations of the poet George Crabbe,[14] to whom the publisher was generous. With the *Bible Illustrations*, however, the steam appears to have gone out of this kind of publication;[15] the *Johnson* made a substantial loss,[16] and the Crabbe project was dropped after several engravings had been prepared.[17]

Encouraged by the success of the Byron *Illustrations*, the three partners went on to issue, between 1834 and 1836, the *Bible Illustrations* also in twenty-four parts, each with four views and eight pages of letterpress text, with the aim, stated in the prospectus[18] and introduction to the first bound volume, of ilustrating 'the most important of all books - THE BIBLE'. Partly, no doubt, to support this pious aim, and partly to increase potential sales, the engravings were designed to be used for grangerizing family bibles, and were accordingly issued in five formats: Imperial quarto proofs at *7s.6d* per part, Royal quarto India proofs at *5s*, Royal quarto at *4s*, Imperial octavo at *3s.6d*, and Super-royal octavo at *2s.6d*. The 'Established and Annotated Editions of the Bible', for which these various styles were suitable, were listed in the prospectus. Each engraving was accompanied by a one- or two-page commentary by the Revd Thomas Hartwell Horne (1780–1862), who had frequently carried out minor editorial and indexing tasks for Murray; the letterpress was printed by Andrew Spottiswoode, who had also been responsible for the letterpress for the *Byron Illustrations*. The plates were intended to show places mentioned in the Bible as they were at that time, and not to give 'Fictitious and Imaginary representations of Historical Events'.[19]

BRINGING THE TEAM TOGETHER

The complications of ensuring the punctual production of monthly parts with such a diverse team may readily be envisaged: the three partners, publisher (Murray), bookseller and wholesaler (Charles Tilt) and engravers (William & Edward Finden); the twenty-seven travellers who provided the on-the-spot sketches; the eleven artists who mediated these sketches for the engravers; and Thomas Hartwell Horne, who had to produce the commentary at the very last moment after seeing a proof engraving, not to mention the plate and letterpress printers.

It is clear that changes of plan occurred as the work went along. For example, the prospectus lists only Turner, A W Callcott (1779–1844) and Clarkson Stanfield (1793–1867) as the artists preparing the finished drawings for the engravers. Turner prepared twenty-five of the ninety-six views, Callcott was responsible for twelve, and Stanfield for thirteen, but J D Harding also prepared nineteen and David Roberts eleven. Similarly four of the 'distinguished Travellers', whose names were given on the prospectus, were not called upon for sketches. In all twenty-seven such travellers provided the sketches, twelve only of these being responsible for more than a single sketch. Twenty-five of the sketches came from the pencil of Charles Barry, who had made a Grand Tour of the area in 1817–1820; Turner worked from many of these. The Hon Capt W E Fitzmaurice, who had served in the army in the area, contributed eight sketches, from five of which he also prepared finished drawings.

It was late in 1832 that the decision was made to publish the *Bible Illustrations*; David Roberts, writing to Murray on 17 October 1832[20] said

> I have no objection to have those drawings copied which will suit Mr Murray but I had rather sell them at three than have them returned at two guineas each. If that will suit Mr Murray he can send me a list of those he requires…

Then, in a letter of 17 November 1832 to Murray, Tilt encloses an estimate, now missing, of the cost of each part, based on 4000 prints of various sizes, 250 proofs, 250 India proofs and 100 'proofs before', and allowing two pages of text for each view. Tilt further estimates that each part would yield a profit of £75. Tilt wrote that he

> reckoned double the number at 3/- [*sic*] to that at 2/6 to be sold for I feel certain that such will prove to be the case – If you abandon the 2/6 edit^{n} altogether I apprehend it would make no material difference in the result – I have a very good opinion of the speculation – which I feel no doubt will pay as it is published at least to be a valuable & constantly saleable property when complete.

He goes on to emphasize that the views should be correct and that the text should be more than 'a mere extract from the Gazetteers'; he suggests as possible authors of the text either Hartwell Horne or Josiah Conder (1789–1855), Editor of the *Modern Traveller*. In fact, as we shall see later, Tilt was wrong in his view of the relative saleability of the cheapest style.

By early December Murray had invited the artists to provide the drawings,[21] and Hartwell Horne to write the descriptions of the views, but, on 11 December, Horne had written regretting that he was so fully occupied for the next two months that he could not undertake the task. His letter is endorsed, presumably in the hand of John Murray III, who had joined the family firm in 1828, 'Decr 17 at British Inst^{n} Mr H agreed to commence work after the middle of February'.[22] On 16 February 1833 John Murray III wrote to Horne, taking the matter up again, and giving him detailed instructions[23]

> The letter-press of each number is not required to exceed 8 Octavo pages - that is two for each view. They [the partners] propose to offer you for each N^{o} which you execute, the sum of £10-10-0 or two Guineas and a half for each description, as they feel no doubt that in your hands the task will be performed in a manner to give satisfaction to the Public, and do ample justice to the Work. –
>
> They by no means wish to consider the text as secondary to the illustrations, and expect that it will prove a valuable and important as well as useful portion of the publication, and one which will materially influence its success. The views will be forwarded to you from time to time as they are engraved, so as if possible to avoid hurrying you, or throwing too much on your hands at once.

Hartwell Horne also supplied a biblical quotation and reference, which was often included on the engraved plate; this had to be provided in good time for the writing engraver, before the prints could be run off.

Although the publishing schedule was tight, it seems from the voluminous correspondence in the Murray archives that Horne was in the habit of letting the publisher know the gist of his description of the views; it is also clear that he did not always receive the views in good time – indeed, from some of the letters one wonders if Horne was able to see some of the views before carrying out his part of the work. For example, in a letter of 20 May 1834, he suggests biblical texts for four plates, which it is clear he had not seen. [One of these was the engraving of Nineveh (plate 48), for which Turner had prepared the watercolour based on a sketch by Claudius James Rich (1787–1820), probably from his posthumous *Narrative of a Residence in Koordistan, and on the Site of Ancient Nineveh* published in 1836.] He then went on

> Have the goodness to let me know what texts you adopt – or, which will be tenfold better, order the writing engraver to furnish me with the correct heading and texts, as soon as you have fixed upon them – No matter how rough. Without this I am really working in the dark.

And he continued in a similar vein for another two pages. His frustration was, no doubt, increased by the fact that he felt it necessary to read quite widely in order to prepare adequate descriptions.[24] In a postscript to a letter to Murray of 13 March 1834 Charles Tilt wrote that Barry was delaying the descriptions of two plates for Part 2, which Horne had submitted to him.

That, in consequence, Horne sometimes made mistakes is indicated in a letter of 18 June 1834 from Tilt, who complained that one of the descriptions for part 5 was for the wrong plate, and continues

> What can be done about this – I fear M[r] Horne has not had the plate sent him & there is not time to write the description now – Today is the 18th & as it happens there are only 28 days for the booksellers in this month –

In the bound volumes, published in 1836, the plates with their descriptions are included in the order of their biblical ascription from Genesis to Revelation; Horne's letters make it clear that this was not the order of the part issue. Reading between the lines of a letter of Augustus Wall Callcott to Murray of 12 December 1832 it is apparent that the order in which the drawings were prepared for the engravers depended on the artists, who might, in turn, have occasionally been delayed by the absence of the appropriate on-the-spot sketch.

THE ARTISTS

While we now have no doubt of the genius of Turner and a few of us may not have heard of Sir Augustus Wall Callcott, it must be remembered that the contemporary regard in which the principal artists were held was rather different. The *Dictionary of National Biography* says of Callcott, for example, 'There are true artistic qualities in Callcott's work, which justified the admiration of such painters as Turner and

Stothard in his day, and must always preserve for him a distinguished place among the earlier masters of the English school of landscape'. That Callcott considered himself Turner's equal is shown by his letter to John Murray III of 12 December 1832:

> I am certainly most willing to assist in your projected work... but it will not certainly be possible for me to get 12 drawings completed in the short time your father specified... before I can finally consent to inlist myself in this service (as you term it) I must see the sketches already in hand and must have it expressly understood that such an arrangement shall take place with respect to the division of the sketches as shall insure an equal appropriation of the better subjects between Mr Turner & myself – This will be best insured by our having an opportunity of carefully looking over the sketches and then alternately taking our choice of subjects –

Nevertheless Callcott might have felt it necessary to 'keep his end up' with Turner, for, in his letter of 14 January 1833[25] to the younger Murray, he wrote

> I have written to Mr Turner on the pertinacity with which he stickers for his pound of flesh, and reminded him that he had two drawings when I had only retained one on sending back the [*tear in letter*] sent to me. But do not be alarmed at my starting on this course – I only do it if possible to make him ashamed of his selfish apprehension that I am to be the favourite and to make him pay the post. that he may not chuckle at the thought of having the advantage of me by threepence.

Many letters to and from Albemarle Street show how important to the success of the project were the younger Murray's diplomatic skills – as, indeed, was the action behind the scenes taken by Maria Callcott.[26]

In the catalogue of a recent exhibition on Turner and the romantic vision of the Holy Land Mordechai Omer repeats Ruskin's description of the process of selection of the sketches[27]

> Turner told me... that he and Callcott had a certain number of Bible sketches to realize between them: they agreed to pick them alternately, drawing lots for the first choice. Callcott won the choice and selected at once a sketch of Ararat; the sketch of the *Pools of Solomon* was left to the last, and Turner said he kept it on his breakfast table for a month before he could make up his mind how to treat it.

This selection must have taken place gradually during the progress of the work, for Callcott, in his letter of 3 January 1833, wrote

> but I do not think it would be right to proceed further with apportioning the subjects than may be necessary for the specimen plates without Mr Turners acquiescence.

Whenever he could Turner chose sketches of open panoramas,[27] and it is noteworthy that fourteen of his twenty-five drawings were after sketches by Charles Barry. The latter's more detailed architectural studies were worked up by Callcott, Roberts and Harding.[28]

Callcott's drawing of Mount Ararat was based on a sketch by James Morier (1789?–1849), Asiatic traveller and author of *Hajji Baba*, published by Murray;

Morier also promised to let the artist have some sketches of local costume so that he could include figures in his drawing.[29] This was the only sketch of Morier's used. That Horace's words may also be applied to Callcott is suggested by his note of January 1833 to the younger Murray sending the Ararat drawing

> You will see that I have ventured to put The Rainbow on it though we are looking to the South. I wish much that Mr Morier should see it before it goes to Mr Finden and sanction the poetical licence I have taken with his subject he will see that I have taken also advantage of his permission to introduce one of the little ruined towers which he says are scattered over the vicinity of this scene and also endeavour to shew a part of the Three Hundred Dromedaries that arrived during his stay in that neighbourhood

In a letter of 6 February 1833 Maria Callcott, who always had her husband's interests in mind and who, perhaps, was more literal than he, wrote to the younger Murray

> Be under no apprehension about the Rainbow I have been reading works on natural phenomena – optics &c for its sake & will undertake that if it sh^{d} be attacked you shall have defence grounded on Latitude Longitude Sir Isaac Newton & the Bible –

On 3 January 1833 Murray drew a cheque to pay Callcott;[30] in acknowledging this the artist regrets that Morier had not been able to see his drawing.[31] He also wrote 'I have NOT heard again from Mr Barry and wish much now to do so as I am entirely without subject to go to work on', and repeated his warning of possibly not being able to satisfy the publisher's time constraint.

In 1818 Charles Barry had met David Baillie in Athens, and the latter had offered to take Barry to Egypt and the Holy Land, and to pay him £200 per year for his drawings of the architecture and scenery they met in their travels. Barry made copies for his own use of the sketches made on the spot;[32] these copies are now in the library of the Royal Institute of British Architects. These sketches were, as we have seen, of great importance to this project, and five of Callcott's drawings were based on them.

Barry returned from the Middle East in 1820, and his sketches must have been fairly widely known, for, on 1 November 1828, Maria Callcott had written to Murray

> I hope your son told you what I said about Mr Barry's drawings. is it not time some thing was done about them? They are very good & made actually in Turkey & places subject to the Grand Turk. Mr Barry is an architect I don't know where he lives but he may essily [*sic*] be found I imagine Mr Baily [*sic*] has given him leave to use his drawings i.e. those made for Mr Baillie –
>
> Will you undertake to find Mr Barry or must I?

This suggests that as early as 1828 Murray was thinking of illustrating Byron, and makes his letter to Edward Finden, mentioned earlier, even more tongue-in-cheek.

Although Charles Barry is mentioned in the prospectus only as a 'distinguished Traveller' providing 'Original Sketches taken on the Spot', his contribution requires us to treat him as one of the artists of the *Bible Illustrations*, and his relationship with Turner is, therefore, of interest. It was in late 1832[33] that Murray brought Turner and Barry together to plan the projected work in the famous drawing room at 50 Albemarle Street.[34] In his letter of 13 December 1832 the architect suggests two possible views for the prospectus: the Valley of Jehosophat and a view of Jerusalem from the south. The former (plate 93) was, in the event, drawn by David Roberts from a sketch by the Revd Robert Master, while the second was the View of Jerusalem from the Latin Convent, which was engraved from Turner's drawing as a specimen plate but was not used in the parts or bound volumes.[35] On 28 January 1833 Barry wrote critically of the artist's work on these drawings

> I have seen Turner's Drawings at Finden's this morning – they are certainly very beautiful as works of art but there are some anomalies about them such as the sun & moon being in the Valley together and in the southern view of Jerusalem the sun in full splendour in the north – I intend to call upon the tickleish Gentleman and see whether I can induce him to correct these and some other trifling departures from fidelity by which the character of the country suffers.

A similar comment is made by Gally Knight, in a letter of 29 January 1834; he thanked Murray for 'the beautiful engraving'. At this date this is likely to have been Turner's Jerusalem from the Latin Convent, 'which is a very good one', but Knight remarked that it was drawn before his sketches had been seen, adding that his view of Jerusalem from the Mount of Olives, 'though of inferior execution, conveys a better idea of the position of the City, the situation of the Temple, & the nature of the surrounding country'. On the other hand, Fitzmaurice, in a letter of 7 May 1834 thanking the younger Murray for a copy of Part 3, wrote

> I must say that the places which I have visited myself, I can speak most forcibly to the likeness of. It is impossible for any thing to be more beautifully executed or be a more perfect fac simile than the Pool of Bethesda [plate 19, drawn by Turner from Barry's sketch]

On 13 February 1833 Barry told the publisher that he would call on Turner that morning to 'give him my opinion & advice on the view of the Garden of Gethsemane'. In fact plate 78 Olive Trees in the Garden of Gethsemane was drawn by Harding after a sketch by Mrs Bracebridge. And Barry's criticism did not stop at visual matters; he told Murray that he did not like Hartwell Horne's text for Jerusalem the Mosque of Omar (plate 75). As an architect he objected to wrong dimensions given for the mosque.[36]

Barry went further than this and was prepared to go behind the back of Turner; in a letter of 31 March 1834 to the younger Murray he wrote

> The information required respecting the Pool of Bethesda [plate 19] and the Garden of Gethsemane I have already sent to Finden – Although after much consideration I determined not to alter the scale of the figures in the view of the Garden I have still some misgivings on the subject I intend therefore to call upon Messrs. Finden either

> today or tomorrow to compare the original sketch (in which I think a figure is given) with the Drawing and determine with them what is best to be done.

Barry, the architect, would have been better pleased with a photograph, if the technique had been available then. A Byron scholar has described John Murray II as a 'timorous Tory';[37] what was his reaction to all this? Ruskin recorded a report from the Revd William Kingsley,[38] to whom Turner had spoken in later years; the artist said that

> the publishers thought he was mad, and required him to put nothing into the drawings beyond what might actually be there; and he had in his hand the sketch of Rachel's Tomb [*Ramah, and Rachel's Tomb*, plate 49, drawn by Turner after a sketch by the Revd Robert Master], and asked whether he might put wolves into it. He [Murray] said to me, 'Perhaps you have found wolves in others'.

Murray was on the side of literal treatment.

Unlike Turner, who was never able to visit the Middle East, David Roberts spent almost eight months there in 1838–9, returning to Britain with a large collection of sketches from his travels. Many of these were published in his *Holy Land, Syria, Idumea, Arabia, Egypt & Nubia* (1842–9) by Francis Graham Moon, who described himself as 'Publisher in Ordinary to her Majesty'. The illustrations were hand-coloured lithographs, the draughtsman being Louis Haghe, at that time associated with the lithographers Day & Son; these illustrations helped to make Roberts's name.[39] A later edition in six volumes was published by Day & Son in 1855. It is illuminating to compare a few of these lithographs with the earlier engravings from his drawings; his own views were generally taken from a greater distance than those in the *Bible Illustrations*.

THE ENGRAVERS

The size of this diverse team caused problems not only with punctuality, but also with clashes of personality. Callcott, for example, appears to have had long-standing problems with the Findens. On 30 September 1833 Maria Callcott wrote to Murray

> I have persuaded Mr Callcott (& indeed he was not very unwilling) to let me send you the accompanying copies of some letters which have passed between him & the Messrs Findens relative to the Bible Illustrations
>
> In your son's absence Mr Callcott cannot but feel it just both to him & to you, to shew how his name has been used as a party to a proceeding that nothing can persuade us he would have authorised.
>
> When Mr Callcott first overcame his extreme reluctance to enter into any engagement with the Messrs Findens for either the Byron illustrations or the Bible work, it was principally because he respected you and remembered with very grateful feelings your long friendship for & kindness to me. And even now in withdrawing from the work on account of Messrs Findens unhandsome proceedings, he feels for your sake

> so much interest in it, that he is determined on giving whatever assistance may be farther in his or my power as to procuring subjects &c

While she continues to mention sketches that she has commisioned for the work, this letter suggests a reason why Callcott produced only half as many drawings as Turner, although it is to be noted that his letter of 12 December 1832, already quoted, mentions twelve only.

Mrs Callcott's letter to the younger Murray of 15 March 1833 possibly explains the artist's action in refusing to make further drawings; she wrote

> Your Carmel [plate 17] is in preparation & the moment his [her husband's] hands are loose you will see it & as many as you will be able to use If the Findens do their duty & pay proper attention to the plates – but if they do not you cannot expect any artist who has a sense of what is right will work to have his drawings misrepresented. Remember I have a reason for this hint... You are even worse treated than any body... a person did call here ten days since – neither an artist or a publisher who gave a caution – beginning 'I would advise him to look to the plates' &c &c – & I think I understood that they had been see[n.]

Was she hinting at any more than that the engravers allowed themselves artistic licence?[40] A month earlier[41] she wrote 'For the Enemy, who can he have to help him? Is it Heath [presumably James Heath (1757–1834) the engraver] in revenge for Turner's assistance to you?' The *Dictionary of National Biography* records that Mrs Callcott, in 1831, ruptured a blood-vessel (possibly a cerebral haemorrhage) and became a confirmed invalid; was she also a believer in conspiracy theories?

From the start Maria Callcott, who had been in close touch with the elder Murray for over twenty years, was doing her best to assist the publisher, not only in smoothing her husband's ruffled feathers, but also in getting authentic sketches for the artists to work from. In a letter marked 'Private', probably from early in 1834,[42] which she emphasized was written without the knowledge of her husband, she wrote that she had 'prevailed on a change in Mr Callcotts arrangements to have given you all the drawings you asked before Christmas', and repeats 'that I am most interested in the work – I should be so for your sake if it were for nothing else'.

The Findens, in a letter to Murray of 14 January 1833, wrote

> As it never was the intention, or wish, of either my Brother or myself to give offence to Mr Callcott, and as we believe that he is in some measure convinced that such is the fact. We have been thinking, that, (as you are in communication with that Gentleman) it might be possible to shew him that we are still anxious to avail ourselves of his Talents in the book, and avoid the publicity of any breach by requesting him to make some Drawings occasionally as his convenience would allow him...
>
> We think this measure would be of advantage to all parties, and we submit it to your consideration to adopt, or reject, as it may appear on reflection to be advisable, or not.

It seems fairly clear that Callcott worked on his twelve watercolours through 1833, in spite of earlier friction with the Findens over the Byron illustrations, but on 22 April 1834 Mrs Callcott wrote

> Mr Callcott bids me say that after what has passed on the subject of the Bible illustrations between Mr Finden & him he can not consistently with what he owes to himself engage in any further works for him… & assures you by me that if he can at any time be useful to either of <u>you</u> he will feel much gratified He is sorry you have stopped Mr Stanfields hand for even if he could have resumed his water colours at present he would not have consented to withdraw any thing whatever from Mr Stanfield from motives of professional delicacy…

Callcott's plates, numbered between 3 and 46, appeared only in the first twelve parts, four appearing in Part 7 (presumably the whole of that issue), with only one coming out after Part 9 (due to be issued in October 1834). The plates for which Turner and Stanfield were responsible were more evenly spread over the parts, and Harding's first plate appeared in Part 10, while Roberts, too, came out mainly in the later parts. Probably, after Callcott failed to patch up his quarrel with the Findens, Harding was recruited in his place.[43]

Samuel Prout (1783–1852), who made one drawing for this work (Pulpit in Mosque of Omar, plate 72, Part 18) had had similar problems with the engravers, as he reported to the Murrays in a letter of 15 January 1831, 'Engravers & Draughtsmen are sad plagues'. Later that year he complained that the Findens had not made corrections to plates from his drawings possibly for the *Byron Illustrations*, going on

> I beg leave to assure you that I have the highest opinion of Mr Findens' [*sic*] talents, & a great respect for him persinally, but this circumstance is so painful to my feelings that unless you are at liberty to assure me it shall not occur again, I must decline making the drawings for the second Vol

The two Findens carried out the majority of the engraving, Edward Francis, the younger brother, engraving fifty-five of the ninety-six plates, and William thirty-two. The remaining nine plates were engraved by James Bayliss Allen (1802–57) three, John Cousen (1804–80) and James Stephenson (1808–86) two each, and Samuel Fisher (*c*1802–55) and William Radclyffe (1783–1855) one each.

THE ON-THE-SPOT SKETCHES

There is much less evidence about the sources of the on-the-spot sketches. The publishers had already been in touch with Barry in the preparation of the *Byron Illustrations*, and they approached him first. The several albums of mounted sketches in the British Architectural Library show that these vary widely in size and detail; twenty-five of them were selected.

It is evident from Maria Callcott's many letters to the Murrays that tracking down – and even commissioning – suitable sketches went on throughout 1833, and even later as the parts were being issued. For example, in a letter as late as 22 August 1834, she reported that her friend, Mrs Bracebridge, whom she had briefed before departure, had just arrived back from Palestine, and listed the views that the latter had sketched there; fourteen of these were ticked, but six only were used, the Findens returning those unsuitable.[44] The first drawing based on a sketch by Mrs Bracebridge – Jacob's Well (plate 71), drawn by Harding – appeared in Part 18. Most of Maria Callcott's suggestions for sketches do not seem to have been taken up.

Some of those whose sketches were used were authors of travel books, many published by Murray. Mrs Callcott sends to the younger Murray, with a letter of February 1833, a book by C J Rich, which she has borrowed from the author's widow, who, no doubt lent the sketch of Nineveh (plate 48 in Part 12). The Marquis Léon de Laborde (1807–1869), who provided five sketches, was another travel writer; the English translation, by M J Quinn,[45] of his *Journey through Arabia Petraea to Mount Sinai* was published in 1836. Gally Knight (1786–1846) was published by Murray, as were Morier and Cockerell. Knight, on being invited to contribute sketches to the work, sketches which he later described as faithful but inexpert, agreed on 7 March 1833, and added

> but you give me credit for much more diligence than I possess – When I was in the Holy Land, I was a very indifferent sketcher, young & thoughtless, & went through the country so rapidly as to have little time for more than looking at it –

A sketch of Syracuse, made by Maria Callcott herself on one of her two tours of Italy, provided the basis of a drawing by Stanfield (plate 37 in Part 8), and I was interested to see that Andrew Allen was rewarded by Murray for his sketch the Fords of the Jordan (plate 22 in Part 4) by being given a set of Waverley Novels at a cost of £8.8*s*.5*d*.[46]

SALES OF THE BIBLE ILLUSTRATIONS

The ledgers and daybooks in the Murray Archives show almost exclusively payments from Tilt to the Murrays for their half share in the publication, which father and son, in turn, shared two-thirds to one-third.[47] Since Tilt accounts to Murray for the sales, it seems that he was acting as the wholesaler – and, perhaps, as general paymaster. Tilt, as we know from a letter quoted earlier, had high hopes for speedy and profitable sales of the part issues.

Writing to Murray on 13 March 1834, the month after the first part was issued, Tilt reported that 6150 of the 7818 copies of the various formats of that part had been disposed of, but went on

> There is not that increase in numbers disposed of since the previous statement that I could wish Many I am sure are awaiting the appearance of the [?] work – The orders however are gradually and steadily increasing and I feel that the work will before 3 or 4 parts are out have a very extensive sale

He seems to have been too sanguine, however; as his more detailed account of 8 May 1834 demonstrates, the numbers of the first three parts produced and disposed of rapidly reduced. For example, of the *2s.6d* format, the cheapest version, 5752 (out of 5944) were sold of Part 1, 5237 (out of 5275) of Part 2 and 3356 (out of 3597) of Part 3. The reaction of booksellers to the *Bible Illustrations* may be gauged from the numbers of this version sold to Oliver & Boyd, who took 750, 750 & 300 of these three parts, while Cumming[48] took 750, 425 & 250.

In his covering letter Tilt referred to American sales through one Wardle, who took 250 each of Parts 1 & 2; Tilt hesitated to send Part 3, and went on 'This worthy owes me about £3500 purchases in the year 1833 & I am anxious to have some heavy remittance before I get in deeper'. He continued

> The work certainly does not sell as it ought. It has been sadly injured by Bulls Adverts to the host of Landscape Engravings which has preceded it has greatly damaged the the [*sic*] public appetite for this class of prints

When writing to one of the Murrays in Sheffield on 27 February 1834, their assistant Edward Dundas reported

> To day the Bible Illustrat[ns] made their appearance and are going off well… and I am sorry to learn that Bull's Illustrations are not to appear till the 1st of April as this delay prevents persons from deciding on what they mean to take —
>
> Bull has issued no prospectus as yet (with plate) probably concurring [?] that his orders (allowed to be very numerous) will be countermanded if his Wood 'Engravings' are allowed to be seen

It is not always easy to separate the profits on the Byron and Bible illustrations in the Murray records, but it does not appear to me that his share of that for the Bible work was to be sniffed at. For example, as late as February 1839 the Murrays received £269.8*s*.5*d* from Tilt.[49] In the early months of 1836 Murray was selling the work at one of his sales at the Albion coffee-house.[50]

The illustrated work on Crabbe was abandoned because the Murrays were disappointed in the profits from this type of work, the public appetite for which had been surfeited. I believe, also, that this kind of work was out of Murray's normal publishing practice, so that the main burden of commissioning the publication was in the hands of others: of the Findens for the illustrations, and of Tilt for sales and payments.[51] And yet Murray in a letter of 7 August 1834[52] instructs Edward Finden 'No drawings for Bible Illustrations to be given out to Artists after this. Mr Murray will be responsible for none after this date'; so, clearly, Murray had not let go of the financial reins.

CONCLUSION

Creators are, probably inevitably, fiercely protective of their work, so that creativity and commercial activity are commonly uneasy bedfellows. The *Bible Illustrations* has been studied only in the context of Turner's life and work. I have prepared this brief paper at least partly to elucidate the part played in this tripartite publication by the 'timorous Tory' publisher John Murray II and his son. All sorts of friction arose in the fifteen months between first commissioning and the issue of the first part, some aspects of which can be appreciated from the Murray Archives. In particular, we see John Murray II as an established and respected figure, with his son playing a very important role, both as prime mover and as diplomat, when things go wrong. After five years in the family firm he was no longer feeling his way, but was taking decisions that did not always please his father.[53]

ACKNOWLEDGEMENTS

I am most grateful to John Murray (Publishers) Ltd for so hospitably making me free of their wonderful Archives. In particular I wish to thank Mrs Virginia Murray, the Archivist, not only for all her assistance on my many visits to Albemarle Street, but even more for having suggested the topic of this paper.

NOTES

1. Horace, *Odes* 3.xi.35.

2. See Cecilia Powell, 'Topography, imagination and travel: Turner's relationship with James Hakewill', *Art History*, 5.4 (December 1982), 408–25; see especially note 1 on p 420.

3. Luke Herrmann, *Turner Prints: The Engraved Work of J. M. W. Turner* (Oxford: Phaidon, 1990), points out that it was through the engravings of Turner's work that the artist 'gained his enormous popularity during his lifetime'.

4. Powell, 'Topography', 408; Herrmann, *Turner Prints*, 84–5.

5. Powell, 'Topography', 408.

6. Powell, 'Topography', 412.

7. Eighteen of the sixty-three plates carry Turner's name. Of the other forty-five plates twenty-seven are outline engravings of plans and contents of museums, to which Hakewill attached great importance.

8. Murray Archives [hereafter MA] letter of 1 February 1819 from the artist to Murray, dealing with their plan for this work, mentions 750 small paper and 100 proofs. However, the daybook (10 November 1818 to 27 December 1820) folio 219 shows that 600 Imperial and 750 Royal prints were made for parts 7 & 8.

9. There is in the Murray Archives a manuscript draft prospectus for a new edition of *Childe Harold*, dated 1831 and possibly in the hand of Edward Finden. This was to be 'a splendid edition of Childe Harold – the Publisher having resolved to render the Edition superior to any work extant has spared no expence in procuring faithful delineations of nearly all the scenes described in the Poem'. The draft is endorsed, in another hand, to Mr Stanfield, Mornington Place, Hampstead Road.

10. MA Letter-book (21 November 1823 to 2 March 1839), folio 88.

11. MA Ledger C, folios 30–7, shows that at least 15 000 copies of each volume were produced, some of which were soon reprinted (ledger C, folios 72–6).
12. Herrmann, *Turner Prints*, 191–2. Each volume had an engraved frontispiece and vignette on the title-page; Turner was responsible for eight of each.
13. Herrmann, *Turner Prints*, 192.
14. MA Letter-book (21 November 1823 to 2 March 1839), folio 142–3, lists 'Stories in Crabbe's Works, which appear most fit for Graphic Illustration'.
15. MA Ledger C, folio 152, shows that sales went on until January 1842; eventually Murray sold the drawings for additional income.
16. MA Ledger C, folio 116; the loss was £525.4*s*.6*d*.
17. MA Ledger C, folio 127, notes 'Nov 1838 By balance [deficiency] Not proceeded with £105.0.0.
18. Undated proof prospectus, probably of December 1833, in Murray Archives. Ledger D fol 52 shows that Clowes printed 23 250 copies of the prospectus for £5.13*s*.6*d*. A letter of 27 February 1834 from Edward Dundas, the Murrays' assistant, to the younger Murray, at that time in Sheffield, shows that the prospectus was distributed both with and without specimen prints.
19. MA Letter-book (21 November 1823 to 2 March 1839), folio 106; letter dated 24 December 1832.
20. Murray Archives. Letters to Murray are archived in boxes under the names of the writers; unless additional information is to be given the notes will not indicate 'Murray Archives' as the source.
21. See, for example, MA letter of A W Callcott to Murray 12 December 1832.
22. Murray Archives; it is worth recalling that the British Institution stands at the north end of Albemarle Street, while Murray's is at the Piccadilly end, and that Murray's published the Institution's journal.
23. MA Letter-book (21 November 1823 to 2 March 1839), folio 109.
24. See, for example, an undated letter of 1834 from Horne in MA.
25. Dated by Callcott 'Monday 14th', and endorsed in a different hand 'Jany 14.1832', but 14 January 1832 was not a Monday; in 1833 it was.
26. Lady Maria Callcott, formerly Mrs Graham, had been in regular correspondence with John Murray II from at least 1815; as the author of *Little Arthur's History of England*, first published by Murray in 1835, and still in print in the twentieth century, she was one of the Murrays' best-selling authors.
27. Mordechai Omer, *J. M. W. Turner and the Romantic Vision of the Holy Land and the Bible* (Boston, Massachusetts: McMullen Museum of Art, Boston College, 1996), 41. It is sad that the very few letters from Turner to Murray deal only with invitations to dinner.
28. J R Piggott, 'Charles Barry and "The Tickleish Gentleman": Turner's Bible illustrations', *Turner Society News*, 65 (December 1993), 13–16 (13).
29. MA letter of Callcott to John Murray III of 14 January 1833 (wrongly dated 1832).
30. MA Ledger C folio 152.
31. MA letter of January 1833.
32. Omer, *Turner*, 41.

33. MA letter of 5 November 1832 to John Murray III, in which Barry invites Turner and Finden to visit him in Foley Place to look at his sketches. The six letters from Barry in the Murray Archives have been published in Piggott, 'The Tickleish Gentleman'.
34. MA Letter from Barry 13 December 1832 to John Murray III.
35. Piggott, 'The Tickleish Gentleman', 15.
36. MA letter of 31 December 1833.
37. Dr Peter Cochran in a letter of 16 May 1999 to the author.
38. John Ruskin, *Works*, [ed] E T Cook & A Wedderburn, 39 vol (London, 1903–12), 13, 534, n 50, quoted by Piggott, 'The Tickleish Gentleman', 13.
39. Fabio Bourbon, *Yesterday and Today The Holy Land: Lithographs and Diaries by David Roberts R.A.* (Shrewsbury: Swan Hill Press, 1994), 21; see also Michael Twyman, *A Directory of London Lithographic Printers 1800–1850* (London: Printing Historical Society, 1976), 29-30.
40. In a letter of 5 December 1835 to Murray Edward Finden, excusing the charge for engraving a plate, wrote 'they [his assistants] require mind as well as hands to make the drawings acceptable to the public as engravings'.
41. MA letter of 6 February 1833 to John Murray III.
42. MA – the exact date is not shown on the letter by the writer, but has been endorsed in another hand 'Feby 1833'. The mention of Christmas, when Callcott was due to have finished his drawings, suggests that the letter dates from early in 1834. It does not seem likley that the artist could have completed his twelve drawings between his acceptance of the commission on 12 December 1832 and Christmas of that year.
43. The ledgers and daybooks show very few payments made by Murray; cheques, for which the amounts were not given, were drawn for Callcott on 3 & 24 January 1833 (MA Ledger C, folio 152). It appears that Charles Tilt was responsible for the payments, and so I cannot check the time of involvement of the various artists.
44. MA undated letter to John Murray III.
45. MA Letter-book (21 November 1823 to 2 March 1839), folio 173; undated agreement drafted by John Murray III between 20 May & 28 July 1835 – Quinn to be paid £50.
46. MA Ledger C, folio 152.
47. MA Ledger C, folio 152, and BB3 (1828–1843), folios 137 & 145 show that the Murrays received one-third only of the profits on the *Byron Illustrations*.
48. I have been unable to identify this bookseller.
49. MA BB3 (1828-1843), folio 145.
50. MA BB3 (1828-1843), folio 137.
51. Typical accounts in the Murray Archives carry the annotation 'per Tilt's Account', and, in his letter of 8 May 1834, Tilt wrote 'If you will be so obliging as to give Mr Horne a dft for pts 1 to 4 I will return M^{r} M the money'.
52. MA Letter-Book (21 November 1823 to 2 March 1839), folio 151.
53. See, for example, MA letter of 2 November 1835 from Tilt, who is vexed that permission given by the son for him to use extracts from Byron's poems has been withdrawn by his father.

Reading in Seventeenth-Century Derbyshire: the Wheatcrofts and their Books

MAUREEN BELL

IN THE COLLECTION OF Derbyshire Record Office are two manuscripts deposited by the Parish of Ashover which are of particular interest to historians of early modern literacy. One, by Leonard Wheatcroft, is entitled 'The Art of Poetry, or Come ye gallants Look and buy, here is mirth & Melody', a fat and crumbling volume containing hundreds of poems as well as Leonard's lively account of his courtship.[1] The other manuscript, written by Leonard's son Titus, is called 'Church and School or The Young Clarks Instructor'.[2] This latter contains memoranda (on, for example, local history, charity lands and church goods, lists of changes to be rung on church bells) and it records information useful to the parish clerk in his office. Amongst the contents are three inventories: one of Titus's household goods; another of 'all my Tools in My Shop';[3] and a third is headed 'A Catalogue or Roll. Of the names of All the Books that I Titus Wheatcroft have Feb. 16. 1722. With the Number and price of them, which are as followeth...'[4]

Leonard Wheatcroft, author of the first of these manuscripts, was born 1 May 1627 in Ashover, the eldest son of a tailor. He and his four brothers followed their father's trade. He was a soldier, probably in the local militia, during the 1650s. In 1657 he married Elizabeth Hawley and wrote down, in chivalric mode, the story of his courtship: 'my pilgrimage towards this town called Woman'.[5] In 1658 he was described as a 'yeoman', but in the 1660s he was imprisoned for debt three times, was forced to sell his house and land, and pawned his goods. Elizabeth became an ale-seller and Leonard turned his hand to many occupations. As well as tailoring, he worked for local gentry families as a garden planner, a planter of orchards, grafter of trees, carpenter and tuner of virginals; he probably also engaged in small-scale farming. By the1680s he had in part recovered his position and some of his property: as well as regaining his office as parish clerk,[6] he also became sexton and for two years in the 1680s 'being perswaded by my nightbours' he kept a school.[7] He was involved in a local waterworks project and had an interest in local lead mines at Youlgreave and near Sheldon. Leonard and Elizabeth had nine surviving children. Titus, the writer of the manuscript containing the book list, was their youngest child, born in 1679. He, too, began – at the age of eleven – to work as a tailor; in his teenage years he kept house with the aging Leonard and eventually he followed his father as a schoolmaster and (after Leonard's death in January 1706/7) as parish clerk of Ashover.

The catalogue of books, begun by Titus in 1722 and apparently added to and amended over several years, contains a total of 370 volumes containing approximately 392 individual titles, valued at a total of £32.1*s*.0*d*. About 50% of the titles are religious (Bibles, biblical commentaries, sermons, devotional works) and about 20% are schoolbooks and educational texts (classics, grammar, language and spelling, oratory and rhetoric, dictionaries, copybooks and books on penmanship and shorthand). But about 30% are of other, miscellaneous kinds (poetry, music, romance, morality, emblems, heraldry, history, politics, law, popular medicine, science, mathematics, geography and travel), and it is this portion of the books that indicates something of the recreational reading of the Wheatcrofts. Leonard, as is clear from his own writing, was familiar with popular romances, ballads and songs, and took some pride in his learning which seems to have been acquired without formal education. He was clearly recognised as a kind of local poet laureate, supplying verses for special occasions (horse-races, bell-ringings, birthdays and deaths), and for neighbouring gentry and aristocracy (birthday verses, for example, were presented to the Earl of Rutland) as well as for friends and family. A story from his autobiography, of how he defended his reputation successfully in a contest with a rival poet, gives something of the flavour of his own pride in his learning:

> I was desired of sum jentellmen to cum to Tupton to discours with one Ouldham who profesed himself to be a poet, and was one who had writ severall verses, not only against me but in derision of the fabricke which I had Bulded upon the top of Ashover hill, so according to their desirs we met, where great companey gathered togather, there I did challeng him to whake with me to Parnishus Hill, but we both missing our way, we chanced to light of an all-hous, and after we had drunk awhile we fell into discors concerning the 9 Muses which he could not name, naithe could he tell from whence the came, or what the had done, or what the might doe, so I in the audienc of all the companey gave them their right names and all their right titles, where upon the decked my head round with lorill branches to the great vexation of my antagonist Ouldham. So ever since I am called the Black Poet.[8]

In his autobiography Leonard mentions 'my libry' and although no will has been found it seems reasonable to assume that, in following his father in the office of parish clerk and as schoolmaster, Titus would have inherited his father's books.[9] It would seem that Leonard's books are to be found amongst the first batch of entries.[10] A full analysis of the book list, which as well as the printed books includes more than twenty 'written' volumes, some of them original works by the Wheatcrofts themselves, is currently in progress.[11] While a few of the books, particularly those toward the end of the catalogue, are certainly new acquisitions by Titus made after his father's death in January1706/7 (largely new religious books, sermons and schoolbooks) the majority of the books seem to have been older, some printed in the sixteenth century, and presumably acquired at second hand. Some have a specific local interest, such as works by Immanuel and Obadiah Bourne, rectors of Ashover, and local visitation sermons. The Wheatcrofts had few expensive books: more than two-thirds of the books are priced at less than 2*s* and only about 7% are valued at more than 4*s*. Many of those given higher prices are family manuscripts.

That the size of the Wheatcrofts' collection of books was unusual for men of their class is established by comparison of its value (£32.1*s*) with the evidence from Chesterfield probate inventories collected by Rosemary Milward. Her Chesterfield owners of books range in social class from gentry to better-off tradesmen (gentleman attorney, secretary, surgeon, mercer, yeoman, clothworker, tanner, butcher, chandler, vintner and a widow), and most individuals owned only a few books. The only collection comparable in value to the Wheatcrofts' is that owned by the Clarke family of Somersall, Brampton, a rising gentry family. In 1634 they had books in a room 'called the Studie' valued at £6.13*s*.4*d*; but by 1670 their 'Library in the Study' at Somersall was valued at £30, with other 'old Lawe bookes and other bookes in the Closet in the Dyningroom' worth £3.6*s*.8*d*: a total value of £33.6*s*.8*d*.[12] This is the only one of the 116 Chesterfield wills and inventories considered by Milward which is close in value to the Wheatcrofts' £32-worth of books. John Coope, vicar of Chesterfield, had a library of books and writings worth £24 and William Allott, a surgeon from a gentry family, had books worth £15 in 1670.[13]

Comprehensive analysis of the list is our intention and more work on identification is still to be done. Here, I will concentrate on one specific question which the existence of this catalogue raises: how could these rural craftsmen in a small Derbyshire town amass such a collection of books? In the late seventeenth century Ashover had 190 households and an estimated population of about 800. In the 1640s, 20% of men in Ashover were able to sign their names rather than make a mark.[14] The largest towns in the county were Derby, with 611 households, Wirksworth with 449, Chesterfield with 315, Matlock with 256 and Ashbourne with 229 and, not surprisingly, it is in the larger towns that bookselling first appears.[15] Norman Taylor's article on Derbyshire printing notes seven booksellers in Derby between 1675 and 1722 as well as the printer Samuel Hodgkinson.[16] The *British Book Trade Index* makes clear that several bookselling businesses were already well-established by 1700 in Derby, Chesterfield and Ashbourne and that in the 1720s bookselling became established in Wirksworth. At least from the 1670s onwards Leonard could have had access to the shops of the Thorntons, Thomas Cadwell and Henry Nisbett in Derby; that of Job Brunsley, succeeded by Joseph Bradley, in Chesterfield; and of Robert Hilton in Ashbourne.[17] Rosemary Milward's publication of the inventories of the two Chesterfield booksellers Job Brunsley [d. 1682] and Joseph Bradley [d. 1699] indicates that bookselling was already well-established in Chesterfield by the 1680s, and is a vital source of information to which I shall return.[18] The Brunsley-Bradley shop in Chesterfield and the Nisbett business in Derby carried on into the eighteenth century and between 1700 and 1730 *BBTI* records, in addition to these two businesses, eight more booksellers, most of them apparently established for several years.[19] Numbers of booksellers, and therefore local opportunities for book-buying, certainly increased during Titus's lifetime, and by the 1730s he would have needed to travel relatively short distances to acquire new books.

The obvious place one might expect to find information about how and where Leonard acquired his books is his autobiography. Unfortunately, despite his references to 'my libry' and to his own manuscripts and poems, he makes absolutely no mention of book-buying or borrowing. The only reference to the book trade in the whole autobiography comes near the end of the text, where he writes: 'My next jorney [of 1699] was to Chasterfield July 8 with the Church Bible to get it bound'. Thus the only evidence of Leonard's visit to a shop dealing in books is in connection with his office as parish clerk and occurs when he was 72 years old! The shop Leonard visited was presumably that owned by Joseph Bradley (who died in the March before Leonard's July visit) and which was eventually taken over by his son Job.[20] Rosemary Milward's transcription of Bradley's surviving inventory dated March 1699 gives an exact impression of the shop as it must have been when Leonard visited it in July of that year. Milward argues that the business was declining under Bradley. Whereas in 1682, when Brunsley died, the stock consisted of books in folio worth £64.11*s*.10*d* and 'Other bookes £90.2*s*.10*d*', a considerable stock when compared with other provincial booksellers of the period, Bradley's inventory of March 1699 values his book stock of around 570 copies at a mere £22.10*s*.8*d*.[21] Book-binding was certainly an important part of the Chesterfield business: the Mayor's accounts, quoted by Milward, have Brunsley paid 'for binding old Mr. Woodes Bible and Claspes £1.9*s*.0*d*' and Brunsley's inventory lists binding materials and tools: '1 dozen Bassill skins, a parcel of glue, 1 parcell of Beech, 5lbs of Teare, 12 yards of Harding cloth, parchment and leather, Presse and working tools, a parcel of Paper, Leafe Gould'.[22]

Though this single trip to Chesterfield is the only visit to a bookshop recorded in Leonard Wheatcroft's autobiography, there are other aspects of his account of his life which are suggestive. For although Leonard was based in Ashover for most of his life he travelled widely and often, both in search of work and for pleasure and companionship,[23] and it seems likely that these frequent trips around not only his own county but also into Nottinghamshire and south Yorkshire might have provided opportunities for book-buying.[24] In his youth he went at least four times to London, and his courtship 'pilgrimage' gives an account of one such journey to the capital, to visit his brother, travelling via Derby, Leicester, Bugbrooke, Dunstable, St Albans, Barnet and Mimms. While in London he visited Westminster, Whitehall and the Tower and his journey home took him from Leicester north to Nottingham and home via Alfreton. By his own account 'as for my daly travills and idle jorneys to and fro the came to above 550... miles a yeare, which I believe I went for above 20 years togather...'.[25] Placing his children in work took him to Derby, Rowthorne, Butterley, Glapwell and Chesterfield; family celebrations took him as far afield as Sheffield and, when he was 70, on a walk of more than fifty miles to Barwick-in-Elmet near Leeds. The frequency of his visits to nearby market towns and his fondness for his 'jorneys' suggest, at least, that the tailor and sometime yeoman of a small Derbyshire town had plenty of opportunities for buying books or exchanging them with others. He also had connections with London throughout his life; as well having a brother living there, he apprenticed three of his sons to London tailors, a daughter went to London and they all made occasional visits in later years to their father in Ashover.

One of the interesting features of Leonard's travels is his lifelong enthusiasm for fair-going. He records going to fairs and wakes many times, often recounting that he stayed several days away from home. Some of these fair-goings were avowedly for pleasure, as were other outings he recorded to weddings, christenings, feasts and a bull-baiting; other visits to hiring fairs were at least on the pretext of business, as part of his arrangements for putting his children to work. He was a regular visitor to Chesterfield fairs, usually twice a year (in February and September), and to wakes at Matlock; once he travelled to the large sheep fair at Newhaven and the eight-day fair at Lenton Abbey, near Nottingham.[26] Any of these occasions could have brought him into contact with chapmen and ballad-sellers, and possibly booksellers' stalls.[27] A pedlar who might have crossed Leonard's path was William Johnson, alias Peter, who was arrested on suspicion of felony at Chesterfield fair on 14 September 1661. An inventory taken of his goods by the Town Clerk, constables and beadle shows that he travelled 'with a little bay nag, a hawking bag, and a trunk' containing the usual buttons, ribbons and small goods. Amongst his wares when he was apprehended were a dozen battledores, eight gilt primers and nine other primers 'in a bunch'.[28]

The book trade itself, whether in the form of the established bookshop or the itinerant pedlar, was not, of course, the only possible source of books. The informal circles of friendly as well as professional book-buying and book exchange noted by Michael Hunter and others in the case of Samuel Jeake of Rye might well have had its humbler, though less well-documented, equivalent.[29] Giles Mandelbrote remarks on 'informal private sales' as 'relatively commonplace' in late seventeenth-century

Sussex.[30] The Wheatcrofts, too, might have acquired books from local sales of this kind. Leonard records, for example, that in 1697 'I and my doughter Sara went to Chasterfield to buy sum houshold goods when Rich: Stringfelow broke' and house clearances of this kind may well have provided opportunities for buying secondhand books cheaply.[31] Buying books, of course, was not the only way in which the Wheatcrofts might have acquired them. Titus records in his catalogue a few gifts and loans, and some of his father's books, though unrecorded as such by Titus, might have been gifts. Item 232 in the catalogue, 'the English Empire in Amarica, or a View of ye Dominions of ye Crown of England in ye west-indies', is annotated as follows: 'this Book was <given me by> Jonathan Walker's & I design to keep it for his Sake'.[32] Borrowing might itself lead to purchase: item 295, 'The whole Duty of Man' was noted as 'borrowed of Mr Wm Hopkinson of Stubbinedge' and later were added the words 'bought since cost 2/6'. A volume of three early seventeenth-century sermons by Immanuel Bourne and a catechism by the same author published in the 1640s, probably acquired by Titus in the early 1730s, might have been gifts to his parish clerk from Obadiah Bourne, Immanuel's descendent and successor as vicar of the Ashover parish.[33] Titus was also a lender of books to others: next to item 268, 'the Maides Revenge, a tragedy' is later added 'this I have given'.[34]

The Wheatcroft catalogue provides a unique glimpse of readers from the lower social classes in rural England. That these men were writers, too, is evident not only from their surviving manuscripts, but also from the catalogue's own listing of many more manuscripts, now lost, composed by both father and son.[35] In preparing a thoroughly annotated edition of the catalogue itself we hope to shed some light not only on the book-ownership of these particular men but also on the local literary culture in which they were participants. The tantalizing question of whether or not this Derbyshire family was unique in its enthusiasm for reading and writing will only be answered if and when more records of book-ownership amongst rural artisans and craftsmen are found.

NOTES

1. A manuscript of Leonard's autobiography, with a continuation by Titus, was deposited in 1979 (DRO D2079), and has been edited by Dorothy Riden [ed], 'The autobiography of Leonard Wheatcroft of Ashover 1627–1706', *A Seventeenth-Century Scarsdale Miscellany* (Derbyshire Records Society), 20 (1993), 71–117. The courtship narrative was edited by George Parfitt & Ralph Houlbrooke as *The Courtship Narrative of Leonard Wheatcroft* (Reading, 1986). Cedric Brown of the University of Reading is currently working on the poems.

2. DRO 253 A/PZ 5/1 and DRO 253 A/PZ 5/2. My thanks to the Archivist of Derbyshire Record Office and to the Revd T Johnson of Ashover parish for permission to quote from these volumes.

3. 'My Shop' contains carpenter's tools, small-scale farming implements and 'frames'. The household goods and shop tools together are valued at £34.5*s*.10*d*. The inventories appear on pp 94–105 and the book list on pp 55–69, 90–3 and 107–10 of the manuscript.

4. This book list is mentioned, and some sample entries quoted, in [Charles Kerry], 'Ashover. Memoranda by Titus Wheatcroft, A.D. 1722. With a few Notes by the Editor', *Derbyshire Archaeological Journal*, 19 (1897), 24–52.

5. Parfitt & Houlbrooke, *Courtship Narrative*, 36.

6. Leonard had previously acted as Ashover parish clerk from 1650 to 1663.

7. Riden, 'Autobiography', 94. The recovery was completed only by the next generation of Wheatcrofts. In the summer of 1700 Leonard was visited unexpectedly by his eldest son Leonard who lived in London, and he records with evident pleasure that Leonard junior 'bought that hous and land which I sould, which was to the vallew of one hundred and 20 pounds which was great joy to me and all my nightbours [*sic*] and relations' (Riden, 'Autobiography', 99).

8. Riden, 'Autobiography', 97.

9. Thanks to the staff of Lichfield Record Office for their efforts to find wills for both Wheatcrofts. None has come to light. The assumption that Leonard's 'libry' is contained within Titus's catalogue is strengthened by the presence there of Leonard's manuscript books.

10. Changes in handwriting and the layout of the list suggest that the original list might have ended in the middle of page 65, with the Wheatcrofts' manuscripts followed by a selection of romances.

11. George Parfitt and I are working together on an edition of the catalogue. I am grateful to him for his sharing of the labour and for his contribution to this paper.

12. Rosemary Milward, 'Books and booksellers in late 17th century Chesterfield', *Derbyshire Miscellany*, 10 (1985), 119–45. The yeoman Francis Reynshawe, who might be nearer the social class of Leonard Wheatcroft at the height of his fortunes in the 1650s, died in 1648 leaving only three named books and other old books in a closet, not separately valued.

13. Milward gives no date for the Coope inventory.

14. Andy Wood, *The Politics of Social Conflict: the Peak Country, 1520–1770* (Cambridge: Cambridge University Press, 1999), 154 (evidence from a petition).

15. Household figures are for 1664, from David G Edwards [ed], *Derbyshire Hearth Tax Assessments 1662–70* (Derbyshire Record Society), 7 (1982), xliv.

16. Norman Taylor, 'Derbyshire printing and printers before 1800', *Derbyshire Archaeological Journal*, 70 (1950), 38–69.

17. *BBTI* has also an entry for one year only (1699?) for Hody, selling books in Chesterfield.

18. Milward, 'Books and booksellers', 120–4.

19. Between 1700 and 1730 *BBTI* records in Derby Henry Allestree (1712–1737), William Cantrel (1717–1728), John Hodges (1708–1719), Jeremiah Roe (1720–1778), Thomas Sheppard (1711) and Henry Nisbett (1688–1714); in Chesterfield, Joseph and Job Bradley (whose business continued until 1798); in Ashbourne Thomas Hanworth (1721) and Richard Smith (1727–1732); and in Wirksworth William Holt (1721–1728).

20. According to Milward, Job was 11 when his father died, and his mother, Anna, had died five years earlier. It is not clear who ran the shop until Job was old enough to take over.

21. Milward, 'Books and booksellers', 120–1. Books in folio mean, *pace* Milward, just that: folio books, some of them ready bound for sale, would indeed form a large part of the value of his stock. The total value may be slightly higher.

22. Milward, 'Books and booksellers', 120. Bradley's inventory does not describe the tools, but has 'Bookes that were at Bakewell and tooles in the shop' valued at £2.

23. From 1664 to 1668, having let his house, he lived in Bolsover, working at planting orchards and running a malthouse.

24. In 1670, for example, he went to Chesterfield twice for the fair, to Padley, Winster, Bolsover, Derby and Tupton.

25. Riden, 'Autobiography', 87.

26. See Riden, 'Autobiography', *passim* and note 22, p 107 on Chesterfield fairs.

27. Fair-going by established London booksellers might have been in decline in the latter part of the century; see John Barnard & Maureen Bell, 'The Provinces and Wales' in *A History of the Book in Britain, vol 4 1557–1695* (Cambridge, forthcoming). There is no doubt that provincial booksellers carried on the practice in their own regions; see, for example, Margaret Spufford, *Small Books and Pleasant Histories: Popular Fiction and its Readership in Seventeenth-Century England* (London, 1981).

28. Milward, 'Books and booksellers', 132.

29. Michael Hunter, Giles Mandelbrote, Richard Ovenden and Nigel Smith, *A Radical's Books: the Library Catalogue of Samuel Jeake of Rye, 1623–90* (Cambridge, 1999).

30. Hunter and others, *A Radical's Books*, xxxix.

31. 17 July; Riden, 'Autobiography', 98.

32. [Nathaniel Crouch], *The English Empire in America*, Wing C7319–21 (1685–98).

33. Items 299 and 296. The sermons are *STC* 3418 (1617), 3416 (1623) and 3419 (1622); the catechism is *A Light from Christ*, Wing B3854-6A (1645–7).

34. James Shirley, *STC* 22450a (1639).

35. On the Wheatcroft manuscripts see Maureen Bell, 'Reading and writing in rural England: the Wheatcrofts and their books' (paper given at the SHARP conference, Mainz, July 2000). One other surviving manuscript is known to be in private hands.

Book Availability in Ipswich over the Years

JANET PHIPPS

IPSWICH IS A BUSY TOWN with about 120 000 inhabitants. Because of its position as county town of Suffolk and its proximity to the sea, it has had a varied history, being one of the biggest ports during the busy wool years and going down in prosperity when the river was silted up, at the same time as the wool trade lessened. However, the agricultural revolution, together with the maltsters, who had been in the town since medieval times, kept the town alive as the centre of a large agricultural region. Its close proximity to London, by both road and water, meant that the town was also attractive to many wealthy families. The industrial revolution, with its need for coal and iron, encouraged many industrialists, Ransome and Cubitt among them, to bring industry to Ipswich. In 1801 the population was 11 277 and by 1850 it was 32 000. Ransomes became one of the first large companies to support the Mechanics' Institute in 1824. Once again Ipswich was to become a prosperous town, so attracting more industrialists and entrepreneurs. This prosperity was to last until the closure of the engineering and manufacturing factories and the running down of the docks in the 1950s and 1960s. It was not until the late 1980s that prosperity again came in the wake of the insurance companies who opened their large pretentious buildings in Ipswich. This short-lasting boom ended recently, however, when several of the smaller factories and some of the insurance companies were either sold or taken over. There is now an increase in commuting traffic, however, it being cheaper to buy a property in Ipswich, use the excellent train service into London and still keep relatively sane. However, the shops are not booming (commuters not being the best users of local shops and out-of-town developments being favoured by the busy families). It remains to be seen whether the commuters, who read books when not using their mobile phones on the train, and the increase in interest in reading being developed by reading groups, book prizes such as the Booker, and the media, keep bookshops and bookstalls in business in the town.

When Daniel Defoe visited Ipswich between 1724 and 1726 he wrote

> I take this town to be one of the most agreeable places in England and several things indeed recommend it: Good houses, at very easy rents; an airy clean and well governed town, very agreeable and improving company almost of every kind, a wonderful plenty of all manner of provisions, whether flesh or fish and very good of the kind. Those provisions very cheap, so that a family may live cheaper here than in any town in England of its bigness within such a small distance from London. Easy passage to London, either by land or water the coach going through every day.

What a good job he was not alive to read John Glyde's report on the 1800s: 'by 1800 local government in Ipswich was a byword for corruption and inefficiency, an oligarchy of the worst description'.

When I looked at Ipswich in 1995 as a place to which I might retire I too found a very agreeable town, with good houses at a reasonable price, very agreeable and improving company of almost every kind, plenty of provisions at a reasonable price and its nearness to London was also an attraction. Though I must admit it was not the cleanest town I have visited and whether it is well-governed is a debatable point – according to your politics, view of the motor car and how much council tax you have to pay.

When I actually moved to Ipswich in 1997 I found the people of the town friendly and entrepreneurial. They seemed to have more mobile phones per capita than those I had left behind in Hertfordshire – though less cars, thank goodness. They were also very much into computers and the internet, and discussions on buses and with friends, some of whom (contrary to Mr Blair's preconceived notions) were well over 65, is much of computer programs and e-mail. However, I have yet to find anyone who actually uses the dot-com companies to buy their books – a book in the hand (with no postage) is still better that several books in a warehouse!

The excellent library – a great Victorian edifice – was filled with books, CDs, videos, tapes and computers. An online catalogue covering the whole of Suffolk meant that I could renew, order and search for books in my own home as well as at the main branch and any of the many branches throughout the town and county. There is also a mobile service serving not only remote villages but also residential-care sites to enable the less able to use the library. Like other towns there is also a voluntary door-to-door service for those unable to get out at all.

The Mechanics' Institute eventually became 'The Institute', a haven for members which is in the centre of the town and not only supplies the reading wants of those interested in biographies, travel, local history and the novels of the more popular authors, but also houses a pleasant restaurant, the cleanest and most pleasant loo in town, has a reading group, and many educational and special-interest courses and trips are organised by its staff and members. The Institute has been in the town since 1824, when it had only 210 members and was one of the Mechanics' Institutes; indeed even in 1925, when public education and public libraries had made the original idea of the Institute outmoded, it had a membership of 1862 and circulated no less than 64 000 books. The Institute is one of only a very few of its kind left in the country and a great loss to the people and ethos of Ipswich it would be if it had to close. It now has about 2600 members who find it a bastion of quiet, and supplier of many of their social as well as reading needs. Their stock of journals, ranging from *PC World* to *The Lady,* can be looked at while having a quiet cup of coffee in their pleasant restaurant. Newspapers can be read whilst sitting in a comfortable armchair in front of a warming gas fire – a haven indeed.

Waterstones have a well-organised branch, and we can only hope that the politics which are going on in other parts of the country in regard to this bookshop let it stay that way – of course some books cannot be ordered through them. But we are also lucky in Ipswich in having an independent bookshop, Amberstones. This shop will order any books from anywhere and has a firm and devoted clientele. In 1987, Mr and Mrs Alex Bennett had come to Ipswich and were looking for a change in business, and they opened Amberstones, beautifully decorated in the Art Nouveau style then becoming fashionable again; this bookshop is still open, though Mr Bennett sold to a new proprietor last year. It stocks new books of all types, but does have a specialist interest in science fiction and fantasy, and children's books, J K Rowling supplanting Terry Pratchett at present, of course. It also has an excellent classics section. The College bookshop, which was just opposite Suffolk College, closed down at the beginning of this year and the stock, and customers one hopes, transferred to Amberstones. At present the new J K Rowling book is on sale at Waterstones at £5 less than full price; Amberstones cannot compete with this and it is to be hoped that they can keep their customers by giving the personal service with which Waterstones cannot compete.

There is an excellent and charming antiquarian bookshop, Claude Cox, which is still housed in one of the many medieval houses in the town. It was from the mid-nineteenthh century a secondhand bookshop under the proprietorship of Myfanwy and Thomas Cook; Claude Cox, the father of the present owner, took over from Tom Cook in the 1980s.

There is also a secondhand bookshop run by the Samaritans, containing much of interest to a booklover such as myself, including some *Saturday Books.* And, of course, all the charity shops stocked books of varying quality and quantity – as they still do.

There were also two other secondhand bookshops. One with a specialist stock on railways, the history and nature of East Anglia, and military books, housed in a very run-down medieval building which obviously needed much repair, and the contents of its shop windows sadly needed dusting – this is now closed. The other was a run-down bookshop on the edge of the main part of the town which contained many nice secondhand books, some old maps and an owner with an obvious love of books and great knowledge who loved to chat; this closed recently when the owner retired.

The Tourist Office has shelves filled with books about Ipswich, Suffolk and East Anglia generally. Newsagents and supermarkets supplied their limited number of books and there was a huge and well-organised stall of books at the Eastgate shopping centre – in fact that appeared to be almost all there was at this badly sited shopping centre – which is still well worth a browse. There is also a market stall which is well worth a look at.

Then there was 'The Works' for those picking up a book to keep the kids happy or because it was there – and cheap at that. Woolworths, too, is also in this market with a large stand of dictionaries and books on popular subjects – gardening, cooking, children's, etc.

Smiths have its usual stock – need I say more? And Smiths station bookstall had four bookstands filled with the notable and the popular of the moment. When I moved to Ipswich these four stands had become only two; but I am glad to report that this bookstall has been revitalised by extending with new shelving (the new commuters bringing in business, perhaps), and can offer a very large choice of journals and magazines as well as a much larger choice of books.

Now that I have lived in Ipswich for three years and have attended local-history classes and met some of the local people, I have learned that bookshops were of great matter in Ipswich and its past had been filled with shops which the present town-dwellers much missed. I decided to look into the background of the bookshops of Ipswich. Having put an advertisement in the local paper and being rung up by a very worried-sounding gentleman who asked 'are you writing a book about the bookshops of Ipswich' I laid his worries to rest and explained that my interest was superficial, my being retired and extremely unwilling to take on anything which sounded like work. He was very relieved, as he is very much into writing books of local interest and bookshops of Suffolk was the next on his busy agenda. Keep a look out - it may be published this year.

My advertisement did, however, also bring forth seeds, or at last people who had worked in two of the most famous of the Ipswich bookshops of the past.

Read & Barrett was established in 1827 and had several floors selling stationery and new and secondhand books, Miss Barrett eventually taking over the shop. It was however slowly run down, and by the 1930s, when Mr and Mrs Charles Wilcox took over, it needed a great deal of sorting out, every room on every floor, including the cellar, being filled with old books. One way of getting rid of books, which would otherwise have cluttered up the shop shelves, was the tray of 6*d* books outside the shop and, although usually marked at more than that today, there are still such trays outside most bookshops. However Mr Wilcox, who had worked in Mudies in London and so had a good grounding in his chosen business, still had hundreds of books, which were too far gone to be even given away, and they went for waste paper. Had you visited the shop during the lunchtime you might have been served by the granddaughter of the house. She remembers the many Americans who visited the shop during the war and has never forgotten the film star who bought £100 of books in one go – a tremendous amount in the 1940s. However, business with America had been going on before the first world war – Read & Barrett were to lose a box containing £10 of books when the Titanic went down.

Miss Wilcox also remembers the smell of the old – and often damp – books which was not popular with her school friends. Of course the granddaughter of the house was not allowed to use the public library – simply not done by the middle classes at that time – and not the respectable working classes either, as my mother insisted, in Tottenham, that we use Boots library. (There was, of course, a Boots library and bookshop in Ipswich.) Mr Wilcox would visit country-house sales, sale-rooms, other bookshops and auctions by taxi. In 1953 they were given notice to quit as Queen Street was going to be widened. It never happened, but Ipswich lost one of its most historic and interesting bookshops. I wonder if it would still be there now if it had not been for this decision by the local council.

The Ancient House seems to have been a bookshop and printers for ever – at least since the end of the eighteenth century, when it was owned by James Haddock. This is a medieval and beautifully pargeted building in the very centre of Ipswich's main shopping area. It became a bookshop, printers and stationers in about 1817, run by Culls, and by 1885 belonged to Pawsey & Hayes, also printers and stationers. It was eventually owned and run by Mr Walter Harrison. His sons also worked in the business and when he died in 1933 they took over a thriving shop and printers. Not only stationery and fancy goods could be obtained there, but there was a large lending library, a children's book department, new and secondhand books, of course, and a busy printers, supplying not only stationery for the private buyer, but printing newspapers, maps and guides, children's books and one-off books bound specially for school prizes. It was also famous for printing seed catalogues. If a customer came in for a book not on the shelves the doughty assistants would rush along the street to other bookshops and purchase the required book, rather than recommending – as we do now – that the customer visit another bookshop. This bookshop also supplied the Ipswich public library with stock. There was also a very good restaurant; so the excellent American coffee-cum-bookshops are not so new after all! Customers could enjoy afternoon tea, lunch or morning coffee and then look at the vast stock of new and old books as well as the stationery and fancy goods – what are they I wonder.

In 1948 the salary for the assistants for a six-day week was about 30*s* (£1.50), out of which 6*d* a week was put aside for the annual outing to the seaside, which all the staff took – going, of course, by charabanc. They did not, however, have to pay towards the staff Christmas dinner, which was kindly supplied by the management.

The shop was often very cold, the older books often smelled none too pleasant, and the customer was, of course, always right. In those days, too, customers would be able to pay for books on account and also – heaven forfend – take books 'on approval', and return them if they did not like them after all. The life of a bookshop assistant in the 1950s was not easy, nor well paid (I received £2 a week as a junior in London). However, there were plenty of staff and as each department had its own staff and a manager, these staff were very knowledgeable about their own speciality.

The Harrisons also owned the College Gateway Bookshop. In those days the college gave the bookshops a list of the books students would need for their course – if only!

During the war Harrisons lent its printing plant to Cowells, which was just along the street. Cowells had been founded as a printers in 1818 by Stanley Cowell, and when he died in about 1875 W S Cowell took over. In 1905 one shilling a week was the wage of an assistant in the shop. This printer became famous for colour printing and in 1952 printed one of the first of the large-format colour books for children, *Orlando the Marmalade Cat.*

Hatchards eventually took over the Ancient House Bookshop and it became a modern bookshop. Hatchards went the way of many good bookshops and was taken over, and, in Ipswich at least, the bookshop was closed down altogether. Though whether they could have survived with the opening of a large branch of Waterstones in 1993 is debatable.

During the period from 1800 to the present day many bookshops opened (and closed), but Ipswich has never been without a large selection of bookshops to meet every need. Organisations such as the Social Settlement Society, concerned with education as well as welfare, meant that the poor, as well as the rich, were interested in reading. And, although Ipswich was one of the first towns to open a free public library and pay libraries were abounding, people did like actually to 'own' books, just as we seem to now.

Had you lived in Ipswich in the 1800s you might well have ordered your books through David Morley, who also dealt in stationery (and law stationery in particular), and possibly even practised as a solicitor. In 1837 he would have easily been able to supply you with secondhand copies of at least one Bible, Burn's *Justice*, *A History of England*, Virgil, Geography, Iver's *Voyage to India*, *The History of the French Revolution*, Bloomfield's *Poems*, Lewis & Clarke's *Travels* and Coxe's *Lectures* to name but a few.

John Raw's shop was opened in 1817, and in the 1850s William Hunt's bookshop, in the centre of the town, displayed a painting by William Holman Hunt – was he a relation I wonder?

By 1859 there would certainly have been a great number of books by Charles Dickens bought and borrowed, as he visited the town and gave readings to the people of Ipswich. He had already stayed at the Great White Horse Tavern and based the lovely part of *Pickwick Papers,* where Mr Pickwick finds himself *en déshabillé* in the same bedroom as a lady, on the room where he stayed – which contained not one, but two four-poster beds. You can still stay at the Great White Horse Tavern if you visit Ipswich.

In 1885 you would have been able to obtain both new and secondhand books from shops in Dial Lane, in the centre of the town, to the outskirts – east, west, south and north from at least seventeen shops among whom – could you resist the name? – was Mrs Scoggins.

From 1900 to the end of the first world war some of these shops managed to stay open and five more were to open (and close) before the 1930s. The 1950s brought a second explosion of bookshops, with at least ten shops selling books, both secondhand and new and, in the 1970s the choice of bookshops (though many would have also sold other goods as well) was enormous with almost twenty different outlets.

John Glyde's shop was also a post office and a free library. John Glyde was a well-known historian and writer born in the early 1800s, and was a much respected man about the town. He owned and ran a bookshop and post office, as well as his own printing company. Coincidentally he lived and worked until 1844 in the shop which now houses the Samaritans' very successful bookshop – perhaps his ghost still overlooks the bibliophilic transactions there. It is hoped that soon there will be a blue commemoration plaque outside this shop. When he died at the age of 85 he left £500 for the public library to buy books by local authors to lend to the people of Ipswich.

Caxton's published encyclopaedias and educational books and these were sold door to door in Ipswich. This company, together with Odhams, would have the representative call at the door with a suitcase of books, and the buyer could pay for them by instalments. In the late 1940s and early 1950s Mr George Scoggins could be found driving about Ipswich and East Anglia in his little black Ford selling Caxton's educational publications on the doorstep. This house-to-house selling has not entirely stopped and Dorling Kindersley use the Tupperware method of parties to sell their books and software to people in their own homes even now.

The 'rep' is, of course, often the bane in the life of the bookseller, as well as being the supplier and Miss Wilcox remembers having to deceive the 'reps' about the buyers being unavailable, much as my mother used to send me to the door when the Odhams 'rep' came to sell my father yet more heavily bound and expensive books.

George Reach's shop was also a lending library, as were many of the bookshops at that time. A ready readership, paying about a penny a borrowing, later to become 6*d*, could be found among the people of Ipswich. The public library was not always the most acceptable place to go, and it did not, of course, accept all those who might wish to read; therefore there were many such pay libraries right up to the 1960s when public libraries realised that they were in the business of getting business!

Seemingly 'unsuitable' shops selling books is not new, of course; those that sigh with dismay at the supermarkets selling books and magazines must be reminded of Boots, which not only sold fancy goods, and was also a pharmacy, but had a popular lending library and sold books as well. Of course there was also Harrods which, together with the Times Library, would have sent books to subscribers in Ipswich. And many of the shops not only sold new and secondhand books but also secondhand goods to eke out a living. Department stores used always to have a book department. And there were, and still are, the book clubs. By the 1960s Boots had already gone as a book supplier, W H Smiths was thriving, but even up to the 1970s the Chain Library had enough customers to keep it open.

Finding in the Yellow Pages under 'Bookshops' the name 'Secrets' I made my way across town to find the shop and ask the owners how long they had been there and which books were their speciality. The bus stopped right outside the shop; I looked at the window and there I saw displayed slightly unusual leather goods and some very minute red underwear. I did not bother to go in! This shop supplied books I was not interested in at all – though for the purpose of this paper it is relevant that Ipswich can supply any books on any subject.

Now that the College bookshop has closed, the nearest bookshop to the College is the Samaritans' bookshop. I hesitate to mention a charity bookshop in such august company, but this does provide a service; it is well set out and books are priced sensibly – in fact an antiquarian bookseller comes in and looks at any stock which seems out of the run of the ordinary and prices it accordingly; he also has first choice of anything good which may come into the shop. One of our customers specialises in books about music and helps us to price these, again getting first choice of any he wishes to buy. Amberstones and some antiquarian bookshops give books which they cannot move to this bookshop. Recycling does not stop here, however, as books which do not sell after several years, but which have a decent spine, can be sold to a company which specialises in supplying books by the yard to theatres and public houses, etc. Books do furnish a room! Some unsold books can be passed on to a boys' home which had a library built for it, but was given no money for books. Books which cannot be sold are sent to various suitable places or, as is sometimes necessary, for pulping. Amberstones is grateful that we have moved to a shop near them, as this attracts book-loving customers to both shops in a less salubrious part of Ipswich and Cox's often recommends us to customers who do not find what they want on their shelves.

Ipswich is a town with a dock and is visited by sailors of many nationalities. At the Samaritans' shop we have visits by many Russian sailors in particular, who wish to purchase English books and we are happy to oblige them; they do not seem to worry much about the cost of the books. They especially like children's books, particularly ABC books for teaching English to their children. But they also ask about other books which we do not have. We often suggest they visit Claude Cox's shop, and Amberstones, of course. I have never had to direct them to Secrets, I am glad to say.

I have not mentioned the Church shops, one of which, The Church Centre Ltd, is still thriving in Ipswich, though it not only sells and lends books, but also other religious supplies – candles, and such like. From the 1940s the Christian Science Reading Room, SPCK, of course, and the Christian Literature Crusade all supplied the need for religious publications.

A good book-supplier will do anything to obtain a book for a customer. With enthusiasm he or she will even recommend other shops which might be able to supply the customer's needs. The talent in getting the right book to the right customer – or the right customer to a book they have found – is symptomatic of the trade.

With changing circumstances and an increasing population, Ipswich has always had good bookshops. Market forces being what they are, there are perhaps fewer specialist bookshops, and the large conglomerates have unfortunately taken over to a large extent. However, I am sure there will always be a place in this town (however full of mobile-phone and internet users) for the ever-changing book trade.

ACKNOWLEDGEMENTS

To Naomi Sanger, Mrs V J Offord, David J Barton, Valerie Boylett, the staff at the County Record Office, Ipswich, the staff at Amberstones Bookshop, *The Historical Essay of the Ipswich Institute,* Robert Malster's *Ipswich Town on the Orwell, East Anglian Daily Times, East Anglian Daily Star*

Mapping the Migration of Paper: Historical Geography & New Zealand Print Culture

SYDNEY J SHEP

AMONGST BOOK HISTORIANS, the name Lucien Febvre requires no introduction. This pioneer of the *Annales* school of historiography brought to research on the French book trade a perspective beyond simple textual bibliography. He extended the repertoire of analytical possibilities by taking a sociological approach and reinstating an undergrowth of rich extra-textual archival sources; it was an approach which later gained currency in Anglo-American bibliographical studies through the equally pioneering work on printing-house practice by D F McKenzie.[1] Less known amongst book historians, however, is Febvre's significant contribution to the development of the field of human and historical geography. Predating *The Coming of the Book* (*L'Apparition du Livre*) by several decades, his *A Geographical Introduction to History* laid the groundwork for his later resonant call to study 'the geography of the book'.[2] This paper examines one aspect of that geography in the context of colonial print culture: the New Zealand paper trade between 1835 and 1843. It investigates the distribution networks amongst papermills, paper merchants, and stationers contracted by the Church Missionary Society in London, and William Colenso, New Zealand's most famous early printer. It looks at some of the temporal and spatial factors which influenced Colenso's printing habits and argues that the geography of the paper trade informed patterns of local printing and helped to shape New Zealand's early print culture. It also suggests that by adopting the methodologies and contemporary research tools available to historical geographers, the new generation of book historians and print culturalists can begin to map an international geography of communication.

Febvre was highly influenced by the mid-nineteenth-century work of Jules Michelet, whose *Tableau de la France* (1869) was grounded on the assumption that history must, in the first instance, have a geographical basis. 'He saw in the past of peoples a whole play of subtle, multiple and complex geographical influences.'[3] Amongst these factors, Febvre included communication routes, whether commercial, religious, intellectual, or political, and argued that they played a significant role in what he termed the genesis of the state, that social construction generated by a collectivity of common interests. The study of commercial trade routes, he argued, should not be confined to a simple geographical mapping of 'the details of the track, nor on considerations of place or situation, but on the importance and nature of the traffic which feeds the route'.[4] Mapping the migration of paper offers one window upon the complex trading networks established amongst New Zealand, Australia, Britain, America, and Canada in the nineteenth century and brings into the foreground the inherent transportability across space and time of that container of information, the book.

My current work-in-progress studies the role of paper, that often invisible substrate, in the development of New Zealand print culture. Paper history tends to fall between the cracks of history of the book and print culture, even though its material centrality must be obvious, though perhaps too obvious, to most. On the one hand, paper exists as a substrate, functioning as the vehicle for language, frequently rendered invisible in the process as we overwrite its surface with a palimpsest of meaning. On the other hand, paper's deeper structure and internal language are always there, always communicating more than meets the print-fixated eye, always waiting patiently to be read. Paper's own language is a fascinating study. Through its creation, dissemination and survival, we can track rhythms of exchange, cultures of literacy, economic developments and political crises. Its materiality influenced local reading and collecting habits, it played an integral role in the marketplace of knowledge, it dictated the rhythms of everyday life. All too often, however, the study of paper is assumed to belong to specialists in the history of technology or scientists in the conservation laboratory; rarely is it considered an integral part of the print culturalist's analytical tool-kit. As the seminal American paper historian Allan Stevenson observed some forty years ago 'Inasmuch as what one buys when one buys a book (new or old) is usually mainly paper, it is surprising how little scientific attention has been given to this ingredient by bibliographers and other scholars in the description and discussion of books'.[5]

Like the books into which it is fashioned, paper is a transportable commodity which moves through time and space, irrespective of national boundaries, of what is written on it, or of what role it serves in transmitting knowledge or information. Increasingly, it appears that an understanding of the complex relationship between the supply and demand of paper is pivotal in determining the development of colonial print culture, something Robert Gross has recently referred to in the colonial American setting as 'the marketplace of print constrained by scarcity'.[6] Furthermore, a wide range of local, regional and international circumstances surrounding the pattern of trading networks regulating that supply and demand, and connecting New Zealand with overseas markets, is a crucial part of the story which cannot be addressed in a simplistic national-based study or one strictly delimited by national boundaries. Amongst these factors are paper suppliers, availability and cost, rag and raw materials trade, transportation routes, shipping patterns, weather patterns, winds and currents, outbound cargoes, government interventions, religious denominations. This paper will deal with some of these factors through the lens of the first 'book' printed in New Zealand, the New Testament in Maori, printed in 1837 by William Colenso.

Printing on New Zealand soil commenced in 1830, yet the first commercial papermill was not in production until 1876, despite the Church Missionary Society targeting New Zealand as a potential site for the production of its India or Bible papers as early as 1819.[7] This delay between printing and papermaking, replicated in virtually all colonial settlements, occurred with good reason. Besides the enormous capital investment required for a papermaking machine (£3-8000 and £20-50 000 for an entire mill set-up) location was everything: proximity to a sustainable fibre source, an abundance of preferably clean water, and a reliable transportation network to ensure that finished goods reached their appropriate markets. Between the arrival of printing presses and belated papermaking technology, the New Zealand printing industry was reliant upon overseas paper supplies, initially from Britain, then later continental Europe and America. Even when New Zealand had her own papermills, their output was primarily brown and grey wrappings, newsprint and paper bags; writing and printing papers were not produced domestically until the 1950s. The movement of paper was dependent upon a number of factors. From the originating country, mill-production schedules, availability of raw materials, taxation and tariff regulations, and the distribution lines between mill, paper merchants, brokers, agents, wholesalers, and clients entered into the supply equation. Shipping schedules, cargo space, naval blockades and weather patterns all affected supplies on the voyage out. Locally, printers complained that 'It costs more to convey a newspaper to some of the remote inland districts than to the uttermost parts of Europe'.[8] Early missionaries were, perforce, their own commercial travellers, evangelising the word by becoming, whether on foot or on horseback, the living networks of reading distribution. The increased demand for reading materials, particularly by the indigenous Maori, put pressure on sources of supply of even the crudest sorts of papers.

William Colenso arrived in Paihia, the Church Missionary Society's northern station, at the end of 1834. He was trained in his native Cornwall, and worked in London for a short time for the British and Foreign Bible Society printer, Richard Watts. Enlisted as mission printer by the CMS, Colenso prepared for the long three-month voyage to the Antipodes. He neglected, however, to oversee the inventory of printing equipment and supplies to be shipped out. Upon arriving in New Zealand, his precious Stanhope printing press was landed by Maori war canoe along with various crates and bundles, but when he sorted out his supplies, he was horrified to find that there were no printer's cases, no composing sticks, leading, rules, furniture, or galleys, no imposing slab for composing and locking up his formes, no ink rollers and, significantly, no paper. For a printer commissioned to produce five thousand copies of the complete 356-page New Testament in Maori, this was a daunting prospect. While Colenso could, ingeniously, improvise to make up the absence of equipment, the absence of paper was disastrous. However, rather than waiting for a shipment of paper from England or Sydney, Colenso went ahead and printed a Maori translation of the *Epistles of Paul to the Ephesians and the Philippians* in an edition initially of twenty-five copies for the missionaries and Home Office, then later two thousand copies for general circulation. He used writing paper secured from the personal supplies of Revd William Williams and general stationery stocked at the mission store at Kerikeri. The binding for the first copies consisted of pink blotting paper backed with stronger paper donated from the limited personal reserves of local missionaries' wives.

The circumstances of this first opportunistic publication became the pattern for much of Colenso's early printed output. Rather than being able to complete a large work like the New Testament all at once (even if he had enough type or a sufficient labour pool to accomplish the task), he ended up printing, binding and issuing the Scriptures in parts. These single-section hand-stitched pamphlets in strong brown paper wrappers were later bound together, frequently interpolated with hymn sheets and prayer books, irrespective of different formats, sizes or papers. As edition sizes increased in the attempt to keep up with local demand from mission stations, settlers and Maori alike, printers were compelled to use whatever papers were at hand, often relying on writing, letter and brown papers or a combination thereof when printing papers were unavailable. In early 1840, for instance, when paper was at a premium, Colenso printed 1400 copies of the first sheet of a 12-page Catechism on post 8vo, and completed the remainder of the edition of 12 000 on demy 12mo. Colenso could not be too particular about his sources, nor the variety of paper suitable for a particular job. Papers originally intended for one application were often called upon to serve a quite different and at times inappropriate function in times of scarcity. Often the distinction between print and manuscript based on size or type of paper was confused. When available, Colenso would use demy printing paper for the bulk of his book and jobbing printing, as well as for binding endpapers and repairs; when unavailable, demy writing, cartridge, post and foolscap filled the gap. Sometimes, he was reduced to brown and deal papers, heavy loan papers and coarse, retree sheets. Some of these inferior papers wore out too quickly, made printing ultimately uneconomical, and exacerbated the increasing problems of supply and demand of finished products.

Throughout his printing career Colenso, along with his missionary brethren, continued to protest at regular intervals about the lack of paper in general and the lack of suitable printing paper in particular. Both impinged negatively on his manufacturing ability and were a formidable influence on the dissemination and preservation of the word of the Lord. In such a scarcity economy, the value of paper was high and Colenso's printing habits had to change. European printers were accustomed to procure a single run of paper from a single mill for a particular book project and use it immediately; alternately, they were faced with 'a considerable diversity of papers, mixtures arising from certain practices of gathering and distribution within the paper trade'.[9] Colenso had to make do with whatever arrived from the Home Office as the evangelising and educational impulses of the missionaries caused increased demand for a range of sacred and secular works in the newly transliterated Maori language. His services were even called upon by the British government's representative who asked Colenso in 1840 to print the Treaty of Waitangi, the nation's founding document. Later in the century, Colenso's heirs indented specific papers on an annual basis with all the attendant problems of project management, storage and insurance. By the time regular direct steamship service arrived in the 1880s, orders could be put through on a more frequent basis and printers could even buy 'right', that is directly from overseas suppliers in England or America rather than through their local general merchant/stationer/postmaster, or the New-Zealand-based representative of overseas paper merchants.

The issuing of the Bible in parts became a common practice, indeed a necessary publishing strategy. It was not until 1868 that the entire Old and New Testaments, that is a complete Bible in Maori, was printed, significantly not in New Zealand, but in London. But book printing was never the mainstay of the colonial printers. Although newspapers were an important part of the colonial printing trade, jobbing printing – broadsheets, pamphlets and advertising ephemera – was the economic staple of those early pioneers of information technology who provided the crucial communication lifeline to geographically isolated settlements. Fine-quality printing, book and writing papers were unnecessary for this type of printing, type was not left standing for extended periods, edition sizes were small and less labour-intensive, accounts could be settled promptly and efficiently, sophisticated transport networks were not required as the product was for a highly localised consumer. For Colenso to attempt book printing in this formative period is a tribute to his tenacity; his methods for resolving the often insurmountable obstacles are a mark of his inventiveness.

By 1837, the year in which Colenso printed his 5000 copies of the New Testament, sufficient quantities of machine-made demy-size Bible paper, olive and blue demy coloured paper for endpapers, millboard for covers, and brown paper for wrappers were finally available from the mission public store at Kerikeri. Colenso required a total of 262 reams 8 quires, or 125 904 sheets of paper for the job and was

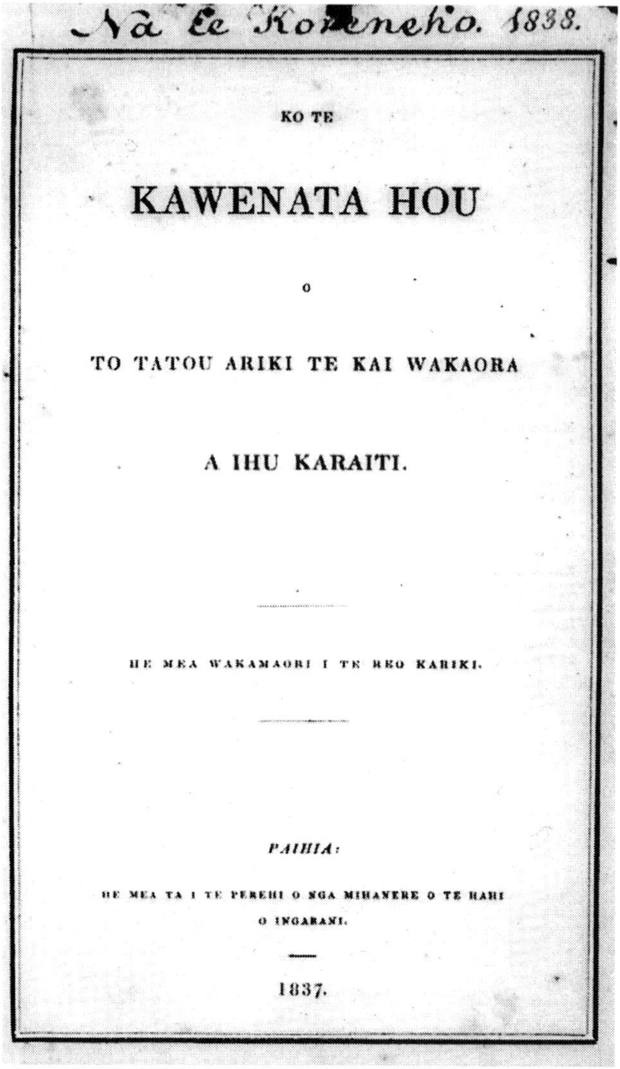

Nā Te Koreneho. 1838.

KO TE

KAWENATA HOU

O

TO TATOU ARIKI TE KAI WAKAORA

A IHU KARAITI.

HE MEA WAKAMAORI I TE REO KARIKI.

PAIHIA:

HE MEA TA I TE PEREHI O NGA MIHANERE O TE HAHI O INGARANI.

1837.

Title-page of William Colenso's Maori *New Testament* (Paihia, 1837) – original size 215x135 mm photograph reproduced by kind permission of Alexander Turnbull Library, Wellington, N Z (reference no F-5695-1/2) entirely dependent upon the Home Office to provide for him. These papers were obtained by the Church Missionary Society as part of their standard business practice of supplying their own London-based publishing enterprises as well as their mission stations worldwide. The Society ordered stock through a chain of middlemen who were either specifically paper merchants, stationers, printers, or general provisioners. To date, most of the hand- and machine-made papers identified as being available to the earliest Protestant New Zealand printers originated primarily from papermills in the southern counties of England from Devon to Buckinghamshire to Kent; that is, those closest to the extensive commercial distribution networks and transportation hubs of the London metropolis. It is noteworthy that New Zealand onshore printing begin at a precisely significant watershed moment in the British papermaking industry. From 1830 there was a marked decline in the number and location of mills and a general geographical contraction as large-scale machine mills opened closer to the main trading centres and gradually squeezed out their handmade, vat-based competitors.[10]

The extant financial accounts of the Church Missionary Society offer an invaluable window into their daily business operations. The cash books document individual transactions with named suppliers and often include variety, quantity ordered and cost of the paper. During Colenso's printing career, three suppliers dominate the paper landscape: Dickinson & Co, Isaac Pratt, and Messrs Tipper & Co.[11] John Dickinson, Liveryman of the Stationer's Company, early inventor of cylinder papermaking machines, rag merchant, owner of numerous mills and advocate for the abolition of paper duties, manufactured primarily printing paper for books and was renowned for producing thin, tough and opaque machine-made Bible papers. He had clients as diverse as the Clarendon Press, the Society for the Promotion of Christian Knowledge (SPCK), Bradbury & Evans, Moxon, Blackie & Son, Sampson Low, and the Bible Society.[12] It was Richard Watts, printer for the British and Foreign Bible Society, who printed the Church Missionary Society's various publications *(Annual Report*, *Missionary Record*, and *Missionary Register)* and with whom William Colenso was first employed. This same Bible Society also published 20 000 12mo copies of the second edition of the Maori New Testament in 1841, once it became apparent that the New Zealand mission press could not keep up with demand. The machine-made papers for both the first and second editions, the one printed on the frontier, the other in the metropolis, were undoubtedly drawn from Dickinson's mills at Apsley and Nash Mills in Hertfordshire, north of London, both convenient for transport on the Grand Junction Canal and the London to Birmingham railway line. Over the nine years of Colenso's involvement with the mission's printing output, three large orders of approximately 650 reams of paper, costing £660.15*s*, were placed with this firm.

If paper supplies were not purchased directly from Dickinson & Co at 65 Old Bailey, London, they could have been part of the commonly mixed-lot mill consignments sold on by London stationers such as Pratt or Tipper. Isaac Pratt might have been a relation of the Revd Josiah Pratt, first Secretary of the CMS, but he was certainly in business as a wholesaler of writing, printing, packing, and coloured papers. He despatched numerous shipments to mission stations around the world, claimed commissions and export drawbacks (refund on stamp duty paid per ream by the papermill), provided the bulk of the paper to Richard Watts for the various CMS publications and kept the London office and school in stocks of letter, copy, and scribbling paper. Undesignated paper shipments were made to New Zealand at a total cost of £115.4*s*.2*d* in four separate instalments. The Tipper firm of Blackfriars and Leadenhall Street was variously printer, bookseller, stationer, warehouse operator for Whatman papers, and millboard manufacturer and dealer. In eighteen separate transactions on account of New Zealand concerns, they sent out a total of £210.14*s*.8*d* in coloured paper, millboard, writing paper ordered by individual missionaries, and the generically termed 'paper for NZ'.

Between dispatch and arrival at the Antipodean mission store, paper had a merry journey. Packed in bales, deal cases, or casks by shipping agents, paper was subjected to insurance costs, freight charges of approximately 50*s* per ton, entry and wharfage charges at points of transshipment or final port of call, and haulage. In this era of global telecommunications and mass-transportation networks, we often forget that New Zealand at the 'uttermost end of the sea' was the furthest of Britain's colonies, 21 000 miles away. Emigrants faced a minimum three-month voyage out by sail and the danger of being becalmed was ever-present. Weather patterns, winds and currents all influenced shipping routes and therefore supply schedules. The proprietors of Wellington's *Evening Post* newspaper accepted a delay in paper shipment with stoic resignation: 'sailing ships must take their own time and submit to winds and waves, and we must wait awhile'.[13] Inevitably, there were numerous tales of shipwrecks with cargoes of paper, stationery, and books lost. The 1830s marked the first attempts to codify hydrographic research started by Captain Cook, but it was not until 1850 that the first accounts were published which actually charted the best sea routes to follow at which time of year for the greatest efficiency and economy. Between requisitioning, obtaining, dispatch and arrival, supplies like paper from Britain or America could take anywhere from eighteen months sailing around the Cape of Good Hope, or six months if available in the neighbouring colony across the Tasman Sea. Before becoming an official colony of Britain in 1840, New Zealand was a dependency of New South Wales, Australia, an important transshipment and nodal point in the volatile paper and book trade. 'The dependence of New Zealand and Australia as a market and source of supplies is clear, and the prosperity of the new colony fluctuated in harmony with the condition of the Australian economy.'[14] As the Australian paper historian Carolyn Mills has remarked, even 'early colonial governors were sometimes forced to buy paper from visiting ships from personal funds to enable them to lodge the bureaucratic documentation required by the home government, and to keep the colony operating'.[15] Supplies of paper in such shipmasters' speculative cargoes were erratic and might have not reached New Zealand at all, juggling as they did with the personal effects of immigrants and the more lucrative cargoes of outbound primary materials such as timber and flax, and inbound manufactured goods.

Sailing ships were said to be the cheapest form of warehousing, particularly once steamships were in the ascendant, and the Church Missionary Society invested in some of these floating warehouses early on in the development of their overseas mission stations. The purchase of the schooner 'Active' in 1827 and the cutter 'Karere' in 1834, for instance, ensured cargo space and regular shipping schedules between Sydney and the Bay of Islands where the first mission press was established; each trip took a minimum of two weeks for the 1200-mile route. With impenetrable bush, mountain divides and the absence of any rail and road links, New Zealand coastal shipping was the communication and economic lifeline of the geographically isolated mission stations and settler communities. Whether by short-haul or long-haul vessels, paper finally arrived at Paihia. Colenso's Day, Waste and Paper Books, his printing-house ledgers, as well as the quarterly or biannual accounts of the mission store in Kerikeri record incoming and outgoing supplies, documenting shipping source, variety of paper, and price sold on to individual missionaries or the stations increasingly scattered throughout the country.

These same printing-house records detail the composition, printing and binding of the Maori New Testament. If Colenso was dependent upon overseas paper supplies to see this publication through to completion, he was equally reliant upon itinerant pressmen to assist with the job. All the book trades were dependent upon a steady stream of intellectual capital, but many trained specialists colony-hopped and the possibility of continuity, let alone expansion of the trade, was frequently fraught with instability. Fortunately in February 1837, Colenso engaged the services of two journeyman printers, James Powell and Charles Upham. Powell continued until mid-July before he moved on; Upham, who gained enduring fame in Colenso's ledgers by spoiling seven quires of paper at a cost of 7*s*, stayed until the New Testament was completed on 30 December. Colenso celebrated the landmark event with an annotation in his Day Book 'Finished printing New Testament 5,000 copies demy 8vo; Glory be to God, alone!'[16]

Printing the Bible was only half the job, however. During the previous two years of pamphlet and broadsheet production, Colenso was equipped to bind single-section pamphlets in brown-paper wrappers with a minimum of inconvenience. Binding 5000 copies of a substantial multi-sectioned work was quite a different story. In a demonstration of inter-denominational cooperation, Colenso sent the Revd John Hobbs, superintendant of the Wesleyan Missionary Society station in Mangungu in the Hokianga, 1000 copies of the New Testament in sheets along with 72 reams of brown paper for binding and packing them. A similar pattern of division of labour had already been well established among the various Protestant mission stations. After binding 260 copies in cloth and leather between January and June 1838, on 13 July, Colenso sent 500 Testaments for binding to the CMS general merchant and banker in Sydney, Messrs R Campbell & Co, via the schooner 'Jess'. This was the first of five lots totalling 2803 copies or 56% of the edition contracted to the Sydney binder Brennand between 1838 and 1840. Each order took between four and six months from dispatch to return. Each copy cost 1*s* to bind and was accounted for in New Zealand at 4*s* per copy, although the majority were given away as part of the mission's evangelising mandate rather than sold. In addition to the binding, the mission was charged entry and wharfage at 2*s*. 10*d* per case of books, each case containing an average of 500 copies, plus insurance and freight. In September 1839, for example, the ship 'Achilles' sent from London to Sydney with goods valued at £2000 transshipped to New Zealand, picking up a case of 498 bound New Testaments, with total freight costing £210.8*s*.[17] Customs clearance charges and import taxes along with fines, fees, licenses, and land sales were among the necessary strategies for the young New Zealand government to finance its outgoings, given chronic underfunding by the British government. Since paper and books were amongst the colony's major imports, they remained an easy source of income until the duty on books was remitted in 1846 after complaints from the missionary societies about such a tax on knowledge; tariffs on manufactured stationery and many kinds and sizes of paper remained in place to protect the tenuous local papermaking and paper-trade industry right into the twentieth century.

With the contract for regular off-shore binding of complete Testaments secured, Colenso returned to the part-book system in January 1839 and bound 200 Testaments in parts, dividing each book into five sections and binding them separately in paper wrappers, 'papering up' as he termed it. As he explained to the Home Office, 'we thought it expedient to divide some Testaments into parts for the readier distribution in visiting distant places, for schools &c'.[18] In April 1840, he also contracted with a newly arrived bookbinder, one W Wilson of Kororareka (Russell) across the harbour from the mission press, to bind 250 copies of the New Testament at *8d* per copy. Colenso provided all materials including 10 quires of demy endpapers, cord, needles, thread, millboards, bone folder, sewing presses and press keys. In the scarcity economy of the colony's early years, paper often changed hands through established networks of sale or barter with local missionaries or mechanics. This same Wilson sold Colenso 8 reams of demy printing paper when supplies ran short in 1841–1842, while Colenso waited for a major shipment of 200 reams of double demy transshipped through the colony as well as 220 reams of first- and second-quality demy printing paper direct from the Parent Committee in London. It is quite possible that this interruption to supply was consequent upon a major cash crisis faced by the CMS in 1841 and 1842 when they used up all their reserves, had considerable debts to tradesmen, and had to obtain loans from members of the Parent Committee to continue their operations at home and abroad. The result was a dramatic restructuring of the organisation, a rationalisation of all activities including printing offices and libraries, and the expectation that all missions should be self-supporting and focus on evangelical principles rather than the temporal affairs of the people.[19]

Once the New Testaments were bound, Colenso acted as his own distributor, packing and shipping orders to other mission stations, selling or issuing copies from his combined print shop and book shop, and loading up copies like a commercial traveller to sell on his numerous walking tours to other stations or through the interior. He records a number of transactions with various seamen such as Commodore Wilks of the American Squadron and Captain King of the Royal Navy, or Maori including Patuone on his baptism, Kihi in prison, or 'a Native for an English Bible'.[20] Copies were also sent to the Home Office in London where they were distributed locally or through a small circle of booksellers and stationers who supplied books and periodicals to the overseas mission-station libraries, furnished binding services, received commissions on sales of CMS publications, and used their shops to collect donations for the evangelical work of the Society. Messrs L B Seeley & Sons of Fleet Street filled orders on a monthly basis; Messrs Hatchard & Co of Piccadilly bound most of the books for the Australasian mission and had a Mission Box to collect donations, as did the bookseller Messrs James Nisbet & Co of 21 Berners Street. Preliminary evidence suggests that, as with the paper trade, these preferred suppliers and distributors often had links to the Society as practising members within the church-going community or had family connections. They were also geographically clustered around the major book-trade landscape of central London and thus close to the CMS Head Office in Salisbury Square.

By tracking the 'biography' of the Maori New Testament, including the migration of its paper, we can begin to appreciate the complex range of factors influencing Febvre's notional geography of communication. To map these complexities and move beyond a simple documentation of place and time, the methods of historical geography offer some visual solutions. The preeminent British paper historian, Alfred H Shorter, was a professional historical geographer who enriched the field of paper research by examining the complex array of circumstances surrounding the development of handmade and machine-made papers. Writing from the late 1930s through to the 1960s, he often included static maps to convey his snapshots of mill histories county by county.[21] Had he contemporary electronic mapping and analytical tools at his disposal, he could have developed further the digital terrain of paper history, documenting, for example, the migration through time and space of personnel, technology, equipment and expertise, and, by extension, the transmission and reception of ideas through the print medium, patterns of consumption and reading based on access to the material object, as well as the imaginative and metaphorical landscape or what James Raven refers to as the cultural topography[22] of print and the book trade.

Recently, Bertrum MacDonald and Fiona Black have proposed using the spatial, syncretic, and graphical interface of Geographic Information Systems (GIS) for book history.[23] GIS is a computer-based technology of significant use to historical geographers and one which comes closest to John O Jordan and Robert L Patten's vision of publishing history as hypertext: 'what will be needed in the future is not more of the linear paradigms of production that commence with the writer's idea and proceed straightforwardly through composition to publication and reception, but the conceptions of the activity of producing and consuming books that decentre the principal elements and make them interactive and interdependent; publishing history, in other words, as hypertext'.[24] New technologies like GIS offer a robust and flexible model for connecting various disparate databases suited to the print-culture field, to examine relationships between these databases, and to provide integrated, interactive and potentially multimedia solutions. GIS also allows a significantly wider range of questions to be posed and answered by New Zealand print-culture historians than has hitherto been possible. That being said, the long-term practicability of using GIS for a web-based, public-domain electronic atlas has been questioned. Humphrey Southall and his Great Britain Historical GIS Project team now at the University of Portsmouth are currently developing other spatially orientated solutions. Citing the cost and complexity of proprietary GIS software, the time investment and need for highly specialised technical support, plus the lack of precedents for the historical application of GIS, they are developing alternative approaches to create low-cost, quality multimedia publications which are cross-platform, viewable with standard software or freeware, and most importantly, which do not erode or compromise cartographic control in the pursuit of interactivity.[25] Despite this cautionary note, the spatial modelling focus of GIS or other such visualisation systems can furnish a powerful analytical tool for examining and capturing the complexity of paper history and its relationship to print culture. Such an approach is being tested at Victoria University of Wellington as part of a project to create an electronic atlas of paper history.

For the new generation of colonial book historians, both the spatial and temporal dimensions of print culture are essential for understanding that 'colonial culture was fundamentally *both* local and metropolitan', a provincial culture defining itself as and against a distant cosmopolitan centre.[26] Or, as the Australian book historian, Wallace Kirsop, has recently put it 'centre and periphery are part of a continuum and [the] distinction between Old and New Worlds is at bottom artificial, the trite expression of a location fallacy. In the end the metropolis-frontier can be transcended'.[27] Paper may be for some an invisible substrate, but for me, it offers tangible, tactile proof of the development of New Zealand's printing industry and New Zealand print culture; it is also pivotal in understanding the fundamental internationalism of the book as a transportable object and transnational container of information.

NOTES

1. Donald F McKenzie, 'Printers of the mind: some notes on bibliographical theories and printing-house practices,' *Studies in Bibliography* 22 (1969), 1–75. and *Bibliography and the Sociology of Texts,* Panizzi Lectures 1985 (London: The British Library, 1986); see also John Feather, 'Cross-channel currents: historical bibliography and l'histoire du livre', *The Library*, 6th ser, 2 (1980), 1–15; G Thomas Tanselle, 'Printing history and other history', *Studies in Bibliography* 48 (1996), 269–89.

2. Lucien Febvre & Henri-Jean Martin, *The Coming of the Book: The Impact of Printing 1450-1800,*. [trans] David Gerard (New York & London: Verso, 1990), chapter 6.

3. Lucien Febvre, *A Geographical Introduction to History*, [trans] E G Mountford & J H Paxton (London: Kegan Paul, 1925), 11.

4. Febvre, *Geographical Introduction*, 325.

5. Allan Stevenson, *Observations on Paper as Evidence* (Lawrence, Kansas: University of Kansas Libraries, 1961), 2.

6. SHARP 2000 conference, Society for the History of Authorship, Reading & Publishing, 3–8 July 2000, Mainz, Germany.

7. Revd Josiah Pratt to Revd Samuel Marsden, 8 May 1819, Hocken Library, MS 56c/153.

8. *Typo*, 6 (27 August 1892), 68.

9. Stevenson, *Observations*, 20–1.

10. Alfred H Shorter, *Studies on the History of Papermaking in Britain*, [ed] Richard L Hills (Aldershot: Ashgate Publishing, 1993), 12, 31, 34, & 266.

11. Church Missionary Society Cash/Day Books 1834–1838, 1838–1841, 1842–1844. Church Missionary Society Archives, University of Birmingham, Special Collections, F/F3.

Further occupational and location data are extracted from the electronic database *British Book Trade Index*, compiled by Peter Isaac.

12. Joan Evans, *The Endless Web: John Dickinson & Co. Ltd 1804–1954* (London: Jonathan Cape, 1955), 67–8. Peter Bower notes that the majority of early British machine-made papers were made for printing; see *Turner's Papers. A Study of the Manufacture, Selection and Use of his Drawing Papers 1787–1820* (London: Tate Gallery, 1990), 124.

13. *Typo*, 3 (29 June 1889), 59

14. Muriel Pritchard, *An Economic History of New Zealand to 1939* (Auckland: Collins 1970), 56.

15. Carolyn Mills, message posted on SHARP-L electronic discussion list, 10 March 2000.

16. Colenso, Day & Waste Books 1835–1843, Alexander Turnbull Library Micro-MS-Copy 0697.

17. 'Supplies for New Zealand purchased in New South Wales' in Australasian Mission Ledger 1837–1843, Church Missionary Society Archives, F/FY3.

18. Colenso, Letters,1 (1834–1847), Hocken Library, Dunedin, copy at ATL qMS-0491.

19. Eugene Stock, *The History of the Church Missionary Society* (London: CMS, 1899), 1,482; and *The Missionary Register* (London: CMS, 1841), 7.

20. Colenso, Printing Office Accounts, Auckland War Memorial Museum Library, Auckland (MS 76 William Colenso Papers Box 2, F10 of 20).

21. See in particular his *Studies on the History of Papermaking in Britain.*

22. James Raven, 'Memorializing a London bookscape: the mapping and reading of Paternoster Row and St. Paul's Churchyard, 1695–1814', in *Order and Connexion. Studies in Bibliography and Book History*, [ed] Robin C Alston (Cambridge: Brewer, 1997), 178.

23. Fiona A Black, Bertrum H MacDonald, & Malcolm W Black, 'Geographic Information Systems: a new research method for book history', *Book History* 1 (1998), 11–31; Black & Macdonald, 'Using GIS for spatial and temporal analyses in print culture studies: some opportunities and challenges," *Social Science History* 24. 3 (2000), 505–36; 'From dream to reality: an examination of GIS methodology in the history of the book in Canada project', paper to the Social Science History Association Conference, Pittsburgh, 26–29 October 2000.

24. John O Jordan and Robert L Patten, 'Introduction: publishing history as hypertext', in *Literature in the Marketplace. Nineteenth-century British Publishing and Reading Practices* (Cambridge: Cambridge University Press, 1995), 11.

25. Ben White, 'Electronic atlases: in theory and in practice', on website http://www.geog.port.ac.uk/jtap_ehap/soc_cart_article.htm (accessed 22 June 2000); also in The Society of Cartographers' *Bulletin* 31.2 (Dec 1998). Dr Paul Ell of Queen's University, Belfast, has marshalled the resources of the Historical GIS team in a recent development, the British contribution to the Electronic Cultural Atlas Initiative, which includes thematic teams on such topics as newspapers, trade routes, photographs and historical atlas; see website http://www.qub.ac.uk/cdda/.

26. David D Hall, 'Introduction' and 'On native ground: from the history of printing to the history of the book', in *Cultures of Print. Essays in the History of the Book*, (Amherst, MA: University of Massachusetts Press, 1996), 6 & 27.

27. Wallace Kirsop, 'Metropolises and frontiers: books in the English-speaking world', *English Studies in Canada* 25.3/4 (1999), 497.

Index